JAZZ GUITAR ICONS

BY WOLF MARSHALL

Cover Photos: Kenny Burrell, © Brad Shirakawa; Joe Pass, © Marc Marnie/Alamy;
Les Paul, © Photofest; Wes Montgomery, © Val Wilmer CTSIMAGES;
Charlie Christian, © Jan Persson Archive CTSIMAGES

ISBN 978-1-4584-1497-7

HAL•LEONARD®
CORPORATION

7777 W. BLUEMOUND RD. P.O. BOX 13819 MILWAUKEE, WI 53213

In Australia Contact:
Hal Leonard Australia Pty. Ltd.
4 Lentara Court
Cheltenham, Victoria, 3192 Australia
Email: ausadmin@halleonard.com.au

Visit Hal Leonard Online at
www.halleonard.com

ISBN: 978-1-4584-1497-7

Published by:
Hal Leonard Corporation
7777 W. Bluemound Road
P.O. Box 13819
Milwaukee, WI 53213

In Australia Contact:
Hal Leonard Australia Pty. Ltd.
4 Lentara Court
Cheltenham, Victoria, 3192 Australia
Email: ausadmin@halleonard.com.au

Printed in the U.S.A

First Edition

Visit Hal Leonard Online at
www.halleonard.com

CONTENTS

GEORGE BENSON

© Photofest

George Benson personifies modern jazz guitar… and then some. He is unquestionably the most important jazz guitarist to emerge since the death of Wes Montgomery in 1968 and the most visible and striking practitioner of the medium in our culture. It is almost impossible to stroll through a mall, sit in a trendy restaurant, or switch on a contemporary jazz radio station without hearing George (or one of his imitators) weave funky bop-flavored guitar lines over a sultry synthesizer wash. So profound is his influence.

George Benson's music and persona transcend the strict confines of the jazz genre. What other jazz guitarist would feel equally at home swapping blues licks on stage with B.B. King, recording with Miles Davis for the horn man's first guitar experiments, sitting in and tearing it up with the King of Swing, Benny Goodman, vocalizing and melting nubile hearts with a stirring pop ballad, or delivering an onscreen acting cameo on "The Love Boat" or "Mike Hammer?"

George Benson has done it all with panache and conviction. A brilliant instrumental-vocal artist and an iconic international pop star, Benson is respected and admired for both aspects of his success. This is the sound of dues paid in full. From humble beginnings in the streets of Pittsburgh to the limelight of the world's top venues and the din of sold-out crowds, it has been a long and eventful journey for the musical giant once called "Little Georgie" Benson.

INFLUENCES

George Benson's earliest influences came not from jazz but from R&B. His first experience was singing pop songs and winning talent contests at the age of four. George's stepfather, who owned a guitar and amp, introduced him to the instrument and arranged for the boy to study and develop basic skills on the ukulele. At age six, Benson heard guitarist Charlie Christian with the Benny Goodman band and was drawn to the electric guitar. He cites Christian's "Solo Flight" as particularly influential.

George acquired his first guitar a couple of years later and mastered it well enough to accompany himself during his preteen career as "Little Georgie." Hank Garland's *Jazz Winds from a New Direction* was the first jazz guitar album that caught his ear. He also learned from records by Grant Green, Barney Kessel, Eddie McFadden, Kenny Burrell, Jim Hall, and most significantly, Wes Montgomery, who became a personal mentor. Another important influence was alto saxophonist Charlie "Bird" Parker, from whom he absorbed the bebop language by transposing Bird's blistering lines to the guitar.

STYLE

George Benson has incredible chops and an amazing ear for improvisation. His fluid single-note passages are clearly bebop-based, marked with an execution and virtuosity associated with the greatest jazz wind players. When playing these single-note phrases, Benson favors a linear approach, using a variety of position shifts up and down the fingerboard instead of remaining parked in standard guitar "boxes." He also favors his first three fingers and rarely uses his pinky. This accounts for the slippery horn-like phrasing and greater range of his jazz licks. He augments his single-note playing with Wes Montgomery-inspired octaves and block chording.

George is often identified by several specific textures he employs regularly. Among the most well known are the ubiquitous three-note chords—heard in "Breezin'"—which he plays like Wes played octaves. He also favors intervallic textures and breaks up two-note chords and octave lines with wide melodic leaps, sometimes articulated fingerstyle.

Blues is an important part of Benson's style and is often found in his improvisations as characteristic pentatonic blues-scale licks, string bends, and vibrato. He further decorates his playing with telltale R&B elements like repeated sixteenth-note riffs and rhythmic motifs. Many of George's single-note phrases are enhanced by his "scat singing." This is a style that Benson owns. It involves singing along with improvised melodies in unison to create a unique two-part texture, as heard in the solo of "This Masquerade."

ESSENTIAL LISTENING

George Benson's discography is copious and encompasses five decades of prolific music-making. Among recommended highlights are the serviceable compilation *This Is Jazz 9: George Benson* (Epic Associates/Legacy), *The George Benson Cookbook* (Columbia), *Giblet Gravy* (Verve), *Breezin'* (Warner Bros), and *Beyond the Blue Horizon* and *Body Talk* (CTI).

ESSENTIAL VIEWING

George Benson is featured in a number of DVDs currently on the market. Among these are *Absolutely Live Benson* and *Live at Montreux*, 1998, both distributed by Eagle Rock Entertainment. Benson shares his guitar insights in a telling instructional video that's aptly titled *Art of Jazz Guitar* (Hot Licks, 2006).

Benson is well documented online as well. Current clips cover the broad range of his talents and phases of his career with numerous live versions of his pop hits and impressive extended blowing performances on "Affirmation" and "Take Five" as well as rare studio out-takes of Stevie Wonder's "Lately." Benson collaborations on video are diverse and include a tribute to Wes Montgomery with Lee Ritenour, an edgy "Breezin'" with Carlos Santana, a gentle country/blues take on "Help Me Make

It Through the Night" with Chet Atkins, and gorgeous straight-ahead jazz renditions of "Round Midnight" and "Stella by Starlight" with McCoy Tyner.

SOUND

George Benson's sound is the epitome of modern jazz guitar tone: warm, rich, and resonant, but with plenty of punch. Accordingly, he has played a variety of arch-top electrics throughout his career. He was seen briefly with a late thirties Gibson ES-150 with a single bar pickup (a la Charlie Christian) in his early years before settling on a top-of-the-line sixties Gibson Super 400CES with two humbuckers. This was most likely his main guitar during his Columbia period of the mid sixties. Benson endorsed Guild guitars in the late sixties and early seventies. It was common to see him at the time with either an Artist Award model or a Stuart X-500—the flagship instruments of the Guild arch-top electric line.

In the early seventies, George acquired a luxurious sunburst D'Angelico arch-top acoustic that he fitted with a floating De Armond pickup. This guitar became a favored instrument in the seventies. He alternated between numerous Gibson, Guild, and D'Aquisto arch-top electrics and the D'Angelico through 1976.

© Photofest

Benson plugged these arch-tops into various tube amps, usually preferring a Fender Twin Reverb model. For the landmark *Breezin'* recording, George experimented with a new combination: a Gibson Johnny Smith model and a solid-state Polytone amp.

In the mid-seventies, Benson signed an endorsement deal with Ibanez, which produced the signature George Benson guitar line that continues to the present day. This includes the traditional GB-20 (with a large body and a floating pickup) and the unusual GB-10. The latter has a smaller (Les Paul size) hollow body and two floating pickups. The GB-10 has a greater resistance to feedback and a better response at high volumes than normal arch-tops and in short order became Benson's primary stage instrument. He presently plays an Ibanez GB-12 "anniversary model," which is basically a beefed-up version of the GB-10.

George Benson has been a Polytone user since the 1976 *Breezin'* sessions. In the eighties, he endorsed the Polytone 104 bi-amp combo model with 160 watts, two separate power amps, and two 12-inch speakers. He used a Polytone Mini-Brute V with a single 15-inch speaker on the *Absolutely Live* concert (on DVD). Benson currently employs a Polytone run

in series with a Fender Hot Rod Deville amp for a balance of solid-state and tube tone in the studio. George strings his guitars with heavy-gauge flatwound strings. Nowadays, he has signature flatwound sets made by Thomastik-Infeld. The heavier GB114 set is gauged .014 to .055, and the lighter GB112 is gauged .012 to .053.

LICKS

FIG. 1: BENSON BURNER!

This fiery single-note lick exemplifies the guitarist in his hungry years when he was striving to make an impression on the jazz community. Musically, it splits the difference between bebop, swing jazz, and jump blues and is delivered with a ferocity that transcends all three. It is played over the last eight measures of an up-tempo 12-bar blues in G. You'll notice a number of physical moves around the fingerboard in this phrase, typical of George's linear approach. Characteristic Benson harmonic substitutions include C minor over a C7 chord in measure 2, F minor over an E7 chord in measure 4, and Eb minor in measures 5 and 6 over Am7 and D7 chords. By contrast, the last three measures have a more down-home blues sound in G.

FIG. 1.

FIG. 2: JUMPIN' WITH GEORGE

This colorful lick uses broken octaves, a favorite Benson intervallic texture. These types of lines were frequently heard in his modal period of the seventies with CTI on such releases as *Body Talk*, *Beyond the Blue Horizon*, and *Bad Benson*. The concept is simple: play Wes Montgomery-type octaves as single notes while holding the fingered shape intact. These two-note shapes are then slurred around the fingerboard to form interesting and largely rhythmic patterns and riffs. This lick is in E minor and is played over a modal vamp in a moderate rock groove. The octave jumps in this case are from high to low. That is, play the higher note of the octave shape first. George plays them in reverse as well, and you should try this too. Any single-note melody can be subjected to this octave-jumping procedure with good results, so try your hand at creating your own patterns after you've mastered this phrase. The patterns in this lick are made more interesting by the rhythmic displacement of the octave jumps. They stress the upbeats, which generates a funkier feel. The regard for rhythmic twists is central to Benson's riffs and general conception. He is a highly rhythmic player in any setting.

FIG. 2.

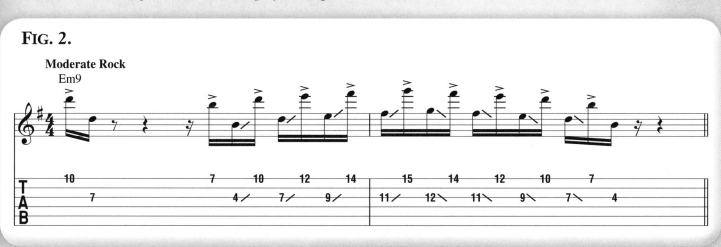

FIG. 3: A BREEZY CHORD LICK

This signature phrase exploits a central component of George's *block chord* approach. Of these he has several forms, but this is arguably the most common. It involves a three-note chord voiced as root-5th-octave or root-4th-octave. The ambiguous harmonic nature of these voicings makes them as utilitarian and serviceable as octaves in Wes Montgomery's style. Translation: you can use them to harmonize melodies over a variety of chords in the key center. This lick is in D major and has both major mode and blues connotations. Note the slurring in the phrase. These slides emphasize the rising half-step motion into the 5th (A) and the 3rd (F♯) tones, a typical embellishment in blues melody. Check out the specific applications of the chords in this lick. The root-5th-octave voicings are used for the chords on string set 4–3–2, while the root-4th-octave is found on the top three strings. This phrase is played over a D–G/A vamp in a moderate R&B groove. It's articulated with the fingers but can also be played with the pick or pick and fingers (hybrid picking). Benson is adept at all three approaches and alternates depending on the mood and intent of his musical statement.

FIG. 3.

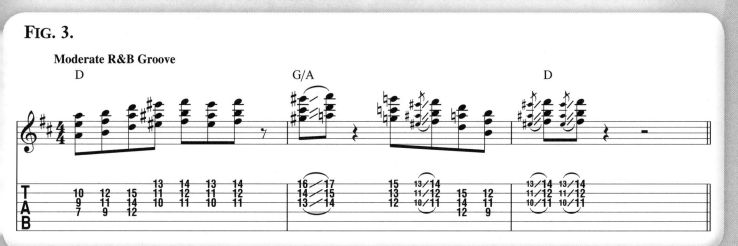

ED BICKERT

© Paul Hoeffler CTSIMAGES

reputation as a popular sideman with a highly identifiable personal sound and conception.

Bickert was playing jazz full time when he began to make his mark in the genre. An early career milestone was his appearance on the original version of "Swinging Shepherd Blues" by the Moe Koffman Quintet (1957). He also worked with trombonist Rob McConnell's 22-piece Boss Brass big band and performed in a small trio, still his most musically conducive setting. To this day, Bickert is arguably most effective in a trio where he supplies the harmony and melody. This setting affords him the freedom and space to improvise, explore, and expound on his unique chord and single-note sounds.

Bickert's trio, with regular cohorts Don Thompson (bass) and Terry Clarke (drums), became the house band at Toronto's Bourbon Street nightclub in the seventies. During this period, his group gained an international reputation backing traveling jazz performers such as Zoot Sims, Art Farmer, Milt Jackson, Frank Rosolino, Red Norvo, and Paul Desmond. The latter artist proved pivotal to Bickert's increasing exposure and recognition.

Forget Labatts beer and the fish farms; guitarist Ed Bickert is Canada's leading export. Bickert and his cool-toned Telecaster have been the pride of Toronto and Canada's premier jazz guitarist since the seventies. What's that you say? A Tele as a jazz axe? Yes, in the hands of Bickert, it is. As a consequence, his unique style and sound have earned him scores of admirers and fans, many of whom are counted among the world's most accomplished musicians. You can put giants like Paul Desmond, Jim Hall, Charles McPherson, Red Norvo, and Tal Farlow on this short list, for starters.

Edward Isaac Bickert was born in 1932 in Hochfield, Manitoba, Canada. He was raised in Vernon, British Columbia and struck out for the big city of Toronto at age twenty. But not so fast; let's go back a bit. Bickert had discovered the guitar as a child, turned semi-pro as a teenager, played with various dance bands, toured locally, and quickly wound up in the studio scene when he relocated to Toronto. He worked at Toronto's CFRB radio station—first as an engineer before picking up sessions as a studio guitarist. He gradually established a lucrative lifestyle where he played recording dates by day and jazz in clubs at night. By the mid-fifties, Bickert had an enviable

Bickert's big break came when alto saxophonist Paul Desmond (the composer of "Take Five" and a member of Dave Brubeck's most famed lineup) returned to the active jazz scene and, at the recommendation of Jim Hall, enlisted his efforts in the studio and on stage. The classic album *Pure Desmond* (1974) hails from this period. This recording found Bickert alongside luminaries Desmond, bassist Ron Carter (Miles Davis, Kenny Burrell, et al), and drummer Connie Kay (Modern Jazz Quartet) in a pianoless ensemble where his showcased guitar was the sole harmonic instrument. In this context, he was free to lend his unusual sonorities to the arrangements—a situation he described as "a good spot for me." Bickert's memorable partnership with Desmond further resulted in the much-lauded live record *Like Someone in Love* (1975).

In the wake of his auspicious outings with Paul Desmond, Bickert went on to record notable albums with luminaries Rosemary Clooney, Frank Rosolino, Ruby Braff, Lorne Lofsky, and several important dates under his own name. His most definitive and expressive work as a leader is featured in live and studio trio sessions with bandmates Thompson and Clarke and in small pianoless groups with drummer Barry Elmes.

Influences

Brought up in a musical family, Bickert picked up the guitar at ten and learned a few chords from an older brother. Initially attracted to country and pop music, he ultimately became enthralled with jazz and jazz guitar via Les Paul, Django Reinhardt, Oscar Moore (with the Nat King Cole Trio), and other artists heard on radio broadcasts from the American West Coast.

Largely self-taught, Bickert eschewed scale studies and theory early on, learning most of his moves by listening to his favorites and simply noodling. His dictum, simple and direct, resounds with powerful implications: "I just played stuff I liked to play." Wes Montgomery embraced a similar philosophy. Come to think of it, so did Eddie Van Halen, Chuck Berry, and Stevie Ray Vaughan. It's a mindset that informs a number of great innovators. In those years, Bickert was working out "the stuff he liked" from players he admired, such as jazz guitarists Barney Kessel, Tal Farlow, and Jimmy Raney, and pianist Bill Evans. While involved with the studio world, he studied informally and briefly with Tony Bradan and additionally looked for insights in guitar method books from Johnny Smith and George Van Eps.

Style

Ed Bickert's musical MO, like his gear, is deceptively simple and utilitarian. Like kindred spirit Jim Hall, he prefers to build a solo in the storytelling sense, relying on his intuition and his ears and applying space and textures as musical events, instead of technical excess and intricacies. That said, Bickert prefers to have the freedom, and with bassist support, to dole out colorful chord voicings and alternate progressions at will. That's another reason he gravitates to the trio format.

Bickert is readily identified by his cool guitar tone, relaxed execution, harmonic sophistication, and bop-inflected conception. His fluency with complex harmony and modern chord progressions allows him to improvise with these resources as easily as most guitarists play basic blues licks. Bickert's light, largely polyphonic attack resembles a keyboard approach more than a conventional guitar attack and shapes his tone and delivery. To paraphrase the old cliché, nonetheless true: it's in the hands. Bickert employs hybrid picking almost exclusively, usually holding a flat pick between the thumb and index finger and plucking freely with his remaining fingers when needed for larger chord voicings. This enables him to achieve a very smooth, organic sound in which single notes, double stops, full chords, and contrapuntal lines are woven together freely.

Bickert is fond of using enriched chords with multiple alterations, extensions like 9ths, 11ths, and 13ths, chromatic harmony, and polychords (chord on chord voicings). He's particularly adept at applying ambiguous rootless chords to his arrangements. These incomplete but complex sonorities are typically dissonant chords with the root purposely deleted, making more notes on the guitar available for tonal color and movement. In live performance with a trio, it is presumed that the bass would supply the fundamental root tones as needed. This is a crucial aspect of Bickert's approach to chord arranging and improvising.

One of the best ways to access the Ed Bickert guitar style is through an examination of his approach to well-known standards from the Great American Song Book. These tunes are the lifeblood and core repertory of the jazz genre, and of these there are many definitive examples in his discography. In this context, Bickert's well-known abilities to re-harmonize, apply modern substitutions, alterations, and extensions in place of conventional chords, and re-think oldies with a new vision on the fly are at the forefront. Perennial classics like "Gone with the Wind," "Easy Living," "I Hear a Rhapsody," "Nica's Dream," "What Is This Thing Called Love," and "Trist" as well as the blues have received strong interpretations from Bickert on record and stand as definitive examples of his harmonic/melodic style.

Ed Bickert & Don Thompson
At The Garden Party

Sackville SKCD2-4005

Though his harmonic sense and chord-melody style generally get most of the attention, Bickert's single-note playing is consistently inventive, melodic, and eminently swinging with clear allusions to Jim Hall, Joe Pass, and the music of his early non-guitar role models Duke Ellington, Miles Davis, and Gil Evans. In Bickert's style, harmony and melody are often melded as one. Many of his single-note jazz lines are reinforced by comping figures, chord punches, brief punctuating progressions, and rhythmic fills, usually composed of dyads and triads (two- and three-note chords).

ESSENTIAL LISTENING

The Guitar Mastery of Ed Bickert (DSM, Canadian import) is a superb two-disc collection gathering live trio performances from 1979 (the Montreux and Northsea Festivals) and quintet studio tracks with second guitarist Oliver Gannon and saxophonist Fraser MacPherson from 1993. Another essential Bickert recording is *At Toronto's Bourbon Street* (Concord Jazz).

Also recommended is Bickert's sideman work with Paul Desmond on *Pure Desmond* (Columbia) and *Like Someone in Love* (Telarc), and on Rosemary Clooney's American Song Book sets: *Sings the Music of Harold Arlen*, *Sings the Music of Irving Berlin*, and *Sings the Music of Jimmy Van Heusen* (all on Concord).

ESSENTIAL VIEWING

The Ed Bickert guitar sound and approach are well represented on a series of live performances currently posted online. Among the many gems are his takes on standards like "You'd Be So Nice," "Easy to Love," "Lollipops and Roses," "Never Been in Love Before," and "Do Nothing Till You Hear From Me," as well as an intriguing introspective but swinging blues like "Ed's Blues."

SOUND

The Ed Bickert guitar sound has long been a source of consternation for many jazz aficionados. Unlike his mainstream colleagues, Bickert jettisoned the traditional arch-top electrics decades ago and has played a solid-body guitar—a mid-sixties Fender Telecaster—exclusively throughout his career. Bickert originally arrived in Toronto with an Epiphone Triumph, later moved up to a single-pickup Gibson ES-175, and finally chose the Tele for its versatility. Though he still owns the more typical ES-175 electric arch-top and strives for a dark, bop-approved hollow-body timbre a la Jim Hall or Joe Pass, you're invariably hearing the iconic blond Tele with a rosewood fingerboard, seen since the seventies, on all of Bickert's recordings.

For many years, Bickert played his Tele with its original single-coil neck pickup engaged and the highs rolled down for a warmer jazz sound. In time, he replaced the Tele's stock neck pickup with a humbucker, which he feels provides a more balanced tone and response. Bickert generally strings his guitar with a light-gauge set (by jazz standards): .011-.046. He prefers a medium-gauge Fender pick and most often plays with his pick and three fingers (hybrid picking).

Originally, Bickert plugged his Tele into a Standel Custom 15 amp with a single 15-inch speaker. He later replaced it with a small Roland Cube 60 solid-state model and recently acquired a small Evans boutique amp—the choice of numerous contemporary jazz guitarists.

LICKS

FIG. 1: TRIO STYLE INTRO

This intro phrase is typical of Bickert's guitar-trio conception. Here, he creates an impressionistic suspended feeling by superimposing chord changes over a steady pedal point (played by the bassist) on Bb, the root or tonic of the dominant chord in the Eb major tonality. The bass note provides an anchor for his more active drifting sonorities. Bickert bases his approach on a repeated iii–VI–ii–V progression in Eb: Gm7– C7–Fm7–Bb7. Note the colorations of the chords. He generally uses simpler, less dissonant voicings for Gm7 and Fm7, saving the greater harmonic pull of dissonance and complexity for the dominant seventh chords C13b9, Bb7#5b9, C7b9, and Bb13. Check out his rootless voicings for C7 and Bb7 as well as his *quartal* approach to Fm11. The latter is voiced as a stack of perfect 4ths in measure 3.

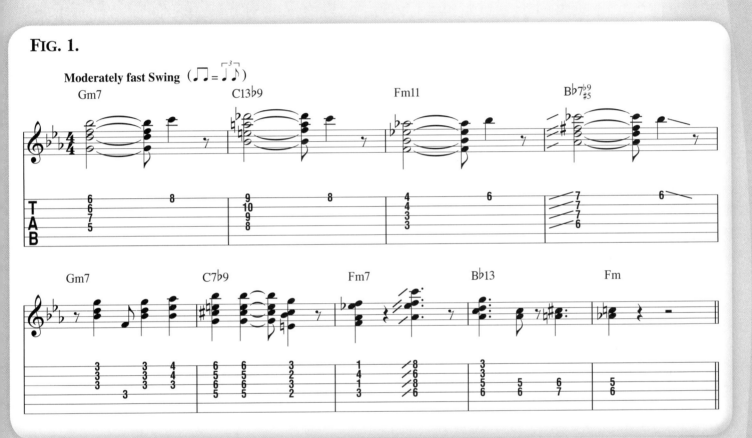

FIG. 2: CHORDAL MASTERY

Several telling chordal maneuvers are contained in this phrase. Note the variety of consonant versus dissonant sounds. The opening Gm7 has a diatonic *cluster* sound and is followed by a diminished voicing that harmonizes a B–C melody on the F♯ diminished chord. The Fm7–B♭7 pattern in measures 3–4 features a simple slurred dyad figure and two complex voicings of the altered B♭7 chord moved in minor 3rds. This motion captures the diminished sound of an altered seventh chord and is voiced in *polychordal* fashion—like the great modern jazz pianists—here triad on triad. Check it out. On closer inspection, you'll find that the seemingly complex chords are a combination of minor and major triads melded together. For example, the B♭13♭9 on the downbeat of measure 4 is made of a Gm triad on the top three strings (B♭–G–D) and a G major triad (G–D–B) on the next three strings—an interesting and colorful sound. In measures 5–6, we find a familiar Bickert pattern expounding on the E♭7–D7–D♭7–C7 progression. Here, slurs and pull offs are used purposefully to produce a smooth legato effect and the upper-partial 13th dissonances are added in dyads to each *rootless ninth chord*. Bickert closes with a favorite inversion pattern in which he builds diatonic sonorities on F minor to color the basic Fm7–B♭7 change. Note his trademark use of quartal harmony (chords in 4th intervals) and modal extensions in this section.

FIG. 2.

FIG. 3: CHORD SEQUENCES

This classic Bickert passage contains two ear-catching sequential ideas. It begins with a chord line that suggests the popular "Bye, Bye Blackbird" theme of jazz. This is stated as a passage filled with common tones, pedal-point variants, and subtle shifting chromatic harmonies. Note the sustained C note, which connects Fmaj9, A°7, and Gm11 in the first full measure. Then, check out the B♭ tone held in the next measure through Gm7 and C7♭9♯11 (another favorite rootless voicing). Similarly, common tones are found in the bass end of the voicings. It all makes for smooth and satisfying motion in the complex progression. Also notable is the treatment given to the second chord sequence in measures 3–4. Here, rootless voicings are used for D7 and C7 with common tones throughout. The typical closing pattern, Cm11–F13–B♭maj7–E♭9–F, is played with a series of rootless chords. Note the unusual cluster voicing of Cm11 in this section as well as more standard extensions for the remainder of the progression. The final chord is a quartal stack, which places a root F note on top of an intentionally ambiguous 5th and 9th voicing.

FIG. 3.

KENNY BURRELL

© Paul Hoeffler CTSIMAGES

The American recording strike of 1942–1944 prevented much of this music, while it was in its developmental stages, from reaching the wider jazz audience. Thus, when bebop emerged fully formed in 1945, it was initially seen as a revolution and a spontaneous mutation. In the course of the decade that followed its "debut," bebop became the prevalent style of modern jazz and began to inform virtually every subgenre to follow. There are undisguised allusions to bebop in cool jazz, soul jazz, Latin jazz, Third Stream (or classical jazz), and free jazz. Since the sixties, bebop has affected various jazz-rock fusion and crossover movements as well as the later smooth jazz style.

Kenny Burrell was arguably the first guitarist to fully embody the new concepts, techniques, and aesthetics of the bebop art form when he made his initial appearance with Dizzy Gillespie's band in 1951. Other guitarists of the period, like Barney Kessel and Tal Farlow, had been inspired by Bird and Diz, but their connections to the earlier swing style proved stronger and more lasting. By comparison, Kenny was already on a modern trajectory that led to Wes Montgomery, George Benson, Grant Green, Joe Pass, Pat Martino, Henry Johnson, Rodney Jones, and beyond. In the years to follow, he would not only influence jazz players but many rock and blues guitarists. Names like Jimi Hendrix, Otis Rush, Steve Howe, Freddie King, Andy Summers, and Stevie Ray Vaughan come to mind immediately. B.B. King cites him as his favorite guitarist.

When Kenny Burrell burst onto the jazz scene in the early fifties, he was heralded as the first genuine bebop guitarist. In retrospect, that's truer today than it was back then. At the time, bebop, still new and somewhat controversial, had grown out of the forties innovations of musicians like Charlie "Bird" Parker, Bud Powell, Thelonius Monk, and Dizzy Gillespie to become the lingua franca of jazz and marked the apex of its artistic aspirations. The music was distinguished by its complexity, virtuosity, and increased levels of dissonance, which challenged players to reach beyond the resources they had at hand. With bebop, jazz became a listener's music rather than a dance genre. Thought to be a radical and revolutionary departure at the time, the bebop genre was actually the natural outgrowth of the swing styles that preceded it.

In 1941, jam sessions at Minton's and Monroe's in New York City served as an incubator for the incipient bebop movement. There on any given night, pianist Thelonius Monk, trumpeter Dizzy Gillespie, alto saxophonist Charlie Parker, guitarist Charlie Christian, drummer Kenny Clarke, and others could be found making the earliest contributions to the art form. In those venues, adventurous jazz and swing musicians invented and, through trial and error, perfected the earliest forms of bebop, which focused on advanced chord structures, rhythmic diversity, fast tempos, and brilliant risk-taking improvisation.

After his innovative work in the fifties, Kenny assumed the role of trendsetter and has since been regarded as one of the genre's major innovators and leaders. By decade's end, he was redefining the sonic possibilities of jazz guitar on his groundbreaking guitar-bass-drums recordings and set new standards in the organ-trio medium through his inventive and sympathetic work with Jimmy Smith. *A Night at the Vanguard* (1959) demonstrated what a guitar could do as the sole melodic/harmonic instrument in a combo setting. And Jimmy Smith recordings like *The Sermon* (1958), *Home Cookin'* (1959), *Back at the Chicken Shack* (1960), and *Midnight Special* (1960) produced a template that's followed assiduously to this day. Never content to rest on his laurels, Kenny continued with a number of ambitious and successful experiments mating the jazz guitar to a wider variety of combo and orchestral applications. Moreover, Kenny's landmark efforts in the burgeoning soul-jazz style and his own emblematic pieces (like "Chitlins Con Carne") on *Midnight Blue* (1963) influenced legions of guitar players and other instrumentalists across various stylistic divides and indeed presaged the funk styles percolating and emerging in the later sixties.

Since then, Kenny has touched virtually every form in the genre—from the grittiest folksy blues, funky soul jazz, and traditional gospel hymns to esoteric modal jazz and the loftiest post-bop modern styles, always delivered with taste, musical sensitivity, and his highly identifiable personal stamp. His appropriately titled opus *Guitar Forms* (1965) presented another side of his artistry. It showcased many of his diverse tangents in microcosm—from the acoustic classical guitar/ amplified jazz guitar and orchestral combinations in "Greensleeves" and his solo nylon-string adaptation of George Gershwin's "Prelude #2" to the Spanish/ Mexican-influenced original "Loie," the down-home blues bent of "Downstairs," and the straight-ahead hard bop rendition of "Breadwinner."

Kenny continues to lead and inspire guitarists to the present day. Past his eightieth birthday, he remains an active and compelling performer while also heading up the jazz studies department at UCLA, where he teaches ensemble classes and a course in Ellingtonia. Burrell's legacy is assured and implicit in his overriding credo: "Let your spirit come through and you will always touch others. Give the music your personal best. Be yourself, it works."

INFLUENCES

Kenny Burrell was raised in a musical family. His mother played the piano at home and sang in the choir at the Second Baptist Church in his hometown of Detroit, Michigan. His older brother played the guitar, and his father, a mechanic by trade, enjoyed singing and playing the ukulele and other string instruments.

Kenny's multi-faceted style was shaped through listening and learning by ear. Like most players growing up in the forties, he was inspired by the music of Charlie Christian, the seminal electric guitarist who made a splash with Benny Goodman's big band in 1939–1942. Oscar Moore, with the Nat "King" Cole Trio, also influenced Kenny in his formative period, as did blues guitarists T-Bone Walker and Muddy Waters. However, Kenny's keen harmonic sense and advanced chord-melody style is informed more by arrangers like Duke Ellington and pianists like Nat Cole than traditional guitar players.

Kenny attended and graduated from Wayne State University in Detroit in the mid-fifties. Though the school didn't offer a guitar program, he sought out Joe Fava, a working professional, for private lessons in classical guitar. Working from piano, sax, and trumpet books, he also taught himself to sight-read during this period.

Burrell absorbed much of the jazz language from bebop horn players like Charlie Parker and Dizzy Gillespie as well as earlier swing stylists such as Lester Young, Herschel Evans, and Coleman Hawkins. These influences are felt in most of his bop improvisations.

STYLE

The Kenny Burrell style can be described as striking an ideal balance of the three B's of jazz: bebop, blues, and ballads—its three most essential qualities. Kenny's bebop playing runs the gamut from the proto-bebop style of Charlie Christian in his Minton days to the harmonically advanced music of Bird, Diz, and John Coltrane. Evidence of this can be heard on many of his mid-to-late fifties recordings where he mixes the loping horn-like phrases of bop saxophonists with more conventional swing guitar licks. Bebop informs Kenny's single-note improvisations as well as his chordal style with modern dissonance, chord substitutions, and long, articulate double-timed lines possessing unexpected accents and an unerring sense of swing. Tracks like "This Time the Dream's On Me" and "Lyresto" argue the case convincingly.

Blues is perhaps Kenny's strongest and most pervasive attribute. Though he has made a point of emphasizing this asset in song titles like "Midnight Blue," "Fugue 'N Blues," and "K.B. Blues," it's hardly an affectation or hollow gesture. Kenny embodies the blues. Even when operating in the context of standards and complex jazz arrangements, the blues aesthetic is never far from the surface of his music. Moreover, Kenny has a broad artistic palette with many shades of blue, ranging from simple and earnest folk-like pentatonic riffs to supremely greasy funk and sophisticated swinging bop blues. The proof is found in the repertory. Compare his down-home work with organist Jimmy

Smith to the straight-ahead playing on his collaborations with John Coltrane. No wonder he is a favorite among blues guitarists like B.B. King, Otis Rush, and the late Stevie Ray Vaughan.

Ballads find Kenny in a class of his own. Jazz ballads require particular abilities from their interpreter. Sensitivity, beautiful tone, rhythmic elasticity, the ability to double-time in a rubato context, and infinite shadings of dynamics are some of the basics—qualities Kenny has in abundance. And while Kenny is a highly effective and soulful interpreter of ballads within his single-note playing, it is in his harmonic rendering—especially chord-melody statements—that we find remarkable and uncommon depth, color, and profundity. His earliest balladic chord-melody passages in tunes like "But Not for Me" (1956) and "All of You" (1957) set the bar quite high early on.

ESSENTIAL LISTENING

Introducing Kenny Burrell (Blue Note) gathers Kenny's earliest dates as a leader in a two-CD set. *Kenny Burrell* and *Kenny Burrell & John Coltrane* (both on Prestige) are also highly recommended, as is the compilation *Blue Lights, Volumes 1 & 2* (Blue Note) and his first guitar-bass-drums trio session *All Night Long* (Jazz Time, import), an important 1959 live date originally issued as *A Night at the Vanguard* (Chess).

Midnight Blue (Blue Note) is Kenny's crowning achievement and is an indispensable landmark album that personifies his balance of soul jazz, blues, and ballads. Kenny's multi-faceted work in the Verve period of the sixties is exemplified by diverse recordings such as *Blues: The Common Ground, Guitar Forms, Blues Bash,* and *A Generation Ago Today.* Highlights are presented in the serviceable compilation *Kenny Burrell: Jazz Masters 45* (Verve), which includes Kenny's personal commentary on the music.

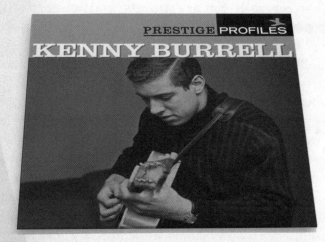

Kenny's work in the seventies is also important. Significant releases include the two-volume tribute *Ellington Is Forever* and *Round Midnight* (Fantasy), *God Bless the Child* (CTI), and *Moon and Sand* (Concord jazz). Later albums, such as *Guiding Spirit* (1989) and *Sunup to Sundown* (1991) (both on Contemporary), *Lucky So and So* (2001) and *Blue Muse* (2003) (both on Concord Jazz), *75th Birthday Bash Live!* (2007, Blue Note) and *Be Yourself: Kenny Burrell Live at the Club Coca Cola, Lincoln Center* (2010, High Note), are highly recommended samples of Kenny's recent work and testaments to his musical relevance.

ESSENTIAL VIEWING

Kenny Burrell is featured in the DVD compilation *Legends of Jazz Guitar* series (Vestapol video/Rounder), both as leader and in a jam with Grant Green and Barney Kessel. Also on DVD are his *Ralph J. Bunche Suite* (UCLA Ethnomusicology Dept) and his appearance in the historic tribute *One Night with Blue Note* (Blue Note).

There are, thankfully, many videos of Kenny Burrell online. Among the choice offerings are "All Blues," "Spring Can Really Hang You Up the Most" (both played on acoustic steel-string), and "Listen to the Dawn" and "Jeanine" (all trio dates from 1990), "Got My Mojo Workin'" and "Organ Grinder's Swing" (1993, with Jimmy Smith's group), "Night in Tunisia" (with Jimmy Smith, Jon Faddis, and James Moody), "A Child Is Born" (duet with Bill Evans, Montreux 1978), "Take the A Train" (with Bill Evans trio), "The Jumpin' Blues" (with Stanley Turrentine and Jimmy Smith, 1985), "Summertime" (with Grover Washington), "Bluebird" (with Tommy Flanagan Quartet, 1991), "Body and Soul" (duet with Flanagan), "Be Yourself"/"Just Sittin' and Rockin'" (a steel-string acoustic solo medley) and "Lover Man" (international jazz festival, 1987), "Things Ain't What They Used to Be" (with Dizzy Gillespie, Sonny Stitt, Thad Jones, and all stars, Japan 1978), "Chitlins Con Carne" (Burrell's Quintet, Dizzy's Club Coca Cola 2008), and several informal newer videos from LA club dates. A compelling new video from a recent Kenny Burrell performance (2010) at the Catalina jazz club finds him jamming the blues with Stevie Wonder on "Stormy Monday."

Sound

Kenny Burrell has one of the most beautiful and recognizable instrumental voices in jazz guitar. Like most jazz guitarists of the fifties, he favored amplified Gibson arch-tops. On his earliest recordings, Kenny used a blonde Gibson ES-175 with P-90 pickups. Kenny is seen in the studio with a single-pickup model on the jacket of *Introducing Kenny Burrell*, ostensibly documenting the guitar he played in the 1956 Blue Note sessions. A double-pickup 175 was pictured on the cover of 1957's *Kenny Burrell*. This may indicate that his earlier single-pickup model had been upgraded to the dual P-90 configuration. During this time, Kenny also added the new tune-a-matic bridge in 1957.

In the late-fifties and early sixties, Kenny moved through a succession of guitars. He briefly experimented with what appears to be a custom blond Gibson L5CES with a bar pickup, Florentine cutaway, and finger tailpiece. This one-off was pictured in the booklet of *Wes Montgomery: the Complete Riverside Recordings*. Kenny used it for his first appearance at the Newport Jazz Festival.

By 1959, Kenny preferred a Gibson L-5 or L-7 (both sporting Charlie Christian bar pickups). The latter was heard on Wes Montgomery's Riverside debut album *The Wes Montgomery Trio* (1959). Kenny loaned the L-7 and his Fender Deluxe amplifier to Wes for the recording session. He also used a D'Angelico New Yorker and an Epiphone Emperor (both fitted with floating DeArmond pickups) before finally settling on the large-body Gibson Super 400CES. The sixties-style Super 400 with an 18-inch body, two humbuckers, and Florentine cutaway has remained Kenny's primary guitar since the late sixties.

Though Kenny played numerous guitars in his long career, the Heritage Super KB is the only instrument to be issued in his name. Based on his trademark sixties Super 400, the Super KB has an 18-inch body, solid carved spruce top and solid figured maple back and sides, Florentine cutaway, five-piece maple neck with a 25 ½-inch ebony fingerboard, gold-plated hardware, and two humbucking pickups. Heritage refinements include an adjustable finger tailpiece, reduced body depth (3 inches), four-point mounted HRW pickups, split-block and full-block inlays, curly maple pickguard, and Kenny's signature on the headstock.

Kenny has preferred tube amplifiers throughout his career. He used various tweed Fender combo models in the fifties, generally employing a smaller Deluxe for recording. For live performance, Kenny played through a tweed Fender Twin or, in early years, a Gibson with

© Raymond Ross Archives CTSIMAGES

a 15-inch speaker. Later, he was known to favor blackface and silverface Fender Twin-Reverb and Super-Reverb amps. He occasionally resorted to a portable solid-state Polytone amp. The current Heritage line boasts two all-tube Kenny Burrell signature amps.

Licks

Fig. 1: Burrell's Bebop 101

This weighty phrase presents Kenny's fleet-fingered modern jazz style of the fifties. Comprised of chromatically inflected single-note lines, which owe an obvious debt to horn players of the era, the up-tempo melody gives you a sample of his improvisation in "This Time the Dream's on Me." This section is played over the bridge, a B7–E7–A7-D7 *cycle of fourths* progression similar to the "Rhythm changes" pattern in G. Throughout, you can readily discern nods to Bird in the lengthy strings of eighth notes and most notably in the wide interval leap and voice-leading melody of measure 4. The chromatic approach via Am7–A♭m7 to the final resolution to G in measures 7–8 is another familiar substitution strategy, often used in turnarounds, indigenous to the bebop language.

FIG. 1.

FIG. 2: BURRELL'S BLUES

By contrast, this idiomatic melody embodies Kenny's blues conception. Inspired by a classic solo from his Blue Note period, it occurs over a swinging, medium tempo groove and a simple 12-bar progression in B♭ This soulful phrase splits the difference between a T-Bone-inspired approach and Kansas City horn riffing. Notice the predominant use of the pentatonic and blues scales for much of the melody as well as the tell-tale arpeggio figures and triplet phrasing, which have for decades distinguishcd the work of the great blues masters—of which Kenny is unquestionably one.

FIG. 2.

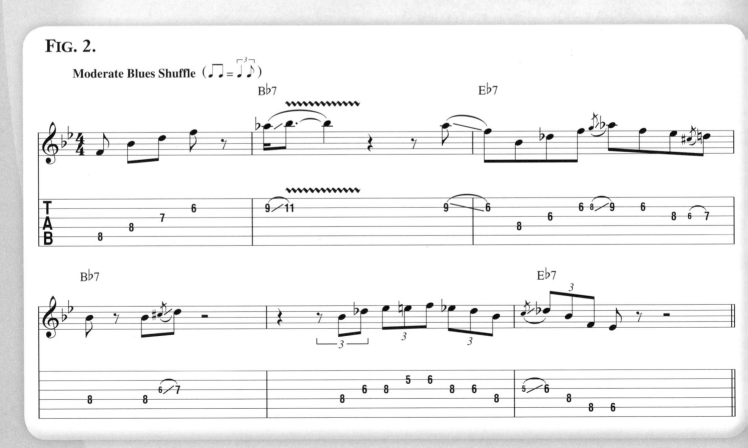

FIG. 3: BALLADIC BURRELL

This is one of the most gorgeous chord-melody moments in his fifties catalog. The phrase is based on the opening section of a standard ballad and finds him setting a hypnotic mood from the outset with a variety of intriguing harmonic devices. Note the contrapuntal effect of his first statement with its independent chromatic melody woven into the inner voice of the D major chord and its inexorable motion to the more remote C13 chord. The chromaticism of E♭maj7 to Dmaj7 is a straightforward modern jazz gesture, but the modal and dissonant extensions on A that follow in measure 3 take on a more exotic impressionistic color. Kenny maintains the heightened musical drama with his use of pedal point and floating ambiguous root-less voicings in measures 4–6.

FIG. 3.

CHARLIE BYRD

© Jan Persson CTSIMAGES

*C*harlie Byrd was one of the most unique and intriguing guitarists in jazz and popular music. He was a promising disciple of Django Reinhardt, a talented composer, and a performer who worked in the theatre with Tennessee Williams' play *The Purification* and on stage with Woody Herman's group. He was a leading proponent of the acoustic guitar as a jazz solo instrument, when everyone else was going electric, and a student of Andres Segovia who sought to merge classical guitar techniques with jazz improvisation. His place in the annals of guitar lore would be assured based just on those merits.

In the 1950s Byrd was already revolutionizing the music with his fusion of jazz and classical guitar elements in a sympathetic trio that included bassist Keeter Betts and drummer Bertel Knox. Their repertory merged traditional combo jazz with Byrd's solo classical guitar pieces. The trio enjoyed great popularity in the Washington D.C. area and soon ascended to the ranks of traveling American jazz ambassadors, sponsored by the State Department. However, Byrd's primary accomplishment will always be viewed as bringing the South American music known as bossa nova to America pop charts and ultimately the world's audiences. In a larger sense, his efforts and success precipitated the now-common genre of world music, then a curiosity and a niche market to most, now a familiar global exchange of cultures. Moreover, with Byrd's recordings, the art of jazz music received another avenue of expression still much in use today, a half-century since Byrd first made his mark with "Desafinado."

2012 celebrates the 50-year anniversary of bossa nova entering the pop culture, facilitated by Charlie Byrd and his collaborator, saxophonist Stan Getz. Their hit single "Desafinado" reached No. 15 on the American Top 40 charts in October, 1962, and was an early cross-over success, one of a handful in jazz. "Desafinado" remained in U.S. pop playlists for 10 weeks and also reached No. 11 on the U.K. charts in 1962. What began as a notion and musical experiment imagineered by Byrd rapidly assumed greater proportions and opened the floodgates for the bossa nova craze that followed. Consider the subsequent outing by Getz and Astrud Gilberto, released as the British Invasion was in full swing. "Girl from Ipanema" climbed to No. 5 in 1964 and won a Grammy for Record of the Year in 1965.

The sound, feel, and approach of bossa nova influenced countless pop stars, performers of all stripes, and famed composers, then and since. The short list includes Frank Sinatra, Ella Fitzgerald, Herb Alpert, Oscar Peterson, Cannonball Adderley, Dusty Springfield, Stephen Sondheim, George Michael, Kenny G, Eric Clapton ("Signe" on *Unplugged*), Nina Persson, Norah Jones, and Diana Krall. Moreover, the success of bossa nova in the U.S.A. set the stage for the importing and international popularizing of local Brazilian composers such as Antonio Carlos Jobim, Luiz Bonfa, Joao Gilberto, Bola Sete, Baden Powell, and Sergio Mendes. It has become evocative of and synonymous with sultry South American beaches, romantic liaisons, and an easygoing tropical lifestyle. In retrospect, Byrd's effect on the world's music has been profound and transcendent and continues to reverberate in practically every corner of the globe.

INFLUENCES

Charlie Byrd began playing the guitar at age nine. He initially studied with his father, who played a variety of fretted instruments. Byrd's early heroes were jazz/swing guitarists Charlie Christian and Django

Reinhardt. He heard and played with Django in Paris in the mid 1940s while in a touring Army show band.

Byrd was initially a plectrum guitarist but became interested in classical guitar and fingerstyle playing in the late 1940s. By 1950, he had devoted himself to the nylon-string instrument. Byrd studied in Washington, D.C. with local jazz/classical guitarist Bill Harris and later with classical master Sophocles Papas. He also studied theory and harmony with musicologist Thomas Simmons. In 1954, Byrd attended a master class in Siena, Italy, given by Andres Segovia.

In 1961, Byrd traveled to South America on a State Department-sponsored tour. There he got the inspiration to combine Brazilian bossa nova music with American jazz elements and his own classical guitar technique. Byrd's early recordings featured compositions by Antonio Carlos Jobim, Luiz Bonfa, Joao Gilberto, and other important Brazilian musicians.

STYLE

Charlie Byrd is immediately recognizable and sonically distinct from his jazz guitar colleagues of the 1950s and 1960s through his use of classically influenced fingerstyle technique and nylon-string acoustic guitar timbre. Originally a plectrum player, he liberally applied finger-picking patterns based on the classical, flamenco, and Spanish guitar techniques and repertory to a jazz context. His fingerstyle articulation of jazz chord sonorities and improvised melodic lines resulted in an uncommon fusion.

Byrd's early background in swing and bop music merged with classical technique made his style unique among jazz players emerging from the traditional swing and bebop schools of the 1940s, and remained so through his lifetime. One example of his merging of classical and popular guitar music was his use of the right-hand index fingertip to strum chords and to create extended tremolo passages as if with plectrum. In other settings, Byrd plucked chords and chord partials to generate impressions of sax/horn section figures or pianistic textures, as in his solo on "Air Mail Special" with the Great Guitars.

Another aspect of Byrd's uniqueness was his application of American jazz sensibilities and classical technique to Brazilian rhythms and repertory. That is arguably his greatest contribution to the form and a combination he kept at the forefront of his music throughout his career. What is distinctive about the bossa nova music Byrd nurtured is the *swaying feel* of the samba pattern, and other Brazilian rhythms with their typical syncopations, as opposed to the *swinging feel* of most mainstream American jazz. Although pieces like "Air Mail Special" proved he never abandoned traditional American jazz, his aesthetic was closely aligned with the South American music he introduced to the U.S.A. in the early '60s. The Brazilian rhythm feeling afforded Byrd and countless musicians of the time a different and more exotic path to explore in their improvisations, still very much in vogue today and indeed an important dialect of jazz and pop music languages.

While improvising in bossa nova tunes, Byrd favored jazz elements. His solos were replete with modern blues licks, swing jazz figures, groove riffs, free modal lines, and bebop melodies. These he phrased as inherently American jazz lines juxtaposed over Brazilian samba rhythms delivered with a classical tone and fingerstyle articulation. Byrd's innate musicianship smoothly reconciled these seemingly disparate ingredients, as exemplified by his many single-note solos in the repertory.

Byrd often interpolated chordal phrases and intervallic patterns into single-note solos. He followed no particular format or template, preferring to expand melodic lines with spontaneous arpeggiations, chords partials, or full chord figures as if accompanying himself. The harmonic source material invariably came from jazz, with its extended and altered chords and characteristic chord progressions, and held true for Byrd's core approach.

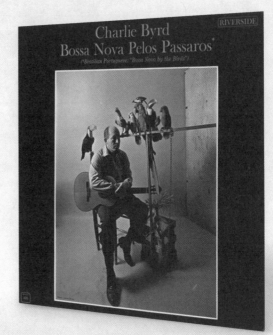

ESSENTIAL LISTENING

Jazz Samba (Verve), a collaboration of Charlie Byrd and Stan Getz, is a must-have recording for any fan of jazz, world, and American music. Released in 1962, it included the early hit "Desafinado" and is widely acclaimed as the seminal bossa nova album. Modern reissues on CD and MP3 contain both the edited pop single and the longer album version. Also recommended are *Brazilian Byrd* (a 2008 reissue originally recorded for Columbia in 1965), Byrd's homage to the master of bossa nova, Antonio Carlos Jobim, and *Bossa Nova Pelos Passaros* (the current Riverside reissue combines material from two classic albums). The latter is a masterpiece of the genre often called Byrd's greatest work.

ESSENTIAL VIEWING

Charlie Byrd Trio: Live in New Orleans (2001), *Charlie Byrd Live at Duke's Place* (1993), and *Great Guitars of Jazz* (2005 with Tal Farlow and Herb Ellis) are highly recommended Byrd performances on DVD. Also worth a look is his instructional video for Hot Licks, in which he details and demonstrates many of his personal concepts and techniques.

Charlie Byrd can be viewed in numerous video clips online. Among the best are his performance with Stan Getz on the Perry Como Show playing "Desafinado" in 1962, various performances with the Great Guitars and his own trio, and clips from his instructional video.

SOUND

Charlie Byrd favored the acoustic guitar for practically his entire career. His main instruments were nylon-string guitars, played with and without amplification systems. His interest in acoustic guitar began early in his career. While on a tour he acquired a Martin gut-string from a pawnshop in the 1940s but did not formally switch to classical guitar until the 1950s.

For many years Byrd played Ovation electric-acoustic classical guitars on stage. In later years his favorite classical was a Japanese-made Kohno. He also played and traveled with Takamine cutaway electric-acoustic guitars. Before making a permanent switch to nylon-string acoustic, Byrd played arch-top acoustics, most notably a custom non-cutaway D'Angelico Excel with a sunburst finish, no position markers, and a floating McCarty finger-rest pickup-pickguard unit.

Byrd used various amplifiers throughout his career. He was seen with small piggyback rigs with Walter Woods heads in Great Guitars concerts. The only amplifier Byrd officially endorsed was a Baldwin combo amp in the late 1960s and 1970s.

LICKS

FIG. 1: BRAZILIAN BYRD

Charlie Byrd's signature blend of jazz harmony, classical fingerstyle articulation, and Brazilian rhythms is at the forefront of this characteristic phrase. The multifarious passage is based on Byrd's intro to Jobim's "Este Seu Olhar" ("That Look You Wear") from *Brazilian Byrd*. Note the free use of plucked chord textures, single-note jazz lines and arpeggio melodies, and sustained arpeggiations. Byrd plucks and

rolls chords in measures 1 and 5–6, while in measures 7–10 he builds arpeggiated figures on F, Gb7, Fmaj7, and F diminished. These are neatly complemented by his sophisticated single-note line in measures 2–5. In this section Byrd addresses the chord changes in a jazz bebop manner, playing arpeggio lines, harmonically related interval leaps and chord-tone skips, and stepwise melody.

FIG. 1.

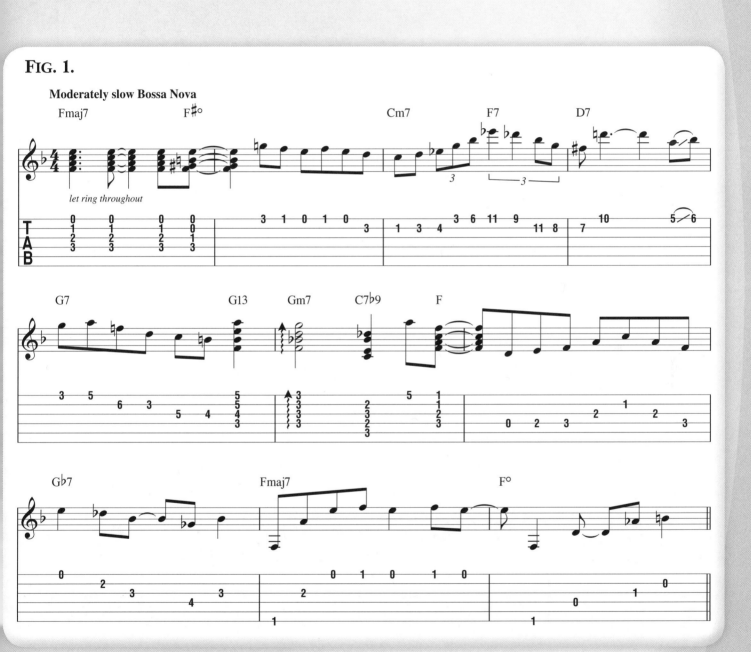

FIG. 2: BYRD IN FLIGHT

Charlie Byrd was a fluent and coherent jazz improviser. This example, based on his solo in "Desafinado" (from *Bossa Nova Pelos Passaros*), makes the case admirably. This is a single-note jazz phrase played fingerstyle. Byrd tends to articulate these types of melodies with a classical rest stroke as in the manner of flamenco guitarists. The passage is played over the standard jazz chord changes of Amaj7–A♯ diminished–Bm7–

E7 in bossa nova rhythm and teems with enumerable Byrd-isms. Noteworthy are the following: a jazz-based reliance on strings of eighth notes delivered with a driving swing feel, numerous blues licks including the closing string bends, chromaticism, and the swing-genre oriented B and F♯ tones (ninth and sixth) and major-pentatonic sounds heard throughout.

FIG. 2.

FIG. 3: BOSSA NOVA CLASSIC

Charlie Byrd's implementation of classical-guitar techniques applied to bossa nova music emerges in this phrase, based on the main riff of "Bim Bom" *(Pelos Passaros)*. "Bim Bom," written around 1956 by Joao Gilberto, is considered to be the first bossa nova song in history. Byrd's interpretation is taken at a fast samba tempo. He exploits his fingerstyle approach throughout, applying standard arpeggiation technique and free strokes to the figurations. Check out the steady eighth-note patterns arranged in *three-against-four* rhythms resulting in typical internal syncopations. Byrd phrases the three-note chord arpeggios in such

a way as to emphasize alternating down beats and up beats, effectively shifting the rhythmic accents along the time line throughout. The chord riff is played in the guitar's nut position and makes copious use of open strings, as is common in the classical repertory. What is less common and distinctly Brazilian is the insistent samba pulse, originally inspired by the swaying footsteps of passing laundresses carrying basket loads on their heads as they crossed a bridge over the Sao Francisco River. Byrd follows with a segue to the main theme that prompts a freer fingerstyle approach to the E7 and A minor chords.

FIG. 3.

CHARLIE CHRISTIAN

© Jan Persson Archive CTSIMAGES

jazz genre, including B.B. King, Chuck Berry, Scotty Moore, Hank Garland, Steve Howe, and Brian Setzer. Indeed, many of his licks are found in the most modern electric blues styles as well as the earliest rock 'n' roll music. In this regard, Christian is unique in the history of jazz. His musicianship is universal, crossing myriad cultural, sociological, and stylistic boundaries. Rarely can that be said of any jazz artist; rarer still can that be said of a jazz guitarist. In retrospect, Christian's legacy today is larger and more pervasive than ever, and his contributions are more profound and worthy of appreciation.

INFLUENCES

A true pioneer, Charlie Christian created his groundbreaking style from diverse sources. He took informal guitar lessons from his father when he was 10 years old and picked up the trumpet a couple of years later. Tenor saxophonist Lester Young had a strong effect on Charlie, who remained a permanent "addict" to his music and was known to scatsing his solos throughout his life. Christian studied guitar with Ralph "Big-Foot Chuck" Hamilton, from whom he learned some basic music theory and the ability to read music. Charlie introduced his boyhood friend, T-Bone Walker, to Hamilton, who taught them together. Hamilton played in the typical chordal style of the period, and it is doubtful that he had any influence on either Christian's or Walker's single-note solo approach. During this time, Walker and Christian, while learning together, played shows as a duo alternating on bass and guitar and most likely developed and shared ideas. Eddie Durham introduced Charlie to the electric guitar in 1937.

*E*veryone playing an electric guitar today owes a tremendous debt to Charlie Christian. Over 70 years ago, his pioneering spirit and quest for "a new sound" led to breakthrough recordings that placed the amplified guitar permanently in the pages of music history. Christian's public exposure came at a time when swing music was at its apex and his employer Benny Goodman was the universally acknowledged "King of Swing." His prominent solos with Goodman's Sextet and the Goodman Orchestra marked the genesis of the electric guitar virtuoso and launched the modern era of jazz guitar. In Christian's hands, the electric guitar became, overnight, an instrument that could contribute to the music on the same level dynamically and artistically as a saxophone, trumpet, or clarinet. Following his appearance and innovations, the guitar was no longer confined to strumming chords in the rhythm section, and a school of stylistic disciples emerged.

Christian's licks and riffs became the lexicon of swing and pre-bop guitar—learned and spread far and wide by players like Barney Kessel, Herb Ellis, Kenny Burrell, Tal Farlow, and virtually every jazz guitarist post-1940. His work also affected pickers outside the

STYLE

Charlie Christian's style was unprecedented in the annals of guitar lore. He combined earthy blues licks with the most urbane jazz lines of the swing genre. His improvisations generally made use of long strings of single notes with articulations and phrasing typical of jazz horn players. A prime identifier is the strong sense of swing in his lines.

Many of Christian's substitutions and note choices, especially those in his extended improvisations during after-hours sessions at Minton's, transcend the strictures of pure swing music and have been called *pre-bop* or *proto-bop*. Christian favored linear playing (motion laterally up and down the fretboard), used down strokes predominately, rested his right-hand fingers on the pickguard, and rarely used the pinky of his left hand.

Essential Listening

Virtually everything Charlie Christian recorded in his short lifetime is essential. At the top of the list are two notable compilations: the single-disc *Charlie Christian—The Genius of the Electric Guitar* (Columbia Jazz Masterpieces) and the four-disc box set *Charlie Christian—Complete Studio Recordings: Columbia, RCA Victor, Vocalion & Blue Note Master Takes* (Definitive Records). Also essential are the various compilations that gather tracks recorded at Minton's, such as *Charlie Christian—Live Sessions at Minton's Playhouse 1941* (Jazz Anthology).

Sound

Charlie Christian chose the Gibson ES-150 for most of his playing. Introduced in 1936, Gibson's first Electric Spanish guitar became immortalized as the "Charlie Christian model." He is known to have played at least three different ES-150s from 1937 to 1942. The ES-150 was a 16-inch non-cutaway acoustic with a carved spruce arch-top. It was fitted with one bar pickup—now generically called a "Charlie Christian pickup"—in the neck position. Charlie adjusted the pickup close to the body, away from the strings, resulting in a warmer, mellower, "stringy" tone with less output. Christian also played the fancier ES-250 guitar announced in late 1939. His friend and colleague T-Bone Walker later favored the 250 in the early forties.

Christian plugged his guitar into Gibson EH (Electric Hawaiian) amplifiers. Of these, he used two models: the EH-150 and the EH-185. The smaller 150 (Style 3) had a 12-inch speaker, six tubes, and an output of 15 watts. The 150 had two controls: volume and a two-position tone change switch for bass or treble sound. The larger 185 had a 12-inch speaker, seven tubes, and an output of 18 watts. Its controls consisted of a volume and a variable tone pot.

What did it sound like? The combination of the bar magnet pickup in the neck position, the resonant hollow body, and the small underpowered amps resulted in a thick, semi-clean tone ideal for Charlie's horn-like lines. Though the amount of sustain and gain would be considered minimal by today's standards, the sound was quite revolutionary at the time and a radical departure from the acoustic guitar sounds heard in jazz previously. The basic tone Christian pioneered in the thirties remains the classic jazz guitar sound to the present.

© CTSIMAGES

LICKS

FIG. 1: CLASSIC CHARLIE CHRISTIAN BLOWING PHRASE

Inspired by saxophone playing, the serpentine contours in this melody are typical of Charlie's arching eighth-note lines and his horn-like conception. These types of licks tend to outline chords, and this one is no exception. Here, Charlie is thinking C7, decorated with all the "pretty" notes. He includes the 9th (D) and the 13th (A) in this phrase, strategically using chromatic passing tones for melodic flow. Two favorite Christian arpeggio motifs are found in this lick: a descending C9 in measure 1 and an ascending C13 in measure 2. The bopping two-eighth-note rhythm as a phrase ending was a common rhythmic motif of swing music and a vital component of the Christian style. Charlie used licks like this in both blues and jazz settings.

FIG. 1.

FIG. 2: SWINGING CHRISTIAN BLUES LICK

The take-off line that begins the phrase was a fixture of the swing style and is now a staple of electric blues. Note the use of rhythm in the punchy repeated notes and syncopation of the first full measure. The string bend in measures 1–2 further exemplifies the blues ethic running through Charlie's playing and clearly presages the work of the first wave of electric blues players. But then, didn't Charlie play electric blues?

Christian's use of the major sixth chord and its related arpeggio permeate this lick. In his style, the 6th tone (F in this example) was favored over the more common ♭7th tone (shades of Albert Collins!). Try this substitution with your own repertory of blues licks for a swing-approved result. The final two measures feature a characteristic Christian phrase ending using both the 6th and major 7th tones.

FIG. 2.

FIG. 3: DEFINITIVE CHARLIE CHRISTIAN LICK IN THE MINOR MODE

Charlie also used the favored 6th tone to color his minor mode improvisations; this lick is a case in point. The melody is in D minor, and its 6th is B. Note that the B is used in both single-note and double-stop phrases. Licks like this are natural in minor blues and tunes written in the minor mode, but Charlie often used them as blues licks in G. This is where the 6th becomes useful from a melodic aspect. It allows the Dm6 to be interpreted as a G9 for more playing possibilities. Double your pleasure! The double-stop riff, with its funky bending in measures 3–5, is an allusion to Charlie's Oklahoma rural blues roots. Subsequently, the idea of bending and slurring double stops inspired countless players—Chuck Berry and B.B. King among them.

FIG. 3.

HERB ELLIS

© Ray Avery CTSIMAGES

and modeled on the Nat Cole trio. He wrote several successful songs while with the band, including "I Told Ya I Love Ya, Now Get Out" and "Detour Ahead." The Soft Winds stayed together for five years and toured extensively.

Following his stint with the Soft Winds, Herb replaced Barney Kessel as guitarist in the acclaimed Oscar Peterson Trio of the mid-fifties. During the five years of this association (1953–1958), he not only contributed to a number of classic Peterson trio albums but also toured with the group for the Jazz at the Philharmonic concerts and participated in important Peterson sessions with Stan Getz, Buddy Rich, and Ella Fitzgerald. When Herb left the trio, it was determined that no other guitarist could replace him, and from that point on, the Oscar Peterson trio—previously a piano-bass-guitar group—became and remained a piano-bass-drums ensemble.

*F*ire, swing, drama, and sophistication are hallmarks of Herb Ellis's eclectic and exciting guitar style. So are deep blues feel, groove, taste, and sensitivity. One of the most soulful and solidly blues-based of the fifties West Coast jazz guitarists, Herb is a role model for countless players—whether they know it or not—and a legend in the genre. In the same milieu that attracted and nurtured out-of-state "transplants" like Barney Kessel, Jim Hall, Howard Roberts, and Joe Pass, the ever grooving Texas-born Ellis was without parallel.

Herb was born Mitchell Herbert Ellis in Farmersville, McKinney (near Dallas), Texas, on August 4, 1921. He began on the banjo and harmonica and picked up the guitar at age ten. Herb played alto sax in his high-school band and later attended the famed North Texas State College, where he helped start a seminal jazz program.

Herb's first professional experiences were with local musicians Jimmy Giuffre, Gene Roland, and Harry Babasin as well as Glen Gray's band, the Casa Loma Orchestra of Kansas City, and Jimmy Dorsey's big band in the early to mid forties. In 1946, Herb formed his own instrumental/vocal trio—the Soft Winds—named after a famed Charlie Christian/Benny Goodman track

In the late fifties and early sixties, Herb established a solo career with albums like *Ellis in Wonderland*, *Nothing but the Blues*, *Herb Ellis Meets Jimmy Giuffre*, *Thank You Charlie Christian*, and *The Midnight Roll*. He settled in Los Angeles and became one of the primary architects of the West Coast jazz guitar school. A fluent, blue-toned jazz soloist and thoughtful accompanist, Herb soon found plentiful work in the Hollywood recording studios and became house guitarist on *The Steve Allen Show* and, later, *The Joey Bishop Show* and *The Merv Griffin Show*. He also participated in numerous jazz-oriented West Coast sessions with the Dukes of Dixieland, Leroy Vinnegar, Victor Feldman, Stuff Smith, Charlie Byrd, and others.

Herb entered a particularly productive and historically important phase in the seventies. He formed a guitar duo with Joe Pass that is considered to be one of the most compatible and influential two-guitar groups in jazz. Their earliest recording, *Jazz Concord*, in 1973 launched Concord Records, subsequently a top label in the genre. Numerous albums with Herb as leader followed in the decade, including *Soft Shoe* (1974), *Hot Tracks* (1975), *Rhythm Willie* (1975), *Pair to Draw* (1976), *Wildflower* (1977), *Soft and Mellow*

(1978) and *Herb Ellis at Montreux* (1979). During Herb's fifteen-year run with Concord, he also continued to collaborate with Joe Pass and other luminaries like Remo Palmier, Freddie Green, Harry "Sweets" Edison, Plas Johnson, and Red Mitchell.

With Joe Pass (and earlier with Charlie Byrd), Herb discovered that two guitars are better than one. In 1974, he upped the ante when he assembled the Great Guitars with Barney Kessel and Charlie Byrd. An awe-inspiring three-guitar jazz ensemble backed by bass and drums, it was the first super-group of its kind and began a rich heritage that later boasted Tal Farlow (who took over for an ailing Kessel in the nineties). With the three elder statesmen of jazz guitar at the helm, the outfit purveyed a potent cross-section of post-Charlie Christian styles, demonstrating their expertise in a diverse range of material—from blues, swing, and bebop to bossa nova and pop re-inventions. Hardly a thrown-together concoction, the Great Guitars was a natural outgrowth of the players' collective histories and shared traditions. Herb's relationship with Byrd goes back to 1964 and their *Guitar/Guitar* collaboration, while his connection with Kessel harkens to the mid-forties and the swing-bebop scene in New York City.

Herb remained active into the nineties and new millennium with such albums as the live concert recording *An Evening with Herb Ellis* (1995), *Burnin'* (1998), and two albums with Duke Robillard: *Conversations in Swing* (1999) and *More Conversations in Swing* (2003). At the same time, numerous re-issues of his classic and previously out-of-print releases began to appear on the market. Today, his music resounds across those generations, remaining influential, appreciated, swinging, soulful, and timeless.

INFLUENCES

Herb's earliest musical influences were the indigenous country sounds heard on local radio shows. Raised on a farm, he initially taught himself guitar by gleaning what he could from a Nick Manoloff book. He was inspired to play electric guitar when he heard George Barnes on the radio. Herb became accomplished enough to enroll in college as a music major. While at college, he heard and fell under the spell of Charlie Christian.

Herb declared himself to be "a direct descendant of the Charlie Christian school." That sweeping influence, which has touched countless other players of his time and genre, is manifest in his swing phrasing, blues content, and rhythmic inventiveness. Herb also admired the guitar playing of Joe Pass, Wes Montgomery, Barney Kessel, Tal Farlow, and Jimmy Raney and further cited tenor saxophonist Lester Young and alto saxophonist Charlie Parker as important role models.

STYLE

Like so many guitarists from the South Western region of the USA—Charlie Christian, T-Bone Walker, Oscar Moore, Barney Kessel, Gatemouth Brown, Freddie King, Albert Collins, and Stevie Ray Vaughan come to mind immediately—Herb Ellis possessed a deep blues feeling coupled with an inimitable sense of swing and command of the jazz lexicon. In fact, the marriage of down-home blues and uptown swing is a prime identifier of his style and sound.

Country blues, as represented by the Southern schools of Texas and Oklahoma, similarly affected his predecessor Charlie Christian, who pioneered the electric guitar and this fusion of styles in Benny Goodman's bands of 1939–1941. The Christian lineage was a cornerstone of forties and fifties swing and bebop electric-guitar styles as purveyed variously by Barney Kessel, Oscar Moore, Tal Farlow, Jimmy Raney, Jim Hall, and Herb Ellis. Arguably, Herb was one of the jazz genre's bluesiest proponents. In his musical pallet reside obvious idiomatic blues gestures like string bends, speech-rhythm licks, and funky double-stop riffs alongside long sophisticated bebop lines from Charlie Parker and Dizzy Gillespie and swing jazz phrases a la Lester Young and Roy Eldridge.

Herb relied on other telling aspects of the blues. One prominent aspect of his style is the use of *call and response* phrase structure, typical of many blues forms. Another is the exploitation of pentatonic and blues-scale melodies in improvisation as well as the heads of tunes, like his own "Haystack Blues." Herb often colored his blues licks and themes with pungent chromaticism, double-timed bebop lines, extended arpeggio melodies, and sax-inspired ornaments and target-note figures. Bottom line: He was as equally at home with long strings of jazzy eighth notes and bop standards as he was with three-chord blues and simple swing riffs.

ESSENTIAL LISTENING

Thankfully, there is now an abundance of classic Herb Ellis music to hear via re-issues. *Gravy Waltz: The Best of Herb Ellis* (Euphoria) is a fine introduction that gathers important out-of-print tracks from the early sixties, including his signature song "Detour Ahead" and a duet with Charlie Byrd, as well as several unreleased gems. *Nothing But the Blues* (1958, Verve) is an undisputed classic—'nuff said. Also worth the search are *Ellis in Wonderland* (1955–1956) and *Herb Ellis Meets Jimmy Giuffre* (1959) (both re-released on Verve). Moreover, no guitarist's library would be complete without at least one Joe Pass/Herb Ellis album. *Jazz Concord* and *Seven Come Eleven* (1973, both on Concord) are highly recommended.

ESSENTIAL VIEWING

Great Guitars of Jazz (with Tal Farlow and Charlie Byrd) and *Detour Ahead* (a musical documentary) deliver superb examples of Herb's playing. Both are currently available as DVDs (Stefan Grossman's Guitar Workshop).

Herb is well represented online with clips from the Guitar Workshop series as well as many rare live performances. Highlights include a *Herb Ellis Medley*, which finds Herb blending a ballad, "It Might as Well Be Spring," with a swinging blues, "Things Ain't What They Used to Be." Also worthy of investigating are "Days of Wine and Roses" (preceded by a brief interview), "Flintstones Theme" with Barney Kessel, "Georgia on My Mind" (a theme song in his career), performances from the classic Oscar Peterson Trio (from *Music in the Key of Oscar*), "I Want to Be Happy" with Ray Brown and Monty Alexander, and various excerpts from Herb's instructional videos.

SOUND

Herb played the same type of guitar for his entire career. Like most straight-ahead jazz pickers of his generation, he favored an arch-top electric-acoustic. Herb played various Gibson instruments—from the ES-150 "Charlie Christian" model to an amplified L5-C (seen in the liner photos of 1959's *Herb Ellis Meets Jimmy Giuffre*). [*Author's note:* Herb's ES-150 was heavily modified over the years, sold to his buddy Howard Roberts in the early sixties who transformed it into the infamous "Black Guitar," and is currently one of my jazz guitars.]

Herb's main instrument was the Gibson ES-175. His first recordings found him playing a 1954 sunburst model with a single P-90 pickup in the neck position. This workhorse was used on the Oscar Peterson Trio recordings as well as his solo albums and session dates. Herb modified the guitar with a Van Eps string damper (adjustable mute) mounted on the headstock and, later, a neck humbucker. He played this instrument from the fifties to 1977 when he began endorsing an Aria Pro II PE-175 Herb Ellis model.

The Aria Ellis model was essentially an upgraded ES-175 with an ebony fingerboard and fancy divided block inlays (like the Gibson Super 400), jumbo frets, a 16-inch body with a Venetian cutaway, Grover keys, gold-plated hardware, an L-5 style tailpiece, and two humbucking pickups. Herb used this guitar until Gibson collaborated with him on the Herb Ellis ES-165, which was introduced in the nineties. The Ellis ES-165 is based on Herb's original ES-175 and sports several refinements, including a single 490R alnico humbucker, laminated maple-poplar woods, gold-plated hardware, and a sixties-style wire trapeze tailpiece.

Herb played a variety of amplifiers in his career. He preferred tube amps in his early years—old Gibsons in the fifties and Emrad Johnny Smith and Benson amps into the seventies. In the mid-seventies, Herb switched to a solid-state Polytone 102 with two 8-inch speakers and a single 12-inch speaker. The Polytone remained his favorite amp through the decades that followed.

Herb strung his guitars with medium-gauge flatwound strings. He used Darco and D'Aquisto brands in the seventies and later preferred Thomastik-Infeld Swing Series flatwounds. Herb favored heavy-gauge picks of no particular brand in a standard pointed shape.

LICKS

FIG. 1: CALL-AND-RESPONSE

This Ellis theme is based on a 12-bar blues melody in A over a rock groove with an implied jazz feel. Note the *call-and-response* phrase structure typical of the blues style. Then note the jazz ingredients: chromaticism in the rising line of measure 1 (pickup to the tonic note) complemented by an A7 arpeggio answer in measure 3. Like many modern jazz and blues tunes, the D7 (IV) is seen through the prism of A minor. Listen for this sound, as well as some funky syncopation, in measures 5–6 and Herb's affectionate nod to Texas twang via a bluesy hammered double stop in measures 7–8.

The completion of the theme is a return to the I chord via a typical V–IV–I pattern. Herb interprets the E as E7#9 in the progression. This simplified cadence links Herb's melodic conception with the simplest form of 12-bar blues. Note the use of arpeggio and stepwise motion in the melody. The ascending A7 arpeggio in measure 9 ends on a G tone, which then becomes the raised 9th of E7. The descending melody that follows in measures 10–11 exploits a strict A minor pentatonic scale, and the closing melody recalls a fragment of the original theme pattern with a pickup containing identical *chromatic approach* tones.

FIG. 1.

Moderately fast Rock

FIG. 2: SWING BLUES

This characteristic solo phrase finds Herb in a funky groove improvising over the first six measures of a 12-bar blues progression in A. It's marked by bluesy, Texas-bred string bending and characteristic major-minor polarity, both of which run through the best blues playing. Check out the *articulated bend* in measure 1 (the first full measure), which is gradually bent to D while picked, as well as the riff-like melody in measure 2 and the simple but effective repeated-note pattern in measures 3–4. The latter lick finds Herb exploring and exploiting the purely rhythmic side of his music. The final arching line is a classic Texas blues melody that T-Bone would be proud of.

FIG. 2.

FIG. 3: BLUESY BEBOP

You'll find a potpourri of Herb Ellis elements in this telling solo line. This melody combines East Coast bebop, Texas blues, and traditional country music. The opening melody is a definitive bop lick inspired by saxophonist Charlie "Bird" Parker. Note the use of *target note* patterns (which target the E and D tones), a favorite ornament (pull-off and slide figure in measures 1–2), and purposeful chromaticism in this section. The soulful line in measures 3–4 contains an earthy half-step string bend and exudes Texas blues flavor.

A country-oriented scalar line in measures 5–6 contrasts Herb's jazz and blues facets. This lick comes off like a bluegrass picker placed in a jazz context. Like Charlie Christian's "Shivers" solo, the winding melody alludes to fiddle tunes such as "Turkey in the Straw" and "Arkansas Traveler." Note the emphasis on the A major scale with a prominent G♯ in the melody and the regular eighth-note phrasing.

FIG. 3.

TAL FARLOW

© Ray Avery CTSIMAGES

INFLUENCES

Born and raised in Greensboro, North Carolina, Talmadge Holt Farlow's first exposure to music was through the indigenous hillbilly and country sounds of the region. At home, his father played guitar, mandolin, and clarinet as a hobby, and his mother played gospel music on the piano.

Essentially self-taught, Tal picked up the mandolin at age nine and quickly progressed to the guitar. His listening was augmented by the mainstream big band, pop, and swing music emanating from the radio. Farlow had no interest in jazz or a desire to be a professional musician until he heard guitarist Charlie Christian with the Benny Goodman Sextet. Christian's late thirties improvisations on the newly-invented electric guitar exerted a tremendous impact and marked a turning point in Tal's life. Thereafter, he purchased a second-hand guitar, installed a homemade pickup made from a pair of radio headphones, and acquired a $20 Sears Roebuck amplifier. He spent his ensuing formative years learning and emulating Christian's riffs and solos from numerous Goodman records.

*T*al Farlow was one of the most important guitar players to surface in the important transitional years between the swing era and the advent of bebop. This was the period in which the electric guitar began its ascendance toward ultimate supremacy in contemporary music. Tal is part of the reason for that pre-eminence.

Tal elevated technical standards seemingly overnight in the fifties while astonishing and influencing legions of jazz guitarists with his extraordinary horn-inspired bop lines and modern conception. After a string of groundbreaking albums in the fifties, his reputation was incontestable and undeniable. He set the pace for subsequent jazz innovators like Howard Roberts, Joe Pass, and Wes Montgomery—all of whom have cited and praised Farlow as an influence. Tal's influence is transcendent and remained a factor into the age of rock, when his chops and ideas inspired players as diverse as Scotty Moore, Hank Garland, John McLaughlin, Alvin Lee, and Steve Howe. Tal Farlow is one of a small handful of legendary guitarists who redefined the sound and approach of the instrument and now resides in the immortal pantheon of guitar greats. His contributions to the art of jazz guitar— make that, *guitar* period—are as large as his enormous hands and have left deep, indelible fretprints for all guitarists to follow.

Other seminal influences included jazz pianist Art Tatum and saxophonists Lester Young, Coleman Hawkins, Don Byas, and Ben Webster. From Tatum, Farlow gleaned a virtuosic and harmonically sophisticated chord conception. From various wind players, he absorbed and cultivated a sax-oriented approach to single-note improvisation. In 1944, while working in New York City, Tal met Chuck Wayne, sideman with the Phil Moore Four and "the first guitarist who was into the new modern music." Wayne gave Farlow some informal tips on jazz guitar.

Later in the forties, Tal was attracted to the revolutionary bebop movement taking place in New York City. He was particularly drawn to the music of alto saxophonist Charlie "Bird" Parker, trumpeter Dizzy Gillespie, and pianist Al Haig, and transferred many of their patented phrases to his instrument. Most of Farlow's subsequent improvisations throughout his career borrowed heavily from the bebop legacy and language. Tal prominently incorporated specific "Bird" licks as part of his regular repertory.

Tal credits his experience with the Red Norvo Trio as significant in developing his speed, single-note improvising skills, and comping abilities. Norvo routinely played standards and jazz tunes at extremely fast tempos, often with complicated guitar-vibes unison lines—something that Farlow had not previously done. His on-the-job training in the trio enabled Tal to burst upon the fifties jazz scene with an unprecedented level of technique.

STYLE

It is widely held that Farlow's playing represents an epic milestone in guitar history. He was arguably the first jazz guitarist to flaunt enviable and formidable technical prowess and one of the earliest to successfully realize and actually apply bebop concepts to guitar. As the early fifties recordings from the Red Norvo Trio demonstrate, Tal was ahead of his time. His ability to improvise long, virtuosic jazz melodies with a genuine horn-based pedigree at excruciatingly fast tempos must have been formed in the forties, when most guitarists were content to recycle Charlie Christian licks. As such, Farlow was a true departure from the norm when first heard—a not-so-missing link to today's technically proficient jazz guitarist—and strikingly different from the simpler swing-oriented pickers of his day. For that, he is most remembered and revered. And for that, he is considered the father of "blowing jazz" on the guitar.

Tal's single-note style was characterized by a modern jazz conception and harmonic sense and fleet, aggressive lines that ventured "outside the box." Naturally endowed with large hands, quick musical reflexes, Herculean stamina, and an Olympian stretch, he was aptly dubbed "The Octopus" by incredulous onlookers. Harnessing this physical attribute to good advantage, Farlow was able to exploit the entire fingerboard in a series of rapid and unerring position shifts within the course of his seamless signature licks—which were frequently several measures in length. Furthermore, his bop melody lines often incorporated unorthodox and unwieldy wide-interval jumps played on a single string, again facilitated with his uncanny stretching capabilities.

Tal employed a standard plectrum style with strong alternating pick strokes and a variety of attacks to articulate most of his lines. He frequently used *legato* technique—pull offs and hammer ons—at fast tempos to impart a smooth horn-like impression to his lines, especially when he wished to connect stepwise passages. Another aspect of Farlow's style was his use of *sweep picking*—a quick single unidirectional stroke to play short arpeggio flurries or chord-like shapes across the strings. This often created a smeared effect akin to glissando runs in saxophone or trumpet phrasing. On occasion, Tal picked with his thumb during solo pieces for a different timbre and softer attack, as on "Lullaby of the Leaves," "Walkin,'" "On the Alamo," and "This Is Always." In the latter, he alternates block chords with thumb plucked single notes during the theme for a prescient Wes Montgomery impression.

In addition to his incredible single-note playing, Farlow also possessed an advanced and unconventional chord-melody style. His use of full modern jazz chords was atypical among guitarists and alluded to an assimilation of pianistic influences and bebop harmony with its emphasis on extended and altered tonalities. With his large hands, Tal played many stretched chord formations that most players couldn't physically reach. He also frequently fretted two strings with the end of a single finger and often used his thumb to fret bass notes on the sixth and fifth strings below these voicings. The resulting chords have confounded many an aspiring jazz guitarist.

Farlow occasionally tuned his A string (fifth string), an octave lower to expand the guitar's range, essentially to have an alternate bass note below the normal low E. This is heard in Tal's famous arrangements of tunes like "Little Girl Blue," "Autumn Leaves," and "Autumn in New York." He replaced his 5th string with a heavier gauge for this trick and generally used thumb fretting on the bass notes while fingering chords above.

Tal was also fond of decorating his lines and chords with *artificial harmonics*, as on the melodies of "Skylark" and "Isn't It Romantic" and the cadenza of "How Deep Is the Ocean." When playing these notes, he would hold the pick with his middle finger and thumb and touch the harmonic with the index finger while plucking the string. As a result of playing in many drummerless trios, Farlow employed a number of techniques to produce a fuller or more varied texture. Perhaps the most notable of these is a percussive "bongo drum effect" (a la Herb Ellis) created by tapping with his right hand on the muted strings of the guitar in rhythm.

ESSENTIAL LISTENING

Tal Farlow (Verve Jazz Masters 41) is a serviceable single-disc compilation culling tracks from his most influential period. Also important are the classic reissues *The Swinging Guitar of Tal Farlow*, *The Tal Farlow Album*, *Autumn in New York*, *The Artistry of Tal Farlow*, *This Is Tal Farlow*, and *Tal* (all on Verve), as well as the later albums *Chromatic Palette* and *Sign of the Times* (Concord Jazz).

In 2004, Mosaic Records released the definitive collection of Tal's most important recordings as a seven-disc box set titled *The Complete Verve Tal Farlow Sessions*. This substantial compilation rivals the similar Joe Pass, Johnny Smith, and Django Reinhardt sets in its luxurious packaging, completeness, and thoughtful liner notes and analysis by Howard Alden. It gathers all of Farlow's tracks for the Norgran and Verve labels and a few Decca dates with Norvo's trio, spanning his innovative work from 1952–1959. Highly recommended.

Also essential are the Tal Farlow Savoy tracks with the Red Norvo Trio, currently issued as *The Red Norvo Trio with Tal Farlow and Charles Mingus: The Savoy Sessions* (Savoy Jazz).

ESSENTIAL VIEWING

Legends of Jazz Guitar, Volume 3 (Vestapol) contains a spirited trio performance of "Fascinating Rhythm" by Tal Farlow, Red Mitchell, and Tommy Flanagan. Tal is also featured on *The Great Guitars of Jazz* (Vestapol) with fellow jazz pickers Herb Ellis and Charlie Byrd. Tal shared many of his concepts and performance tips in *The Legendary Guitar of Tal Farlow* (Hot Licks), a 2006 instructional video, currently unavailable but worth searching for.

Tal Farlow can be enjoyed online in a number of video clips. Prime among these are "All of Me" (with Red Norvo), "Cherokee," and "My Funny Valentine" (with Lenny Breau), "Jordu" and "Flamingo" (with Red Mitchell and Tommy Flanagan), "Autumn Leaves" (1978) and "Misty" (both chord solos), a trio take on "Li'l Darlin,'" "Darn That Dream" (with Louis Stewart), "Lover," "Things Ain't What They used to Be" and "Strike Up the Band" (with Barney Kessel and Charlie Byrd), and "Autumn Leaves" (with Larry Carlton, Larry Coryell, John Scofield, and John Abercrombie).

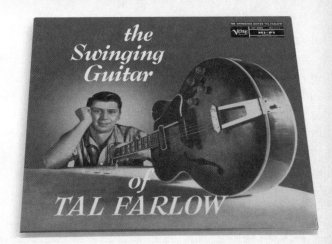

SOUND

A devout "Gibson Boy," Farlow favored Gibson arch-top hollow-body guitars with built-in electronics throughout his fifty-year career. Tal's earliest recordings of note were made with the Red Norvo Trio in 1950–1951. During this period, he played a distinctive modified ES-250. This guitar was a sunburst non-cutaway model with a single "Charlie Christian" bar pickup and a customized short-scale fingerboard. The new fingerboard, built and fitted by master repairman Milt Owen of Hollywood, CA, joined the body at the sixteenth fret. Farlow commented that this modification made the strings feel looser and sound softer, provided two more accessible frets on his non-cutaway guitar, and allowed for an even greater span of the fingerboard. Tal also briefly used a custom-made, bright-red, three-quarter size Gibson arch-top. Designed for the new color television medium, the latter was seen during a TV performance of the Red Norvo Trio on the *Mel Torme Show*.

At the height of his powers and popularity in the mid-fifties, Farlow used a single-cutaway, sunburst ES-350. Known unofficially as "The Tal Farlow model," this was a slightly modified 350. Instead of two P-90 pickups, it was equipped with Tal's preferred "Charlie Christian" bar pickup in the neck position and the customary P-90 at the bridge. Otherwise, this guitar was a standard third-variant model (produced between 1953–1956) with a 17-inch body, individual tone and volume controls, and a three-position toggle switch on the Venetian cutaway horn.

In the early sixties, Gibson launched a trio of prestigious jazz guitars named after the leading players of the fifties: Johnny Smith, Barney Kessel, and Tal Farlow. The official Tal Farlow model was created in 1962 from a sketch made by Tal. Loosely patterned after his ES-350, the guitar has a slightly thinner (3-inch instead of 3 3/8-inch) 17-inch body with a unique scroll inlay on the Venetian cutaway horn, an angular shell pickguard, fingerboard inlays like reversed J-200 markers, a double crown inlay on the headstock (like two adjoining 350 crowns), a trapeze tailpiece similar to the ES-350 with a "Tal Farlow" rosewood insert, and a toggle-switch located near the bridge pickup—an unusual feature on hollow-body arch-top electrics.

The Farlow model was fitted with two humbucking pickups, which accounts for the different tone of Tal's post-1962 recordings. Farlow played a cocoa brown production model from the sixties through the seventies. This original guitar was lost while traveling in 1978. Tal then began playing a 1962 prototype of the Farlow model. This instrument can be recognized by its atypical orange hue and the control knob on its cutaway horn. He also played a standard "Viceroy Brown" (tobacco) sunburst version of the Gibson Farlow model with The Great Guitars.

Like many jazz guitarists in the fifties, Tal plugged into various Gibson tube amps, usually preferring the top-of-the-line GA models. In later years, he favored an old Fender Twin. For live performances, Farlow designed and used a hand-built high stool with a volume pedal mounted under his right foot. This apparatus also housed an octave divider, which produced a second note an octave below the pitch Tal was playing. He applied this effect sparingly in concert.

Farlow used medium gauge flat-wound strings (Gibson or Phil Petillo), kept his action low, played with a light attack, and preferred Gibson heavy picks.

LICKS
FIG. 1: BOPPIN' WITH TAL

This blistering bebop lick is played at a very fast tempo in the key of B♭ major over a characteristic ii–V–I chord progression. The long series of fluid eighth notes is a non-stop line spanning five measures and is typical of the sort of fire Tal created. Tal thinks of complex lines like this as being rooted to a "box" or underlying chord shape. In this case, think of B♭ in the sixth position as "home base." Then select related notes and harmonic extensions above and below to reflect the chord changes of Cm7–F7–B♭maj7. Extended arpeggios are found in measures 1–2 and 4–5. Note the signature wide-interval leap of a 4th—B♭ to E♭—in measure 2. This section briefly jumps into the eighth position to quickly return to the home-base box in measure 4. The chromatic licks in measures 3 and 5 are direct references to Charlie Parker. Bebop sax lines transferred to the guitar are a significant aspect of Tal's style. Also noteworthy are the neighbor-note figure and chromatic passing tones in measure 4.

FIG. 1.

FIG. 2: BURNIN' WITH TAL

This aggressive lick depicts Tal's improvising in a minor key—D minor in this case. The high-velocity phrase takes place over a V–i change (A7 to Dm), which is found in minor blues and countless minor-mode standards and contains a satisfying balance of bebop melody and riff activity. The opening line in measures 1–2 is pure bop. Filled with purposeful chromaticism and arpeggio outlining, it implies the chord sound of B♭m7 superimposed on A7—a familiar bebop substitution. Note the abundant slurs, pull-offs, and slides in this section. Tal changes gears in measures 3 and 4. Here, he drives home a burning six-note riff (A–C–E–C♯–D–F) with a relentless series of pattern

repetitions. Note the shift from the second to the third position in the C♯ to D portion of the pattern. This passage indicates an ascending slide with the first finger on the second string. Tal generally uses a "rolling barre" technique to play across the strings for figures like the C and E notes in the riff. The finger is lifted after the first note is fretted and quickly rolled on to the higher note at the same position. A third notable aspect of the riff is the stretched descending leap of F to A to start repetitions of the pattern. Together, these ingredients provide a capsule view of Tal's highly effective and idiosyncratic fingering—the key to the fluidity of his playing.

FIG. 3: CRUISIN' WITH TAL

Several sides of Tal's far-reaching style are present in this phrase. The line is played in the key of C major in a straight eighth-note feel and is positioned around the home-base box at the eighth fret. The influence of Charlie Christian can be heard in the melody of measure 2—particularly the swing-oriented emphasis of the 6th tone (A) and the F–D♯–E melodic-encircling figure. Both were key aspects of Christian's approach. The line in measure 3 is all Tal, however, and exploits the wide-interval sound he pioneered. Note that the figure requires a wide hand stretch of a tritone—six frets—and produces a diminished arpeggio outline in its course. The consistent use of G♭ (the ♭5th note in C) in measures 3 and 4 imparts a nice, contrasting blues sound to the melody, offset again with bebop ideas in 4–6. Tal's trademark sweep-picked articulation is found in measures 3 and 6. Note both ascending and descending forms of the raking technique in the phrase.

FIG. 3.

FREDDIE GREEN

© Ray Avery CTSIMAGES

What's at the heart of jazz? Here's a hint: Rhythm that moves you. For five decades, guitarist Freddie Green provided the irresistible rhythmic pulse that propelled the fabled Count Basie band to greatness. His style and sound set standards in rhythm guitar, and his legacy has yet to be matched.

Freddie Green played the kind of rhythm that works. Described as music you *feel as much as hear*, his guitar approach is marked by a strong though selfless confidence and an inherent correctness that paradoxically defines and breaks the rules. What does all that mean? For one thing, Green is the paragon of rhythm guitar. He was the ultimate team player. In his fifty-year tenure with the Count Basie band, Green almost never took a solo—chordal, single-note, or otherwise. He played acoustic guitar exclusively and was content to be the timekeeper and glue that held the superlative Basie rhythm section together. Put another way: Green was the master of linking bass with drums while steering clear of the shouting horns and the Count's expressive tinkling fills. And that takes some doing.

Freddie Green rarely gets the accolades he justly deserves. In the history of jazz guitar, there are many obvious giants, but Green's name is not often placed on the short list. Consider the literature. Much of it is devoted, rightfully, to highly visible and often touted single-note heroes like Barney Kessel, Tal Farlow, Jim Hall, Pat Martino, and Grant Green—not to mention influential chord-melody stylists such as Johnny Smith, George Van Eps, and Joe Pass. Important innovators like Charlie Christian, Django Reinhardt, Wes Montgomery, Kenny Burrell, and George Benson made their marks on the genre and are now iconic and venerated. In this milieu, the work of a guitar master like Green remains unheralded, except among a handful of savvy listeners, appreciable players, and well-informed scholars. Why? It's because Green devoted his life and efforts to the essential but virtually invisible role of rhythm player. And it comes back to that central point and governing maxim: the most effective rhythm guitar is unobtrusive. It is felt as much as heard.

The great impresario John Hammond, who was responsible for discovering Stevie Ray Vaughan, Benny Goodman, George Benson, Bob Dylan, and Charlie Christian (among others), heard Green in a Greenwich Village nightclub and swiftly recommended him to the Count Basie Orchestra as a replacement for Claude Williams. Green was hired after a brief audition in 1937 and remained with the outfit until his death in 1987. During the fifty-year association, he epitomized the art of big-band rhythm guitar, distinguishing himself with Basie's ensembles and as a studio player on sessions for luminaries such as Lester Young, Lionel Hampton, Benny Carter, and Benny Goodman. However, Green's work with the Count Basie band remains definitive and legendary, represents the lion's share of his legacy, and is exemplified by his contributions to landmark albums like *April in Paris*, *Atomic Mr. Basie*, *Chairman of the Board*, *Everyday I Have the Blues*, *Super Chief*, *Sixteen Men Swinging*, *First Time! The Count Meets the Duke*, and *The Count Swings, Joe Williams Sings*.

INFLUENCES

Born Frederick William Green in Charleston, South Carolina, on March 31, 1911, Freddie Green began playing tenor banjo in the era of classic jazz. Back in the day, banjo was the preferred accompaniment instrument for the jazz and popular ensembles. In his youth, Green was encouraged by his father's friend, a pro trumpeter, to think ahead; take up the guitar and study music. Following the death of his parents, he moved to New York City at age twelve to live with an aunt. There he attended school and then worked as an upholsterer by day while mastering the guitar by night. During his formative years, Green briefly studied with famed rhythm guitarist Allan Reuss (of Benny Goodman, Paul Whiteman, Jimmy Dorsey fame) in his NYC studio.

STYLE

What's behind the Freddie Green style? For one thing, there is the physical nature itself. Green set up his guitars with very high action and heavy strings (using at least an .012 or .013 on the high E). This made the instrument difficult to play but resulted in much more volume and greater tension on the strings. Green played traditional pick-style rhythm guitar and favored a pulsating *four-to-the-bar* groove, with each quarter note in a measure marked by a firm down stroke.

Guitarist Will Mathews, Green's successor with the Count Basie band, has studied the Green style and techniques closely and done considerable research. His investigations revealed that Green accented his quarter-note pulse by strumming beats 1 and 3 closer to the neck and strumming beats 2 and 4 closer to the bridge. His right-hand technique resembled a sweeping stroke originating from the wrist. Green's left-hand technique has further been likened to a "pumping" motion, synchronized with the right-hand strum strokes. This describes strumming combined with pressing and relaxing of fretting pressure, which naturally produces a percussive effect with efficient left-hand muting. Judicious left-hand muting is central to Green's rhythm guitar style and sound.

Many scholars and experts on Green's style have referred to his most definitive playing as "minimalist." This descriptor alludes to the idiosyncratic fingering of simple three-note chords with only one note in the chord fully fretted to produce a definite pitch. Video documentation of Green's playing reveals that, while fingering full three-note chord shapes, he actually frets only a single note within the chords, generally on the fourth string. The rest of the strings are skillfully muted in a remarkable musical sleight of hand. This minimalism and the exploitation of "one-note chords" are correspondingly thought to distinguish the majority of his rhythm guitar phrases. The advantages for Green, the guitarist, are obvious: easier fingering, similar hand shapes, fewer wrist rotations, and the highlighting of the most important tone in a chord voicing. Additional musical benefits include a less separated sound between chord changes, smoother transitions, less texture in the chord but more presence, and fewer conflicts with piano chords or bass line notes.

Green was renowned for his ability to blend with the rhythm section and the overall ensemble; that was his specialty. He rarely used higher extensions (9ths, 11ths, 13ths) or altered tones (flatted or raised 5ths and 9ths) in his voicings, realizing that these would clash with the horns and piano chords. Instead, Green favored basic seventh chords. He tended to voice these chords in their basic form as tight three- and four-note forms, often in open-position *divided voicings* (chord maven George Van Eps' term) with a deadened string separating the lowest note from the upper two. Other tunes saw him voicing chords as three-note shapes on the lower string sets. While these chords would sound muddy and bass-heavy on an electric arch-top, particularly with the jazz guitar's customary dark tone, Green was able to make the voicings quite effective, usable, and indeed appropriate on an acoustic guitar with his skilled use of minimalist fingering and strategic left-hand muting.

ESSENTIAL LISTENING

Count Basie's classic albums are essential in any collection reflecting the music of Americana. Among the most essential are *April in Paris* (Verve) and *The Complete Atomic Basie* (Roulette Jazz), both of which feature Freddie Green in his prime with a rare prominent chordal moment in "Li'l Darlin" on the latter. Worth investigating is "The Elder," a rare Freddie Green flight with Count Basie containing atypical chord-melody fills, currently posted online.

ESSENTIAL VIEWING

Count Basie's catalog, and Freddie Green along with it, is well represented online. Classics like "One O'clock Jump," "April in Paris," "Corner Pocket," "Things Ain't What They Used to Be," "The Start of Something Big," and "Whirly Bird" are among the highlights. Particularly noteworthy and revealing is the rare Basie Quartet clip, "I Don't Know," from 1968, which provides interesting views of Green's technique in several camera passes.

SOUND

The Freddie Green sound remained consistent during his fifty-year reign. Throughout his career, Green played acoustic guitar and rarely used a microphone, generally only in the studio. Like most swing and jazz guitarists, he preferred arch-top hollow-body instruments. In his early professional years, Green played large-bodied Stromberg arch-top guitars. In time, his favorite instrument grew to be the Gretsch Synchromatic 400, a top-of-the-line large bodied (18-inch width) non-cutaway orchestra guitar, comparable in size and appointments to the luxurious Gibson Super 400. This guitar was introduced in 1939 and is easily identified by the unique bound cats-eye sound holes (instead of the typical F holes), the wider flanged Synchronized bridge, and its graduated Chromatic tailpiece.

By the early sixties, Gretsch's Synchromatic models were phased out, and the company's ads and literature of the period saw Green endorsing the Eldorado: a smaller 17-inch acoustic arch-top. However, Green continued to use his Synchromatic model. In 1985, the revitalized Gretsch Company restored the Synchromatic to its product line as a revamped 17-inch model. In 2002, Fender Musical Instruments Corporation acquired the company and has continued to offer the Synchromatic G400 into the new millennium—largely a testimony to Green's lasting influence, as he is the only notable player to be associated with the guitar.

LICKS

FIG. 1: CLASSIC FREDDIE-STYLE

This rhythm guitar phrase presents a user-friendly pattern with major, minor, and dominant seventh chords voiced in the typical spread form favored by Freddie Green. George Van Eps called these shapes *divided voicings*, referring to the physical division created by the deadened fifth string in the fingering arrangement. These chord forms require the player to mute all other strings with the fret hand. Green's muting is indicated by Xs in the tablature staff. Notes on the sixth and third strings are placed in parentheses, signifying the typical approach of judiciously "ghosting" these pitches while fingering the overall chord shape. (This muting also pertains to chord phrases in Figures 2 and 3.)

Muting is part of the tone, texture, and timbre of the voicings in Green's strummed rhythm style. Moreover, muting keeps errant open strings from ringing and guarantees a clean sound. This example casts the Freddie Green style in a characteristic chord progression, based on the first phrase of the old standard "Tea for Two," and presents a favorite move. The chords in the first two measures exploit the ii–V progression and employ divided voicings in A♭ major. An essential variant is found in measure 4. Here, the divided voicing idea is expanded to create a *first-inversion* major chord (A♭/C) and a chromatic passing chord (C♭°7) headed to B♭m7. This device occurs often in Green's playing and is typical of downward-bound progressions in his style.

FIG. 1.

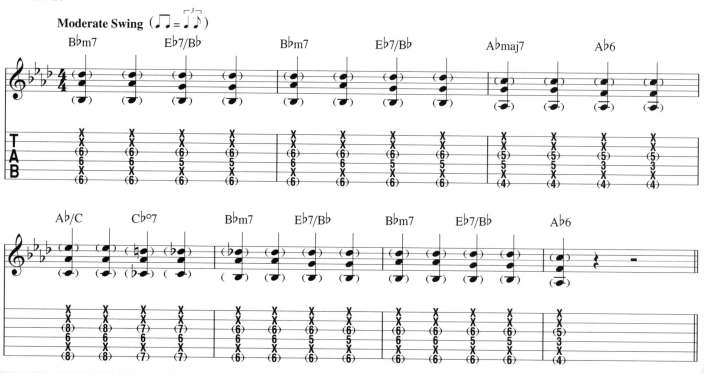

FIG. 2: FREDDIE'S GOT RHYTHM

Many jazz composers have exploited "Rhythm" changes. The process results in a *contrafact*: a jazz composition based on the chord changes of an extant common standard, like the 12-bar blues progression. This excerpt taps into the familiar chord progression of "I Got Rhythm"—which might as well be Freddie Green's lifelong motto. Here, the chords are structured in familiar divided voicings—this time with inner voice activity. They change quickly and ascend up the fingerboard with characteristic connective diminished chords in measures 1 and 2, which produce chromatic "push" chords (B°7 and C#°7) into the ii chord (Cm7) and the first inversion I chord (Bb/D). The sequence in measures 3 and 4, while part of the progression, presents a typical Green descending pattern and is frequently found as a *turnaround* in his style.

FIG. 2: FREDDIE'S BLUES

This demonstrative phrase is based on the first half of a 12-bar blues progression in F—Freddie Green style. The familiar F/C–F7/C move begins the proceedings and sets up the IV chord, Bb7, and a typical minor-to-diminished cadence (Bbm6–B°7) in measure 2. Measures 3 and 4 contain a characteristic Freddie Green variation for the dominant seventh in the blues. Here, a ii–V (of Bb), Cm7–F7/C, is harnessed to color the progression to the IV chord.

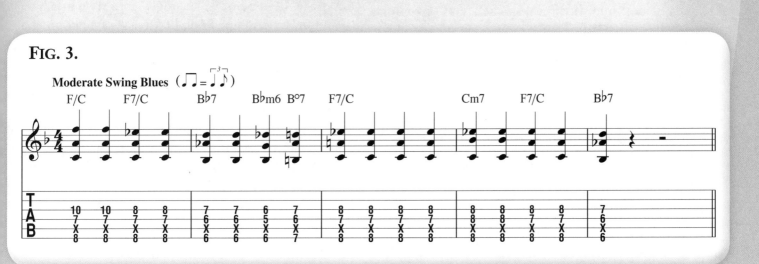

GRANT GREEN

© Jan Persson Archive CTSIMAGES

Grant remains one of the all-time greats of the instrument and an icon to generations of musicians and listeners—whether they know it or not. His innovations have affected virtually every style after 1960 and continue to do so to the present.

INFLUENCES

Grant Green's earliest musical influences were from his father and uncle. Both played blues guitar, and Grant was prompted to take up the instrument and the blues repertory at an early age. He also claimed guitarist Charlie Christian and alto saxophonist Charlie "Bird" Parker as role models. Christian's single-note horn-like style certainly shaped Grant's own conception on the guitar, while Bird's complex bebop lines provided key melodic elements that enlarged his harmonic palette. Green also listened to and assimilated aspects of Miles Davis's and Jimmy Raney's melody-conscious, understated styles. Underneath the lofty jazz elements, one can always detect a solid blues ethic at work in his playing—the result of his earliest influences remaining most profound as his approach evolved over the years.

Green came of age musically in his native East St. Louis area. There he built a formidable soul jazz style as a teenager while gigging with the town's leading gospel, blues, rock 'n' roll, R&B, and jazz groups.

STYLE

Grant Green's unique mixture of bebop, blues, and funk distinguished him as the quintessential soul jazz/hard bop guitarist from the get-go. In the early sixties, he favored a horn-like single-note style in which the guitar functioned much like a jazz saxophone in a group context.

Grant was a master of phrasing. He employed slides and slurs extensively to impart a breathy wind-like quality to his lines, added the occasional string bend at the appropriate moment, and frequently applied finger vibrato, especially on long notes at the end of key phrases. His vocabulary at the time included long sophisticated Bird-inspired jazz passages as well as gritty down-home blues licks, catchy swing riffs, and diatonic modal melodies.

Despite his affinity for complex bebop, Green cultivated a melodic and uncluttered improvisation style that made him very accessible to a rock and pop audience. In this period, Grant's repertory predictably consisted

Grant Green enjoyed two distinct careers in music. The first flourished in the early sixties and found him active in the New York hard bop and soul jazz scene. Grant was the "house guitarist" then at the Blue Note label and was recorded often as both a leader and as a sideman for important artists like Hank Mobley, Sonny Clark, Ike Quebec, Stanley Turrentine, Lou Donaldson, Baby Face Willette, and Larry Young. His playing at the time was fresh, spirited, and pivotal to the new post-bebop streams in jazz. Countless guitarists have claimed inspiration from Green's contributions in this era.

After 1967, Grant Green was a prime exponent of the burgeoning funk movement in jazz. During this phase, his work veered off in a more commercial and pop-oriented direction, yet his playing was no less influential. Grant's current reputation as one of the "most sampled guitarists" arose from this period. Over the last few years, his licks have found new life, albeit as fragmentary borrowings, in the hip hop and modern pop genres as evidenced by the Grant Green samples on tracks by Us3, Public Enemy, 3rd Bass, May May, Youngblood, Cypress Hill, A Tribe Called Quest, and even Madonna on her "Forbidden Love" hit.

of standards and show tunes, pretty ballads, hard bop and soul jazz compositions, and straightforward blues. Unlike most of his contemporaries on the instrument, chord melody pieces are rare in Grant's catalog—the brief unaccompanied intro to "Little Girl Blue" is one such atypical moment.

Grant was fond of placing earthy blues clichés and repetitive rhythmic figures into his solos. He frequently used heady devices like motivic development, rhythmic displacement, augmentation, diminution, and imitation to expand these ideas in his improvisations. Grant was also fond of using short fragmentary snippets and ornamental trill-like figures as embellishment, punctuation, and primary melodic material. He often developed the patterns as riffs in longer syncopated episodes. These elements became fixtures of his style and were heard in modal solos like "Wives and Lovers" and "My Favorite Things."

In the late sixties and seventies, Grant favored a funk/R&B approach and enjoyed playing over rock grooves and extended vamps. These vamps were often lengthy one-chord affairs, which placed a greater emphasis on his rhythmic and textural resources. There, Grant relied heavily on pentatonic and simpler modal melodies (for example, the Dorian mode in a minor tonal center), blues sounds, intervallic motifs, double stops, and tonally grounded but rhythmically charged riffs. His playing in this period inspired many upcoming guitarists of all stripes, including George Benson, Pat Martino, Peter Bernstein, Joshua Breakstone, Melvin Sparks, Carlos Santana, Robbie Krieger, Tony Iommi, Andy Summers, and Stevie Ray Vaughan among them.

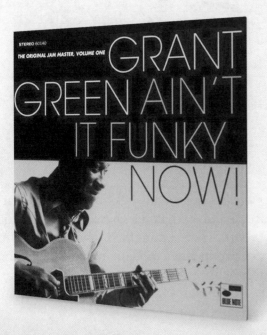

ESSENTIAL LISTENING

The Best of Grant Green, Volume 1 and *Volume 2* (Blue Note) comprise a fine introduction to and overview of Grant's music. These discs neatly separate his two stylistic periods—hard bop/soul jazz of the sixties and funk/R&B of the seventies—and provide definitive examples of his work in varied genres. Also essential are Grant's recordings with pianist Sonny Clark and organist Larry Young. The former are found in *The Complete Quartets with Sonny Clark* compilation and *Born to Be Blue* (both on Blue Note). The latter can be heard on *I Want to Hold Your Hand*, *Talkin' About*, *Street of Dreams*, and *Into Something* (Larry Young as the leader) (all on Blue Note).

ESSENTIAL VIEWING

Grant Green's appearance on the *Legends of Jazz Guitar, Volume 2* (Vestapol videos) is a rare treat and highlight of the program. There he is captured playing the blues ("Blue Mist") in a live 1969 jam session with fellow jazz guitarists Kenny Burrell and Barney Kessel. This video performance is currently the only live clip of Grant Green online—highly recommended.

SOUND

Grant Green played a number of instruments throughout his career. Many photos from his classic Blue Note jazz years (1961–1966) picture him with a Gibson ES-330TD. This was a budget model that landed somewhere between Gibson's entry-level archtop electrics like the ES-175 and semi-hollow thinline guitars such as the ES-335. The ES-330TD, made from 1959 through 1972, had a thin (1¾ inches deep), fully hollow double-cutaway body with a neck-to-body juncture at the sixteenth fret, two P-90 pickups, and a trapeze tailpiece. Grant played the earliest version (manufactured between 1959 and 1962) with a stock sunburst finish, dot-inlaid fingerboard, and black plastic pickup cover.

Grant also played a blond Epiphone Emperor and a sunburst Gibson L-7, each equipped with a floating "McCarty" finger-rest pickup system. These older non-cutaway arch-top acoustic guitars are featured on the covers of *Born to Be Blue* and *The Complete Quartets with Sonny Clark*. By the mid-seventies, Green acquired a James D'Aquisto hand-made arch-top guitar. This was the New Yorker Deluxe model with a single-cutaway body, a low-impedance Bill Lawrence pickup, and mother-of-pearl "GG" inlays on the fingerboard. Green strung his guitars with light-gauge flat-wound strings and employed a small heavy pick.

Grant was photographed often during various sixties Blue Note recording sessions. Many of these photos are published in Sharony Andrews Green's book *Grant Green: Rediscovering the Forgotten Genius of Jazz Guitar* (Miller Freeman). By viewing the shots, it's possible to draw some general conclusions about his sound in the period. Though pictured with a variety of amplifiers at the time, Grant seemed most frequently to use an Ampeg combo amp (seen on the cover of *The Complete Quartets with Sonny Clark*) and a larger Fender narrow-panel, tweed combo amp (most likely a late-fifties Pro, Bandmaster, or Bassman). In the early seventies, he began using a Gibson Les Paul LP-12 amp with four 12-inch speakers and two 10-inch horns.

LICKS

FIG. 1: GREEN BOP

Grant Green was one of the most solid bebop jazz guitarists in history. Many of his innovations are based on the direct transfer and adaptation of horn licks from sax and trumpet players to guitar. This process of borrowing is part of the jazz tradition and standard practice for all instrumentalists from all instrumentalists. This phrase exploits some of Green's favorite bop melodies through chord changes. The underlying tonal center is E♭ major, and the changes reflect typical harmonic patterns found in standards and jazz compositions. Several factors are noteworthy. *Chromaticism* is used generously throughout for melodic flow and to add necessary tensions to basic scales and arpeggios. The *voice-leading figure* in measure 2 is a signature lick and is followed by an essential altered-scale line in measures 2–3. The slurred motif in measure 3 is a direct quote of his idol, Charlie "Bird" Parker. Like many seasoned bop players, Green uses the *F harmonic minor scale* to generate motion from C7 to F minor. That's what you'll find in measures 4–5. The intervallic melody at the conclusion is one of Grant's favorite phrase endings.

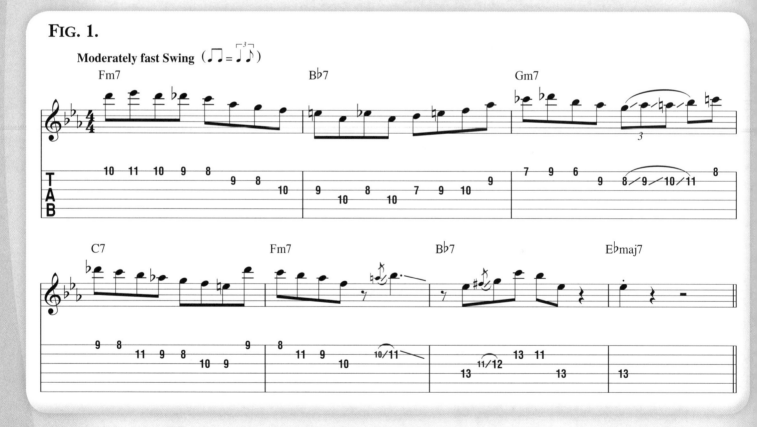

FIG. 1.

FIG. 2: GREEN BLUES

This lick is played over a moderately fast and fiercely swinging groove in B♭ and is typical of Grant's blues conception. The phrase combines a Charlie Christian-inspired swing feel and note choices with an unmistakable leavening of bebop. Note the typical Green inflections in the line: the raked arpeggio in the first measure, and the legato embellishing figure in measure 2. Also telling in measure 2 is the *voice leading figure*—a favorite lick in the Green arsenal. Measures 3 and 4 contain a characteristic approach to the IV chord. Here, Grant begins with a rising A♭maj9 arpeggio, producing a modally based B♭13 sound, and concludes with a descending altered scale line. The melody in measures 5–6 is a classic Christian line reinterpreted by Grant.

FIG. 2.

FIG. 3: GRANT FUNK

This lick exemplifies the sort of excitement Grant generated over a driving one-chord rock vamp. The phrase is played in F minor and makes use of many noteworthy traits of his later years. Chief among these are the reliance on minor pentatonic and blues scale licks, riff-based melodic structure, rhythmically based patterns, imitation, and double stops. The repeated legato figure in measure 3 is a staple of his style and was ubiquitous in his improvisations post–1966.

FIG. 3.

JIM HALL

© Raymond Ross Archives CTSIMAGES

Lyricism is a quality often attributed to jazz guitar legend Jim Hall. There is definitely something resonant and fitting in that descriptor. For many listeners and admirers, Hall's burnished tone and understated approach connote the sonic equivalent of watercolors, haiku, or gentle poetic lyrics. Known as much for the notes he doesn't play, Hall is a complete original. That delicate, sensitive style, with its exquisite note choices, introspective moods, and disciplined restraint, has been his calling card and lasting legacy as generations of ostentatious technicians have come and gone through the turnstiles of history.

In his nearly fifty-year musical sojourn, Hall has distinguished himself as one of the most unique and recognized stylists in the jazz genre and one of its most sought-after sidemen and collaborative partners. The proof is in the pudding. Just check out any of the many Jim Hall solo releases since 1957. Or consider his contributions to the music of the giants. Hall has worked with some of the greatest names in jazz spanning various epochs and stylistic tangents—from venerable classics like Sonny Rollins, Ella Fitzgerald, Lee Konitz, George Shearing, Paul Desmond, Art Farmer, and Bill Evans to current modernists such as Larry Goldings and Pat Metheny.

Accolades abound. The legendary Sonny Rollins calls him "the greatest guitarist in jazz," while Pat Metheny echoes the sentiment with his own accolade of "the greatest living jazz guitarist." Great minds think alike. Some esteemed critics compare Hall's significance and stature with that of Charlie Christian and Django Reinhardt, while Paul Desmond ("Take Five") has compared him to Pablo Casals. Others have referred to his unique and multi-faceted blend of depth, abstraction, finesse, and taste as cubism reduced to guitar playing. Picasso would have loved that analogy.

Hall's music is transcendent. Though he has influenced legions of jazz guitarists, in the ranks of traditionalists he has found a particularly receptive audience among newer exponents—interested, like him, in pushing the envelope. Put pioneers like Bill Frisell, John Abercrombie, Mick Goodrick, John McLaughlin, Bill Connors, John Scofield, and Pat Metheny in this group. Outside the jazz genre, Hall has crossed over to touch disparate players in pop, blues, and rock like Denny Dias (of Steely Dan), Jon Mark, and Boz Scaggs.

INFLUENCES

Jim Hall grew up in a musical household and became involved with music at an early age. His mother played piano, his grandfather the violin, and his uncle the guitar. Hall received his first guitar at age ten and by thirteen was working as a professional musician, obtaining considerable on-the-job training with bands in his local Cleveland area.

Like many guitarists of his day, Hall was initially drawn to the instrument through Charlie Christian—particularly "Grand Slam" and "Solo Flight"—and was also inspired by Django Reinhardt, George Van Eps, and Oscar Moore. His later guitar favorites included Tal Farlow, Barney Kessel, Jimmy Raney, Howard Roberts, and Wes Montgomery.

Hall has also cited saxophone players Ben Webster, Sonny Rollins, Dexter Gordon, Coleman Hawkins, Lucky Thompson, Al Sears, Paul Gonzalez, Wardell Gray, and Don Byas as influential as well as bandleader/composer Duke Ellington and pianist Bill Evans.

Hall graduated from the Cleveland Institute of Music with a bachelor's degree in 1955. There he studied music theory and concentrated on classical composition. Upon completion of CIM, he moved to Los Angeles where he attended UCLA and studied classical guitar with local legend Vicente Gomez. As a result of his experiences with contemporary classical music, Hall was affected by modern composers Bela Bartok, Paul Hindemith, Claude Debussy, and Igor Stravinsky as well as atonalists like Alban Berg and Arnold Schoenberg.

Hall was also influenced by rhythm guitar. Brazilian guitar music ranks high in his esteem. He points to the bossa nova and samba styles of Joao Gilberto and Antonio Carlos Jobim as well the classically tinged style of Laurindo Almeida, the fantasies of Egberto Gismonti, and the compositions of Heitor Villa-Lobos. He also admired the rhythm guitar playing of Freddie Green, Barry Galbraith, and folk rocker Richie Havens.

STYLE

Hall's relaxed, economic style placed him in the ranks of the cool jazz movement when he first made his appearance in 1955. However, true to his vision, he never aligned himself with one particular musical trend. Instead, his novel use of varied textures, unusual intervals, rhythmic devices, and fresh jazz-based melodic lines seemed in the following years to be well-suited to a number of styles—from straight swing to contemporary post-bop, avant-garde jazz, and classically-oriented third stream.

Hall's basic musical pallet draws on the traditions and timbre of forties and fifties jazz guitar. His sound is the same warm arch-top tone associated with players like Charlie Christian and Wes Montgomery, and he strives for a similar harmonically advanced melodic and chordal approach. This is reflected in his penchant for Christian-influenced legato lines with horn-like contours, sweep-picked arpeggios often implying extensions like 11ths and 13ths and substitute harmonies, and a loping behind-the-beat sense of swing. Though rooted in traditional post-bop, Hall is also comfortable with modernistic dissonance and frequently exploits angular intervallic lines.

Hall's solo improvisation approach is noteworthy. Thematic development is one of his guiding principles, and he is renowned for the ability to create extemporaneous melodies of great unity and balance at will. It is often remarked that his improvised solos sound so logical they seem composed.

Hall is fond of employing ghost notes to decorate a phrase and to impart terraced dynamic inflections. He uses space, timing of melodic entrances and exits, rhythmic punctuation in the form of staccato versus legato articulation, subtle pitch bends, and across-the-barline phrasing as part of his regular MO. These ethereal qualities translate into the nuanced and delightfully idiosyncratic style he has created.

Jim is also an expressive and sensitive chord-melody player, as exemplified by such moments as his unac-companied intro in "I'm Getting Sentimental Over You." Offering a capsule view of his well-textured lead-rhythm conception, this chord-melody prelude contains interesting contrapuntal lines and ad lib counter melodies that expound on and transform his pure chordal statements. Hall favors post-bop harmonies with quartal and quintal chords (built from 4ths and 5ths, respectively), often rootless, and smaller two or three-note clusters for their coloristic orchestral effect and often works these esoteric sonorities into the larger tapestry of more conventional jazz chording. These elements are well showcased in the duet and trio work of his repertory.

JIM HALL & PAT METHENY

ESSENTIAL LISTENING

Jim Hall's debut album on the Pacific Jazz label, *Jazz Guitar* (1957), is an all-time classic worth the search. The program finds him delivering a sparkling set of standards in a drummerless trio context typical of the era. His duo records with Ron Carter, *Alone Together* (Milestone/OJC, 1972) and *Jim Hall Live!* (A&M/Horizon, 1975, currently issued by Verve), are considered definitive live jazz guitar albums and contain further strong representations of his playing. Also recommended are his duet albums with pianist Bill Evans, his contributions to Sonny Rollins' *The Bridge* (RCA, 1961), and his early work with Art Farmer as well as his recent collaboration with Pat Metheny: *Jim Hall and Pat Metheny* (Telarc Jazz Zone, 1999).

ESSENTIAL VIEWING

Legends of Jazz Guitar, Volume 3 (Vestapol) contains several exemplary tracks from Jim Hall in trio, combo, and duet settings. Particularly engaging and evocative is his trio rendition of "I'm Getting Sentimental Over You" filmed in glorious period-perfect black and white while performing with Art Farmer's group in 1964.

Jim Hall can be seen in numerous online videos. Highlights include many rare vintage clips: with Sonny Rollins and company from *Jazz Casual* TV show of the early sixties, with the Jimmy Giuffre Trio in Italy (1959), in duets with Barney Kessel and Attila Zoller, fronting the Jim Hall Trio in Germany (1967 and 1973), his appearance on *The Guitar Show*, and other gems. More recent videos feature him with his own trio as well as playing in groups with Pat Metheny and with Bill Frisell from the 2009 Umbria festival.

SOUND

When Jim Hall began his professional career, he originally used a Gibson L5. On a gig, he found it "tubby" and instead made his public debut with a black Les Paul Custom. Hall was pictured with his Paul in 1956 publicity photos with the Chico Hamilton Quintet. This instrument had an Alnico pickup in the neck position, a P-90 in the bridge position, and was fitted with a Van Eps damper at the headstock.

Around 1957, Hall jettisoned the Les Paul and acquired the arch-top electric guitar that became his main instrument for nearly three decades: a sunburst ES-175 previously owned by Howard Roberts. This was an early fifties model with a single P-90 pickup, which was, like his earlier Les Paul, equipped with a Van Eps damper. Hall was first spotted with the 175 during his stint in the Jimmy Giuffre Trio in 1957–1959. He played this trademark guitar well into the eighties, as seen during his performance at the Great American Music Hall in 1982.

© Ray Avery CTSIMAGES

Hall made some notable modifications to his ES-175 over the years, including the replacement of the P-90 with a humbucking pickup and custom surround, the fitting of a narrow wooden pickguard, and the installation of a new fingerboard with block inlays.

In the seventies, Hall also played a custom sunburst James D'Aquisto arch-top with a single neck humbucker. This is the instrument pictured on the cover of his famed *Live* album of 1975 and was his primary instrument from the early eighties to 2003. D'Aquisto also built a blonde acoustic arch-top and a classical guitar with a cutaway and a jazz neck for Hall.

Hall hooked up with luthier Roger Sadowsky in the new millennium. These days, he plays and endorses Sadowsky guitars and has two namesake models in the current Sadowsky line. The first is a signature guitar sporting a 16-inch body with 2.75-inch depth, five-ply flame maple construction in a "Jim Hall sunburst" nitrocellulose finish, a maple neck with an asymmetric peg head bearing Hall's signature and ebony tuners, a 24¾-inch scale ebony fingerboard with no position markers, a single gold-plated humbucker in the neck position, and an ebony tailpiece with string ground. Hall has played this instrument exclusively since 2003. It was first seen in a spring 2004 performance with Charlie Haden at the Blue Note in New York City. Sadowsky also offers a Jim Hall model guitar that differs from the signature guitar in its more traditional look with scraped binding and choice of five finishes.

For the first twenty years of his career, Hall plugged into an early fifties Gibson GA-50 tube amplifier with a brown leatherette covering and two slotted holes for the two speakers (an 8-inch and a 12-inch), rated at about 25 watts. He used this amplifier into the seventies. Hall switched to solid-state Polytone amps in the eighties. In 2001, he favored the Polytone Mega Brute model, rated at 100 watts RMS, with a single 8-inch speaker, active tone controls, and three-spring reverb.

Hall prefers a medium gauge pick and light gauge flatwound strings. He currently favors Sadowsky light-gauge flatwounds (.011–.050 with an unwound .020 gauge G string). Hall rarely uses effects. One such occasion is viewable online in a clip from 2007 where he uses an octave box to mimic a steel-drum sound on "St. Thomas."

LICKS
FIG. 1: RHYTHMIC SWING

This swinging phrase reveals Hall's swing roots and, at the same time, his mutation of the traditional. Note the highly rhythmic treatment with purposeful syncopations in measures 2 and 6 and punchy staccato phrasing in measures 3, 4, and 7. Hall's thematic development approach is evident in microcosm in measures 6–8. Here, he spins out an intervallic motif with chromatic passing tones expressed as melodic leaps. The line closes with a Charlie Christian-inspired swing theme, which sets up the next statement.

FIG. 1.

FIG. 2: INTERVALLIC MASTERY

Hall's ineffable phrasing is exemplified in this offering. He begins with a tongue-in-cheek blues quote. Note the deliberate punctuation and rhythmic variety in the passage of measures 1–3. You'll find staccato notes contrasted with longer notes and subtle microtonal string bends (he used those lighter strings to good effect). The bebop-inflected line in measures 5–7 contains several notable Hall ingredients. Check out the ghosted notes in parentheses, the sporadic accented notes, which provide more weight and purpose in the phrase and suggest a boppish articulation, and the wide interval jumps (7th, 5th, 4th, 6th, etc) that lend an attractive angular contour to the zigzagging melody.

FIG. 2.

FIG. 3: MOTIVIC DEVELOPMENT

Wide intervals and motivic development reign supreme in this characteristically eccentric intro from Hall's celebrated live album of 1975. Who else would break ranks with the traditionalists to introduce an age-old standard with a quirky intervallic interpretation of the I–vi–ii–V changes? And who else would treat the tune as an oblong jazz waltz? The stacked 5th arpeggios are modernistic and intentionally obscure sonorities found throughout twentieth cen-tury classical music (quintal harmony)—sonorities that have found their way into jazz and rock. Andy Summers might have heard this version. The Police's "Message in a Bottle" is close in concept and execu-tion. Here, Hall arpeggiates the consecutive 5ths over a standard progression in measures 1–4 and then moves into a clever variation with a modal pattern (F–Bb–Am7–Gm7) and an elaboration of the rhythm in measures 5–8.

FIG. 3.

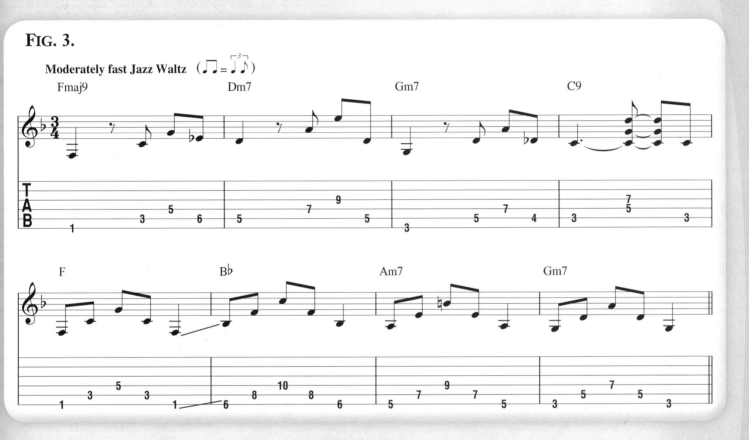

ALLAN HOLDSWORTH

© Photofest

There are few musicians as imaginative, innovative, and adept as Allan Holdsworth—and none as self-effacing. He is an iconic figure to the world's greatest guitarists—and not just jazz-rock fusion mavens. You can put heavyweights like Ed Van Halen, Carlos Santana, Alex Lifeson, Steve Lukather, Eric Johnson, Steve Morse, Joe Satriani, Neal Schon, Steve Vai, George Lynch, and Scott Henderson on the short list of his admirers, but don't expect their accolades to turn Allan's head. He instead is always looking for the next uncommon chord, seeking the musical treasures beneath the surface and never satisfied with what others would deem perfection.

The seventies began with a bang that sent shock waves crashing into all sectors of the jazz world. At ground zero was trumpeter Miles Davis—the restless aesthete and figurehead who started with Charlie Parker in the bebop era, defined its next phase in *Birth of the Cool*, introduced modal jazz into the lexicon with *Kind of Blue*, rewrote the modern jazz rulebook with his sterling quintet of the sixties, and began jazz-rock with *Bitches Brew* in 1970. Jazz-rock or fusion music was born in those electrified progressive grooves, and the world has never been the same since. But that can be said of most things Miles touched—and how does it relate to Allan Holdsworth?

Allan Holdsworth rose to prominence in the wake of Miles Davis's experiments fusing jazz and rock. After 1970, Davis's groups almost always featured a rock-toned guitar—a legacy beginning with John McLaughlin and later encompassing Reggie Lucas, Pete Cosey, Mike Stern, John Scofield, Jean Paul Bourelly, and Robben Ford. Moreover, Davis, captivated by the Jimi Hendrix sound, strove to expand post-seventies jazz into a medium that included and frequently featured overtly rock-influenced ensemble playing and high-decibel electric guitar soloing. And that's where Allan Holdsworth comes into the picture.

British born and bred, Allan Holdsworth is among the most striking of the jazz-rock fusion guitarists to emerge in the seventies. He made his initial appearance in 1973 with Tempest, a progressive rock band that featured Jon Hiseman of Colosseum fame. From that point on, Allan's participation as soloist extraordinaire on a succession of groundbreaking jazz-rock recordings established his growing credentials and rise to preeminence in the seventies. His work with Soft Machine, Gong, Jean Luc Ponty, Bill Bruford, U.K., and Tony Williams speaks volumes and remains astounding.

INFLUENCES

Allan's earliest influences came from his father, Sam Holdsworth, a jazz pianist who encouraged more than tutored his son. In his formative years, Allan was an avid listener of music but preferred bicycling to playing. Nonetheless, he was immersed in and gained appreciation for the sounds of Bix Beiderbecke, Benny Goodman, Oliver Nelson, Artie Shaw, and Charlie Parker.

Allan came to the guitar relatively late in life at age seventeen. A seminal influence was guitarist Charlie Christian but, already looking for unexplored territory, he was also inspired by and swayed to emulate horn players Cannonball Adderley, Charlie Parker, Michael Brecker, and most of all John Coltrane. In time, his guitar playing conception was shaped more by saxophone phrasing and jazz melodic content than standard rock and roll clichés.

Though Allan was increasingly drawn to jazz horn players, he cites Eric Clapton (with Blues Breakers and Cream) as influential in his own "blues period." Allan also credits legendary but relatively obscure English guitarist Ollie Halsall with inspiring his legato approach. Allan and Ollie briefly shared duties in an early lineup of Tempest in 1973.

STYLE

Allan Holdsworth's style is the personification of jazz-rock. Though he is an expert at unusual, and for most guitarists largely unplayable, chord voicings and unwieldy progressions and possesses an advanced sense of harmony, he is most known, especially in the seventies, for his unique single-note solo approach. In fact, like a sax or trumpet player, Allan was regularly employed as a soloist with a clearly defined role: "laying out" in the measures before his solo and otherwise only participating in ensemble figures. In this context, his style and technique are unmistakable, distinguished by long, complex virtuosic lines delivered with the grace and passion and seamless phraseology of a wind player.

As a soloist Allan's wide-ranging ideas run the gamut from "inside" pan-diatonic modal melodies to "outside" atonal and polytonal (triad on triad) sounds and unpredictable often daring note selections. These are generally based on a modernistic post-bop jazz conception, like the Miles Davis and John Coltrane groups of the sixties. The rock side of his style is exemplified in his smooth distorted guitar tone, use of the vibrato bar, and a preference for overdriven amplifiers to emulate the timbre and sustain of a wind instrument. Moreover, in the early years of the seventies, his evolving style still contained numerous allusions to blues-rock with idiomatic string bends and phrasing.

Allan's single-note sound has for years been characterized by his *legato* approach. He often plays remarkable long lines with a minimum of pick strokes, using his prodigious left-hand strength and Olympian stretch to fret notes in a fluid, connected motion. Allan specifies that he has developed his legato technique to a point where he does not play "pull-offs." Instead he *lifts off*, avoiding the typical mewling sound of most players and producing an uncanny unbroken, evenly articulated result.

Another aspect of his single-note style is his ability to stretch his hand to reach wide intervals on a single string. In higher positions, this can mean seemingly impossible distances like 5ths and 6ths. Allan frequently moves these patterns across the fingerboard in both horizontal and vertical motion with his string-skipping approach. He often juggles and inserts mind-boggling wide-interval melodies and extended arpeggio figures played on a single string in the midst of more conventional diatonic passages and chromatic lines for a striking effect.

Allan uses no particular scales or stylistic clichés to produce his uncommon melodies. He plays off the harmony of the moment and is fond of emphasizing higher dissonances and extensions like 9ths, 11ths, and 13ths in the manner of a jazz musician. Allan has mentioned his study and application of partial scales and synthetic scales, which he pursued on a theoretical level while with Tony Williams. However, these were largely etudes and mathematical constructs instrumental in providing atypical material for improvisation and not musical ends in themselves.

Allan developed a distinctive, influential, and immediately recognizable vibrato sound on the guitar. In the seventies, he used both the Vibrola on a Gibson SG and the tremolo arm on a Fender Stratocaster to phrase melodies with numerous pitch bends, glissandi, portamento effects, scoops into notes, and dives and an infinite variety of vibrato nuances—particularly on phrase endings. Allan also used left hand vibrato to embellish notes. On the treble strings, he prefers a linear, classical violin approach (along the string length) but generally favors a more typical side-to-side, slight string-bending technique on the bass strings.

ESSENTIAL LISTENING

Allan Holdsworth's work in the early years is well represented by a handful of exemplary releases. Soft Machine's *Bundles* (issued 1975, See for Miles Records Ltd., French import), Tony Williams Lifetime's *Believe It* (1975) and *Million Dollar Legs* (1976) (currently issued as *The Collection*, Columbia Jazz), Gong *Gazeuse!* (1976, Virgin), Jean Luc Ponty's *Enigmatic Ocean* (1976, Atlantic), *U.K.* (1978, EG Records), and Bruford's *One of a Kind* (1979, EG Records, Japanese import) are among the most definitive.

Essential Viewing

Allan Holdsworth & Alan Pasqua: Live at Yoshi's (Altitude Digital, 2008) is a stellar fusion concert DVD filmed at the famed jazz venue. It finds the two former Tony Williams Lifetime members reunited after thirty years. Also of interest is *Allan Holdsworth* (Warner Bros/Alfred, 2008), a DVD that offers interviews and musical insights from the master as well as band footage with illuminating close-ups.

Film footage from Allan Holdsworth's early years on DVD is understandably scarce but well worth the search. In his seventies videography are a 1974 or 1975 Montreux Jazz Festival performance with Soft Machine, a British 1977 promotional film for "In the Dead of Night" with U.K., and the debut gig of the Bill Bruford band at Oxford, England, in 1979.

There are many must-see Allan Holdsworth video clips currently available online. Among the most compelling are an extended live vintage performance of "Floating World/Bundles" with Soft Machine, footage of his 1984 Tokyo concert, excerpts of the live performances from Yoshi's with Alan Pasqua, a 2007 take on his signature piece "Fred" with Chad Wackerman and Jimmy Johnson, and a substantial compilation of Holdsworth solos from his 2010 tour with Terry Bozzio and Tony Levin, as well as several enlightening excerpts from previously released instructional videos.

ebony fingerboard, replaced the stock Fender tremolo bridge with a DiMarzio unit (with Gibson string spacing), and relocated the volume control lower on the pickguard. Over the years Allan used the vintage PAF pickups from his SG as well as DiMarzio PAFs and Seymour Duncan 59Bs on this guitar. He played the modified Strat as his main guitar into the eighties through the *I.O.U.* album of 1982.

On his earliest recordings and gigs, Allan plugged into various au courant Vox and Marshall amps. Later in the seventies, he began using Hartley-Thompson equipment exclusively for his lead sound, favoring the amp's "red channel" for its overdrive tone. According to Allan, these are deceptively warm transistor amps. Allan prefers playing in stereo and used two heads and two cabinets, each fitted with two customized Goodman GP-12 speakers. In the late seventies, Allan also experimented with Mesa-Boogie, Jim Kelly, and Sundown amps. He used very little signal processing on his lead tone, occasionally adding a touch of delay set below 55 milliseconds for its ambient tonal quality rather than discrete echo.

In his early years, Allan preferred extremely low action, light-gauge strings, and three springs on his Strat tremolo unit.

Sound

Allan began on an unspecified acoustic arch-top f-hole guitar fitted with an after-market pickup. He graduated to a Fender Stratocaster, which he played briefly before switching to a white Gibson SG Custom with three pickups and a Gibson Vibrola tailpiece. The SG was his primary guitar in his earliest professional period and is heard on such recordings as *Tempest* and *Bundles*.

During his stint with Tony Williams Lifetime, Allan began playing a modified early-seventies Fender Stratocaster. This instrument is heard on virtually every Holdsworth track from the mid-to-late seventies. Though Allan appeared to play a number of Strats in this period, it was always this one, repainted a number of times in the half dozen years of its use. Allan removed the three stock single-coil pickups and added two humbucking pickups. He installed a new neck with an

© Photofest

LICKS

FIG. 1: VIBRATO BAR PHRASE

Allan's influential vibrato bar phrasing, in conjunction with his legato technique, is showcased in this phrase. The oblong 7/4 melody is slower and more spacious, allowing room for Allan to take full advantage of sax-inspired vibrato-bar nuances and embellishments. Check out the scooped tones in measures 1–3 and wind-like vibrato on longer notes, such as the sustained E in measure 2 and A at the phrase ending. The scooped *portamento* effect was achieved by pre-diving a fingered note, attacking it, and then releasing tension on the depressed bar, smoothly returning it to its normal pitch.

This characteristic melody also features Allan's *pan-diatonic* approach in his specific triad and chord extensions over E minor. Note the explicit D major sounds in measures 1 and 2, made more explicit with wide-interval jumps to chord tones of the superimposed D major chord (such as the F♯ to D leap in measure 2.)

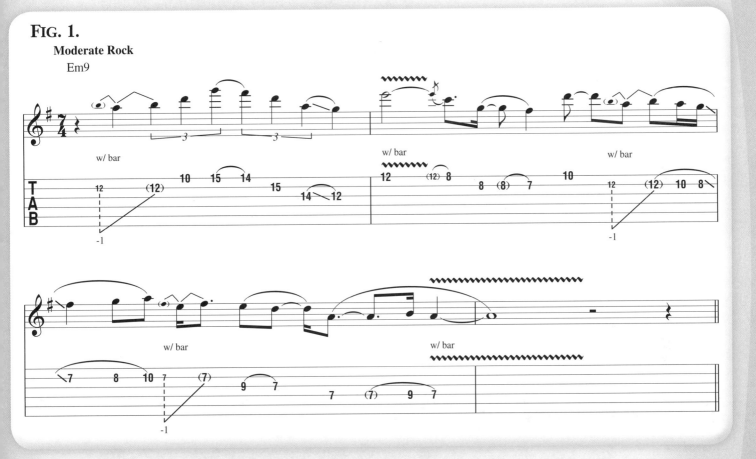

FIG. 1.

Moderate Rock

Em9

FIG. 2: DOUBLE-TIMED SCARINESS

Allan's fusion work of the seventies is exemplified by his collaborations with Tony Williams Lifetime, as on *Believe It*. This was a landmark outing and captured the excitement and innovation for which he is renowned. This phrase is based on Allan's double-timed lines of his early fusion period and presents a number of telling features. The opening lick poses B minor pentatonic sounds over E—a familiar modern jazz extension. This section exploits sixteenth-note groupings and the sound of *perfect 4th* intervals, reflecting the post-bop jazz lexicon of the late sixties. The angular intervallic patterns, arranged as *wide-interval* riffs in measures 3–5, are textbook examples of Allan's expanded melodic sense and his legato execution of 4ths on a single string.

The melody in measures 6–9 illustrates his legato treatment of long scalar lines. It begins in E7 with diatonic lines and makes a smooth transition to G at measure 7. Notice the use of a thematic major-mode motif taken through a cycle of 4ths (C–F–B♭) in measures 8–9 and the use of two different *double diminished* scales (both in symmetrical whole step-half step configuration) in 7 and 9. The first is closely aligned with G7 (D diminished), while the second is "outside" (F♯ diminished) and dissonant. Allan uses a typical chromatic line to make a seamless connection to this dissonant sound and resolves the tension on the last two sixteenth notes.

FIG. 2.

FIG. 3: INTERVALLIC JUGGLING

"Juggling" is a descriptive and apt term Allan uses to categorize some of his uncanny interval-leaping melodies. This phrase, played over alternating measures of 5/4 and 4/4, serves as an instructive case in point. After establishing the tonal framework and mood of the improvisation with a blistering modal line in the first measure, Allan launches into a string-skipping pattern in measure 2 that finds him jumping from string 5 to string 2 seamlessly. Here, he juggles three- and four-note figures (adding up to a seven sixteenth-note time span in his motif) for an intriguing rhythmically and intervallically displaced result.

Another familiar and more subtle aspect of Allan's fanciful melodic juggling is heard in the phrase of measures 3–4, where his stretching for unison tones on adjacent strings produces an unmistakable aural effect. This sort of sonic sleight of hand has remained a fixture in his style. In measures 5–6, we find some typical scale sequences—if anything Allan plays can be called typical. Note the mixture of "inside" diatonic melody with "outside" chromaticism. Also noteworthy is the legato phrasing throughout and the singing whammy-bar vibrato of the final note.

FIG. 3.

BARNEY KESSEL

© Ray Avery CTSIMAGES

Poll winner Barney Kessel was the first notable guitarist to work in the challenging guitar trio format of guitar, bass, and drums—nowadays a standard ensemble. In early 1957, Barney teamed with two similarly recognized musical giants of the era—Ray Brown (bass) and Shelly Manne (drums)—to launch a series of influential and historically significant albums as the Poll Winners. These remain the bedrock upon which future guitar trios are based.

In the years to follow, Barney's resume came to read like a who's who in jazz. He recorded and performed with luminaries like Art Tatum, Billie Holiday, Ella Fitzgerald, Sonny Rollins, Lionel Hampton, Sarah Vaughan, Red Norvo, Stephane Grappelli, and Lester Young, among many others. In addition to his copious jazz credentials, Barney was one of the most sought-after studio musicians in Hollywood, lending his special talents to projects as diverse as pop tracks for Frank Sinatra, Judy Garland, the Coasters, the Beach Boys, and Cher, T-Bone Walker's *T-Bone Blues*, Ricky Nelson, Duane Eddy, and Elvis Presley rock 'n' roll records, numerous film scores, and theme music for television.

Barney Kessel was one of the most important and beloved players to ever touch the instrument. His groundbreaking efforts in the earliest years of the electric guitar helped develop the essential language of the instrument, still very much in use today. Moreover, Barney inspired countless players to follow in his wake—from Larry Carlton and John McLaughlin to Larry Coryell and Howard Alden.

The world of music lost one of its all-time greatest guitarists in 2004 with the passing of Barney Kessel, the iconic player who picked up the gauntlet thrown down by the father of all electric guitarists: Charlie Christian. That Christian and Kessel hung out and jammed together back in 1940—when Charlie was twenty-three and Barney was sixteen and the amplified guitar was new—is the stuff of which legends are made. The account resonates to this day as one of the most compelling stories in jazz, marking an auspicious moment in contemporary music history. The ensuing years of the instrument's and genre's chronologies saw Barney emerge as the undisputed leader of the pack.

Barney Kessel was an innovative and resourceful guitar player who took the Christian legacy to the next level in the post-swing and bop eras of the forties and fifties. His appearance in the award-winning Norman Granz 1944 documentary *Jammin' the Blues* (wherein he is the only white musician) is legendary. Kessel's subsequent contributions to big bands and combos led by the likes of Charlie Barnet, Artie Shaw, Charlie Parker, Oscar Peterson, and Benny Goodman led to an enviable reputation and a slew of accolades from all the prestigious publications, culminating in his glorious five-year sweep of the *Downbeat* polls from 1956 to 1960.

INFLUENCES

Barney Kessel drew inspiration from many sources. His primary and most profound guitar influence was Charlie Christian, but he later mentioned the improvisations of Django Reinhardt and newer players like Pat Martino as impressive. Instrumentalists such as pianist Oscar Peterson and saxophonists Lester Young and Charlie

Parker also inspired Barney. Clearly "Blues for Bird" on *Red Hot and Blues* (1988) bears the imprint of Parker's harmonic approach and melodic phrasing. Along similar lines, Barney cited John Coltrane as an influence during the making of his *Feeling Free* album (1969).

Barney studied composition with famed composer Mario Castelnuovo-Tedesco and composer/musicologist Albert Harris. These experiences enhanced his arranging style and colored the large repertory of Kessel originals on his recordings.

STYLE

Barney Kessel's guitar style was firmly rooted in the jazz music of the late thirties and forties. As one of the key transitional players in the period, his approach naturally embodies the lexicons of the swing and bebop periods. Both jazz genres exerted a tremendous impact on his playing. To a lesser extent, Barney was affected by the post-bop modal and hard bop movements and free jazz.

Barney was an accomplished chord stylist and brilliant single-note soloist. His chord playing suggested the harmonic sophistication, varied textures, and arranging acumen of a pianist and orchestrator. Barney was fond of the modern polytonal substitutions and chord extensions favored by jazz keyboardists and often worked these into his re-harmonizations of standard songs like "Tenderly," "Misty," and "Spring Is Here."

The blues played a large role in Barney's music. Despite the heady bop-inflected lines and colorful harmonic alternatives found throughout his improvisations, visceral blues licks abounded. Barney utilized blues elements in both chord- and single-note form. His flowing solo passages were often punctuated with distinctive string bends, grooving riff-like patterns, slurred seventh and ninth chords, and characteristic double stops.

Barney had several notable phrasing mannerisms that made his single-note improvisations personal and immediately recognizable. Prime among these were the rake-picked smeared figures that decorated many of his bop passages. Another significant Kessel signature was the extended guitar line harmonized in parallel 3rds. Also notable was his strong unflagging sense of swing when rendering long strings of eighth notes like a wind player.

ESSENTIAL LISTENING

The first three Barney Kessel albums on Contemporary provide a splendid introduction to his influential post-swing/bebop approach: *Easy Like (Barney Kessel volume 1)*, *Barney Kessel Plays Standards (Barney Kessel volume 2)*, and *To Swing or Not to Swing (Barney Kessel volume 3)*. Also essential are the first four Poll Winners recordings (also on Contemporary): *The Poll Winners*, *The Poll Winners Ride Again*, *Poll Winners Three*, and *Exploring the Scene*.

ESSENTIAL VIEWING

Barney Kessel: Rare Performances 1962–1991 (Vestapol 13013) is an essential audio-visual chronicle of his most active years. Also vital are Barney's performances in *The Legends of Jazz Guitar* (Volumes 1–3) also on Vestapol.

Online highlights include "I've Grown Accustomed to Her Face" (two versions), "Autumn Leaves," "Misty," "Oh, Lady be Good" (with Ruby Braff), "You Stepped out of a Dream" (guitar duet with Jim Hall), and numerous performances with the Great Guitars. Also noteworthy is Kessel's participation in the blues guitar jam outing "Blue Mist" with Grant Green and Kenny Burrell.

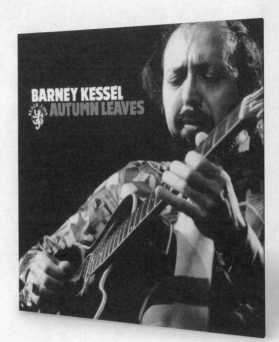

Sound

Barney Kessel's sound was the natural outgrowth of the electric guitar tone fostered by Charlie Christian and embraced by virtually every exponent of the post-Christian school. You can put his contemporaries like Tal Farlow, Jimmy Raney, Hank Garland, and Kenny Burrell in that group, as well as current heirs to the throne like Jimmy Bruno, Howard Alden, and Russell Malone. This is the warm, clean timbre generally produced by a hollow-body arch-top electric with the neck pickup engaged plugged into a tube combo amp.

Barney played the same guitar for almost his entire career: a sunburst Gibson ES-350P made in 1947 or 1948. The P stood for Premier and designated Gibson's first production electric guitar with a single-cutaway body. The ES-350P had a deep (3 3/8 inches), 17-inch arch-top body with f-holes, a 25½ inch scale, and a single P-90 pickup. Over the years, Barney modified

his 350 considerably. He replaced the original P-90 with a "Charlie Christian" bar pickup, added black pre-war-style control knobs from a record player, swapped Grover Roto-Matic tuners for the stock Klusons, removed the pickguard, and fitted the guitar with a new ebony fingerboard with dot inlays.

In 1961, Gibson introduced a Barney Kessel model as part of their prestigious jazz guitar artist line. This instrument had a revolutionary double-cutaway body with sharp Florentine points in a cherry sunburst finish, two humbucking pickups, and a special trapeze tailpiece with *Barney Kessel* inscribed on the central wood and plastic insert plaque. The Kessel model came in Custom and Regular editions. The fancier Custom version was appointed with gold-plated hardware, Grover tuners, bound f-holes, bow-tie inlays, and a stylized eighth-note design inlaid on the headstock. Barney was pictured with this guitar on the cover of his 1961 album *Workin' Out*, but it is doubtful that he played the model for any appreciable time. Like Howard Roberts and Tom Tedesco, Barney played a Telecaster for rock studio dates.

A Kay Barney Kessel model preceded the Gibson deal in the fifties. This electric arch-top guitar was available from 1956–1960 in three versions: Pro, Artist, and Special (from low to high in price). Barney only lent his name to these instruments and did not perform with them in public or on record.

Kessel played through various Gibson, Fender, and Univox combo amps at different points in his career. He strung his guitar with medium-gauge Darco round-wound polished strings and used a heavy-gauge rounded pick.

LICKS

FIG. 1: UPTEMPO SWING LICK

This telling passage is played over the last six measures of a fast blues in Bb and incorporates Barney's mix of bebop, blues, and swing ingredients. It begins with a series of parallel ninth chords—one of Kessel's favorite harmonic devices in the blues. This is followed by a sequence of slurred triads articulated with his patented rake-picking sweeps. A bluesy string bend and single-note Mixolydian lick distinguish the closing melody in measures 5 and 6. Note the swing-oriented use of the 6th tone (G) at the phrase ending, which acts as the 5th of Cm7 harmonically.

FIG. 1.

FIG. 2: DOUBLE-TIMING

More of Barney's inimitable jazz stylings are presented in the second offering, a largely double-timed single-note line colored with chromatic passing tones and idiosyncratic bebop interval jumps. The passage occurs over standard changes in C major and finds Barney combining swing and blues elements in the opening melody. The next is replete with slippery sixteenth notes and exhibits Kessel's tendency to phrase like a saxophone with florid serpentine contours and plenty of typical slurs. The closing thoughts include a rhythmic blues riff over the F7 chord and a favorite bebop/blues lick over the C–C7 chord change.

FIG. 2.

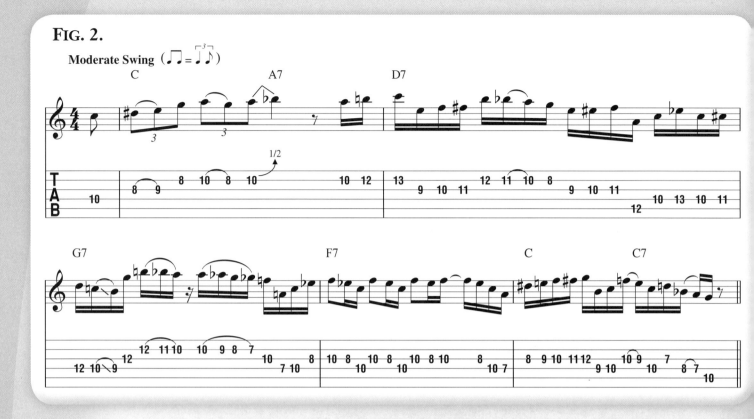

FIG. 3: CHORD-MELODY STYLE

The final phrase is a rubato chord-melody passage in F major demonstrating Barney's use of modern jazz sonorities. Guided by his arranger's ear, Kessel often harnessed colorful voicings and harmonic patterns like these to orchestrate his intros and interludes—particularly in ballads. Noteworthy features include the sequence of 4th sonorities in measure 1, the Bb7b5 substitution for E7 in measure 2, the emblematic piano-inspired Am(maj9) voicing and oblique-motion descent in measure 3, and the characteristic rising melody of parallel 3rds in measures 4 and 5. The final chord is a favorite pianistic voicing, D13#11b9, which expounds on the exotic A minor sound heard two measures earlier.

FIG. 3.

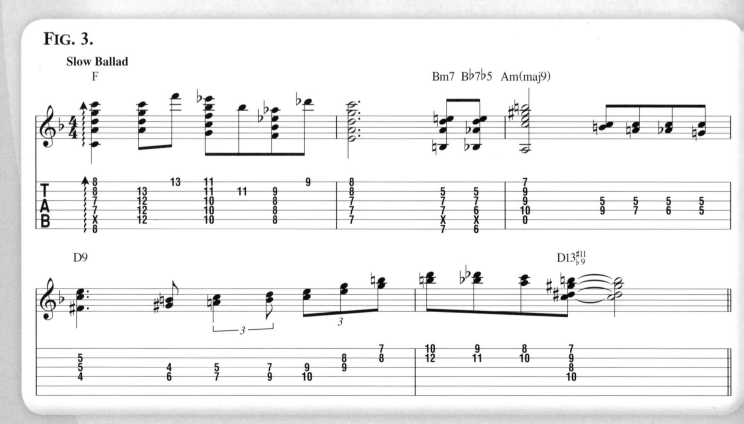

EDDIE LANG

© CTSIMAGES

Eddie Lang was a ubiquitous figure and media star by the late twenties, in demand by top bandleaders and musicians in jazz and popular music settings. As such, he was the first "cross over" guitarist, effective in both rarefied jazz circles and on commercial pop dates. Early on, he made a historic recording with Joe Venuti in 1926 that yielded "Stringing the Blues." And he was the featured soloist with Red Nichols and the Five Pennies. He also recorded with the Dorsey Brothers, Bix Beiderbecke, and Frankie Trumbauer. Future recordings found him in the company of Benny Goodman, Jack Teagarden, and the Boswell Singers, in addition to co-leading his own band: the Venuti-Lang All-Star Orchestra. But, in truth, Lang was a triple-threat player; he was also a fine blues guitarist. In 1928–1929, under the pseudonym Blind Willie Dunn, he crossed racial lines and pioneered some of the earliest jazz-blues duets with the legendary New Orleans guitarist Lonnie Johnson. Lang rounded out his blues credentials with a series of recordings in which he accompanied the legendary singer Bessie Smith.

Eddie Lang was the world's first guitar star. He was the most influential and recognized guitarist of the twenties and early thirties and is forever tied to the era of "classic jazz," when the American art form was in its infancy and ascendancy. Possessing superior technique and prescient artistic conception, he was almost single-handedly responsible for elevating the role of the guitar in jazz and popular music. This has had staggering sociologic and musical consequences. Along with the advent of phonograph recording and the rise of popular music consumption on the radio, there were changes afoot in the sound of the music itself—the guitar, for instance...

Before Lang, the guitar was little more than a curiosity, and the banjo reigned supreme in jazz and pop ensembles. As Lang worked his way up the professional ladder, it was he who was responsible for turning the guitar into the definitive fretted instrument of jazz, swing, and pop music. After Lang, the guitar was a fully realized instrument. In combos, orchestras, and as a solo voice, it replaced the banjo forever.

In 1929, famed orchestra leader Paul Whiteman hired Eddie Lang. Lang appeared with his regular cohort Joe Venuti in a segment of Whiteman's 1930 movie *The King of Jazz*, the first all-color feature film. He also accompanied singer Mildred Bailey in Whiteman's organization. Lang was full-time accompanist for Bing Crosby, one of the band's singers. In 1931, Crosby became the nation's top vocalist. He left Whiteman's band and persuaded Lang to leave and work with him. Their spirited take on "Some of These Days" remains a seminal and historically important jazz classic. Lang appeared on film with Crosby in *The Big Broadcast of 1932*, affording countless guitarists a tantalizing glimpse of his performing style. A year later, he was gone—dead at age thirty-one: the result of complications during a routine tonsillectomy. In his all-too-brief career of less than ten years, guitarist Eddie Lang had permanently and completely redefined the sound of American music.

Eddie Lang's legacy is pervasive and far-reaching. The Lang and Venuti team were an inspiration to Django Reinhardt and Stephane Grappelli in the next phase of "chamber jazz" across the Atlantic. Moreover, Lang inspired countless guitarists including three important American players, George Van Eps, Dick McDonough, and Carl Kress, who were in turn important role models for guitarists in the thirties, forties, and beyond.

INFLUENCES

Born Salvatore Massaro, Lang studied violin and solfeggio (sight singing) with local Philadelphia teachers at age seven. The son of a banjo and guitar maker, Lang taught himself guitar at age nine on a small-scale instrument made by his father. He began his professional career on the tenor banjo in 1922 but soon played the hybrid six-string banjo-guitar (as had Django Reinhardt). By 1923, Lang had made the transition to full-time guitarist. Lang attended the local Philadelphia high school where he met and began a life-long partnership with violinist Joe Venuti. Both musicians influenced each other in the earliest years of classic jazz.

© Pictorial Press Ltd/Alamy

Lang was also influenced by classical music. He recorded a solo guitar version of Sergei Rachmaninoff's "Prelude in C♯ Minor, Opus 3" and was also known to play a similar arrangement of Claude Debussy's "Maid with the Flaxen Hair." Moreover, he cited Andres Segovia as a personal favorite and mentioned his admiration for flamenco guitarists.

STYLE

Eddie Lang is widely acknowledged as history's first important guitarist. In American jazz, he was the form's first guitar virtuoso, setting the stage for the ascendance of the instrument on both sides of the Atlantic. A talented accompanist and soloist, Lang was sought out by leading singers and bands of the jazz age for his innovative single-note playing and tasteful animated chord work.

Lang's single-note style embraced the central tenets of jazz guitar (still in popular use today) with its chord-outlining arpeggios defining chord progressions, chromatic passing tones, exotic augmented and diminished melodies, blues inflections, and horn-like licks and phrasing. He often pursued a sax-like approach with syncopated rhythms, repeated riffs, strong accents, percussive staccato notes, and legato slurs, as in his swinging solo on Bing Crosby's "Some

of These Days." He was fond of varying textures in his solo pieces, often moving from chord-melody playing to virtuosic single-note runs and fills. Lang offset his jazz lines with bluesy string bends and classically based phrases. The former are heard in his solos of "Midnight Call," while the latter is showcased in the elaborate intro of "Rainbow Dreams." Lang colored his lines further with finger vibrato and expressive effects like exaggerated slides and natural and artificial harmonics.

Lang's chord playing style was similarly colorful and influential, exploiting characteristic jazz rhythm-guitar chord strumming, allusions to ragtime and stride piano, impressionistic extended-chord arpeggiations, and a variety of textures, from double stops and triads to larger ringing open-string chords. Unlike other early chord players, he employed numerous quick position changes and advanced chord inversions (sometimes on each beat of a measure). He also incorporated parallel ninth chords, pianistic 10th intervals, and augmented chord passages into his chord statements. Lang's acoustic arch-top tone was fuller and sweeter than his contemporaries, belying the fact that he was primarily a plectrum player. That said, Lang would sometimes hide his pick in his palm and perform fingerstyle, particularly when accompanying singers.

Lang was a diverse performer. Though largely a jazz musician, he tackled Sergei Rachmaninoff's "Prelude in C♯ Minor, Opus 3," producing an intriguing arrangement for solo guitar. He was also drawn to country blues and was a strong early proponent of blues elements in jazz guitar. This earthy aspect created interesting and musically balanced contrast in his uptown style. The third verse (1:47) of "Have to Change Keys to Play These Blues" is a telling case in point.

Lang was a creative force in the creation of jazz guitar duets. His groundbreaking duets with Carl Kress and Lonnie Johnson set the tone and conception for future outings by Herb Ellis & Joe Pass, Chuck Wayne & Joe Puma, George Barnes & Bucky Pizzarelli, Carl Kress & Dick McDonough, Ralph Towner & John Abercrombie, Pat Metheny & Jim Hall, and many others. With Kress, essentially the rhythm-guitar accompanist, Lang played virtuoso soloist. Countless noteworthy moments document their establishment of the art form, including "Pickin' My Way" and "Feelin' My Way." Regarding the latter, his fleet atypical flamenco runs in the introduction of "Feelin' My Way" are a strong artistic contrast to the ragtime-style licks and chording typical of the period, which dominate the piece. With Johnson, Lang was part of a cooperative blues guitar duo, often the accompanist. This context found him milking blue notes, riffs, and string bends in his solo spots. When accompanying Johnson, he played bass line figures and terse chording, as in "Handful of Riffs" and "Have to Change Keys to Play These Blues."

ESSENTIAL LISTENING

Eddie Lang Jazz Guitar Virtuoso (Yazoo) is a serviceable compilation highlighting the guitarist's inventive and innovative chord melody and single-note work as well as duets with Lonnie Johnson, Carl Kress, and Joe Venuti. Also worth searching for is his work with Bing Crosby in the early thirties.

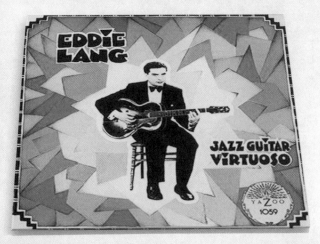

ESSENTIAL VIEWING

Footage of Lang performing is understandably scarce; film was a new medium in his lifetime. However, the internet boasts an important clip of Lang with Bing Crosby performing "Please"—an excerpt from *The Big Broadcast of 1932*. Though brief, the instructive segment has ample and revealing views of Lang's fretting and picking positions.

SOUND

Eddie Lang is closely associated with the acoustic Gibson L-5 guitar, which was the first to use Lloyd Loar's F-hole arch-top design. Preceded by the L-1 through L-4, the L-5 proved to be the most enduring model in the line. It is still in production today, some ninety years later, and has become *the* jazz guitar—first in acoustic form and later as an electric guitar. The first L-5s were made in 1922 and were soon in the hands of guitarists in "dance orchestras." Lang played typical mid and late twenties models with a smaller carved 16-inch body, metal trapeze tailpiece, and dot marker inlays. He was seen with a thirties model L-5 (third variant) in the 1932 movie with Bing Crosby. This guitar is easily identified by its wide pearloid block inlays and metal Grover tuning keys.

LICKS
FIG. 1: GENRE-BENDING INTRO

Eddie Lang was the premier jazz chord-melody stylist of the twenties, but some of his most ear-catching moments pushed the envelope of jazz into unusual tangents, emphasizing a fusion bent that is at the core of the genre. A case in point is this unique passage, which served as an unaccompanied intro in free time to a well-known duet piece from the Kress-Lang team. Here, Lang's playing splits the difference between jazz, flamenco, and romantic Italian music. There are numerous languorously arpeggiated open-string chords complemented by virtuosic Spanish flourishes and modern extended partial-chord figures. Note Lang's use of the *A harmonic minor* scale to define the sound of an altered E7 chord in the opening single-note passage. This is a familiar strategy favored in the years to come by countless jazz and bebop players as well as modern pickers like Al Di Meola and Yngwie Malmsteen. Lang closes the intro phrase with arpeggiated B°7 and E9 chords, reflecting shapes now in common use by many guitarists—jazz, blues, and otherwise. But remember, you heard it first here.

FIG. 1.

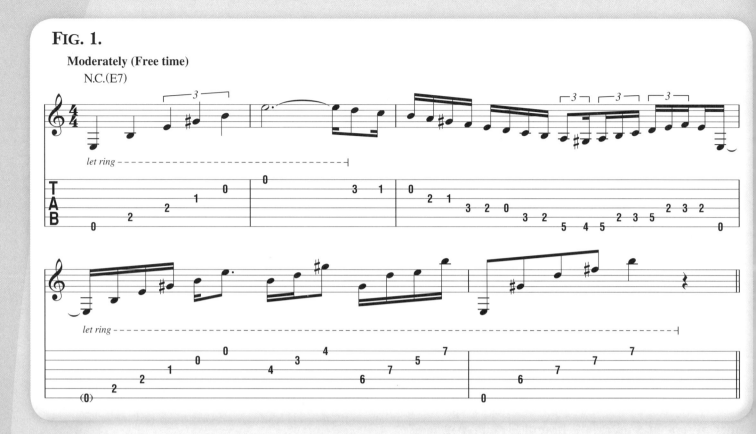

FIG. 2: LANG'S SWING

Eddie Lang was a highly touted recording session star to the jazz world, presaging a lofty status later accorded to Howard Roberts, Barney Kessel, Lee Ritenour, Larry Carlton, and the like. This hustling single-note solo excerpt is one reason why; it graced and decorated a swinging Bing Crosby track from the crooner's early jazz-pop years. Here, Lang phrases and delivers like a jazz wind player. Note the punchy staccato notes and repeated riff figures as well as the recurring leaning on the G♯ chromatic neighbor tone. The expressive bluesy half-step string bends and slow release are evidence of the blues aesthetic at work in Lang's playing. This ingredient formed a strong contrast to his rhythmically charged jazz lines and was a fixture in his improvisations.

FIG. 2.

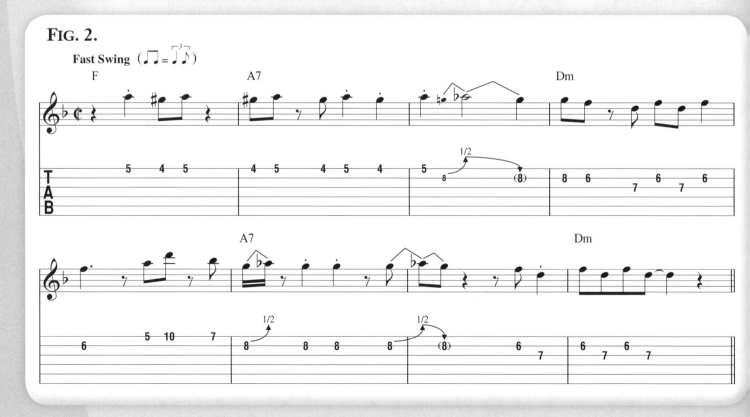

FIG. 3: WHOLE-TONE SCALES AND TRI-TONE SUBS

Eddie Lang developed several variants on the "chamber jazz" theme in his recordings. This acoustic-based format was a natural outgrowth of the Dixieland string bands of the early 1900s. This multifarious phrase exemplifies his work in the medium. Note the long arching single-note intro sequence of skipping 3rds, which has its origins in classical passagework. The diatonic line in D major makes a quick detour to an A augmented arpeggio, embellished with a natural harmonic. The first chord statement in D (measures 7–8) borrows a move from Villa Lobos ("Guitar Prelude No. 5") before maneuvering into the jazz voicing Em7♭5 and an arpeggiation of D/F♯. Lang inserts a quick single-note stepwise run in measure 11 that leads to his conclusion in A augmented harmony in measures 12–13. Note the use of variants derived from the *A whole-tone scale* in single notes, parallel 3rds, and arpeggiations. Also notable is Lang's choice of E♭7 as the final chord. This is the tritone (flat five) substitute for A7 and foreshadows a common procedure in modern jazz.

FIG. 3.

PAT MARTINO

© Jan Persson CTSIMAGES

Today, Pat is supreme among the leading jazz voices of his generation. Following years of accomplishment, he continues crossing and redefining boundaries in his art. A true musical globalist, he's comfortable with routinely blending straight-ahead jazz, bebop and swing, jazz rock fusion, blues, ethnic sounds, avant-garde, and mathematical music in pure improvisation. However, his priorities are communication through the social impact of his playing and the effort of constantly challenging himself to reach greater heights in the moment.

INFLUENCES

Pat's influences are myriad. He cites Les Paul, Johnny Smith, Hank Garland, Joe Pass, and particularly Wes Montgomery as primary guitar influences. Jim Hall, Mundell Lowe, and Barry Galbraith also affected him to a lesser extent. Pat studied with Dennis Sandole and has credited the notable Philadelphia guitarist-teacher with introducing him to the famous Slonimsky tome *Thesaurus of Scales and Musical Patterns* and helping him acquire his personal identity.

Pat also admired jazz instrumentalists like Miles Davis, Art Blakey, Gigi Gryce, Cannonball Adderley, and especially John Coltrane. Coltrane is something of a de facto mentor, acknowledged as a powerful spiritual and musical influence.

Pat has also studied and assimilated the music of modern composers like Karlheinz Stockhausen and Elliot Carter. While much of this study and its fruits in Martino's repertory are not known to his general audience, the challenging sounds undoubtedly affected his strong sense of controlled dissonance.

*P*at Martino is a living legend, a national treasure, and an inspiration to musicians and music lovers of all stripes. His exemplary career now spans five decades, and his personal tale of trial and tribulation is one of the most powerful and miraculous success stories in music history. From his formative years as a sideman (or side-kid) in the rough-and-tumble chitlin circuit and smoky jazz bars to his inevitable ascendancy in the rarefied circles of the jazz world, Pat has remained true to his artistic ideals with staggering results.

An artist more interested in exploring new musical terrain than rehashing old formulas, Pat is a true pioneer and a self-styled alchemist of the guitar. The most obvious and striking aspect of his magic is his seemingly effortless and unflagging ability to transform scales and licks into long, mesmerizing streams of consciousness. Like the magic potions of the legendary alchemist, Martino's unique conceptions are conjured up regularly from a bottomless well of ideas. As a musician, he personifies the five T's: tone, time, technique, touch, and taste. But don't take my word for it; just give any of his discs a spin or ask any knowledgeable member of today's musical cognoscenti. Pat's fans and admirers are legion and have even included players far outside the genre, including Pete Townshend and the late Jerry Garcia.

STYLE

In the world of jazz guitar, Pat Martino is the most striking and unique exponent of the post-modern style, freely blending hard bop, blues, and modal sounds with jazz-rock fusion and avant-garde atonal tangents for an unmistakable outcome. Pat emerged in the sixties in the wake of the Wes Montgomery hegemony and rapidly became one of the most influential and innovative players on the scene.

Martino has a distinctive and immediately recognizable style. Firmly rooted in hard bop jazz traditions, Pat progressed beyond the traditional confines of the genre to embrace atypical directions like jazz-rock fusion (*Joyous Lake* and *Stone Blue*), ethnic Eastern sounds expanded with multi-tracking (*Baiyina*), and eclectic duets with the likes of Joe Satriani, Michael Hedges, and his early hero Les Paul (*All Sides Now*). Despite these incongruous tangents, Pat's guitar voice and conception are never lessened or compromised. Rather, the changing environments attest to the deep musicianship and ability to adapt, which has been his credo since the early days.

Pat's sound, phrasing, originality, facility, melodic sense, and rhythmic delivery are legendary. Most listeners identify him by his complex modern jazz lines, generally arranged in long strings of impeccably articulated eighth notes (fast tempos), sixteenth notes (double-timing at a moderate tempo), or thirty-second notes (slow ballads). Since his earliest recordings, muscular technique, impeccable time, and ornate passagework have characterized his single-note improvisations.

He has a penchant for the minor mode and tends to think in terms of related minor equivalents of major and dominant seventh scales when playing a major-key standard or the blues. Pat credits Wes Montgomery with instilling this conception in him. Of the minor scales he uses to good advantage are the Dorian mode, the harmonic minor scale, the Aeolian mode, and the ascending melodic minor scale (also called the "jazz minor" scale). Pat often employs the various minors as substitutes for altered dominant seventh sounds, as befits a hard bop vocabulary and MO. He also frequently colors his bop-based lines with abundant chromaticism and unusual melodic patterns.

Pat often inserts ear-catching intervallic ideas and dissonant avant-garde patterns into his jazz improvisations—particularly in his post-1970 playing. Many of these were formulated from studies of mathematical music and modern "classical" composers. Some of the patterns arose from his experiments with the chromatic scale and symmetrical divisions of the octave, such as the four-note diminished chord, the eight-tone diminished scale, the three-note augmented chord, the six-note whole tone scale, and the tritone interval, as different points of a star. This concept is expressed in Pat's use of an emblematic twelve-pointed star diagram as a representation of these divisions.

Other singular notions came from ethnic music. In the seventies, Pat referred to a large hand-written tome he had compiled documenting a series of personal studies that employed many unusual and exotic scales and modes from various "world cultures" like Ethiopian, Byzantine, Persian, Hindustani, and Japanese sources in addition to more conventional pentatonic, hexatonic, and diatonic scales.

ESSENTIAL LISTENING

Over his five-decade career, Pat has released a number of important groundbreaking albums. Prime among these are his debut record *El Hombre* (Prestige) and *East* (Prestige) from the sixties, *The Visit* (Cobblestone, re-issued by Muse as *Footprints*), *Consciousness* (Muse), *We'll Be Together Again* (Muse), and *Joyous Lake* (Warner Bros.) from the sixties, *Interchange* (Muse), *The Maker* (Evidence), and *Stone Blue* (Blue Note) from the nineties, and *Live at Yoshi's* (Blue Note) from 2001. Also essential is Pat's reverential tribute to his role model Wes Montgomery, appropriately titled *Remember* (Blue Note, 2005).

ESSENTIAL VIEWING

Legends of Jazz Guitar, Volume 3 (Vestapol video) features an historic comeback performance taped live at Ethel's Place in Baltimore, Maryland. Filmed in 1987, the reading of "Do You Have a Name" features Pat fronting a guitar-bass-drums trio. Recovering from the devastating brain disorder and surgeries that left him in total amnesia in 1980, Pat was seen here performing at about seventy-five percent of his powers and is still stunning. It remains an inspiration and testimony to his courage and tenacity.

Also of great significance is Ian Knox's *Martino Unstrung* (Sixteen Films), a 2008 DVD documentary that chronicles Pat's story of recovery, the details of his medical condition, and his return to musical prominence. It features a compelling live version of Benny Golson's "Killer Joe."

Pat Martino is well represented online. Notable clips include digitalized vintage excerpts of his instructional series, several detailing and demonstrating his remarkable minor-conversion approach, telling moments from seminars and clinics, and many must-see live performance pieces, including "Impressions," "The Great Stream," "Oleo," "These Are Soulful Days," "Welcome to a Prayer," "Sunny" (with guest John Scofield), "On the Midnight Special" and "Going to a Meeting" (modern blues), "Full House," and "Round Midnight." Also worth searching for is a video segment of Pat and Joe Bonamassa playing "Use Me" (Studio Jams #29) in the studio.

SOUND

Pat has used a variety of guitars over the course of his career. His father bought him a gold-top Les Paul Standard in 1956 when he showed initial promise. This was the mid-fifties model with two white "soap-bar" single-coil pickups and a combination bridge/tailpiece. Within six months, Pat replaced it with a top-of-the-line black Les Paul Custom. He began his professional life with this instrument and used it until it was stolen while on the road with Jack McDuff in 1965.

Pat bought a sunburst Gibson ES-175 with a single humbucking pickup in Chicago as a quick replacement. This move signaled a trend toward arch-top hollow-body jazz guitars. The 175 became his main instrument until the time of his first album as a leader, *El Hombre* (1967). Then, he was seen using a Gibson Johnny Smith model. Plagued with feedback problems, Pat switched to a sunburst mid-sixties Gibson L5-CES with a Florentine cutaway for the remainder of the decade.

The seventies saw numerous musical changes, and Pat responded by using a number of varied instruments. He got his first custom luthier-built arch-top when Sam Koontz built him a singular model as a gift. This guitar had a Florentine cutaway, sunburst finish, oval sound hole, and a neck-mounted floating DeArmond pickup. Koontz installed a special door, which closed off the sound hole to prevent feedback.

Pat played a pawnshop prize, a cheap Univox electric 12-string on 1970's *Desperado*. This guitar was re-strung as an eight-string with unisons on the first four courses. Pat played a similarly strung Gibson ES-335-12 sporadically in the early seventies. He also continued to use a Gibson L5-CES and had acquired a second model in a natural finish with a Venetian cutaway. During the mid-seventies, Pat employed a one-of-a-kind arch-top guitar synthesizer with built-in modules. This unusual instrument, also built by Sam Koontz, is pictured on the back cover of *Starbright*. When Pat was playing higher-decibel jazz-rock fusion with Joyous Lake in 1976–1977, he used a solid-body cherry-sunburst Gibson L5-S.

Pat withdrew from performing in the late seventies and began teaching at Los AngeLes's Guitar Institute. There, he used Ovation Adamas acoustic guitars: one an unusual double-neck model with mirror image stringing. On occasion, Pat also played a custom-made Ibanez solid-body electric.

Pat underwent brain surgery in 1980 and, after a long convalescence, gradually returned to performance. He played and endorsed a Polytone solid-body guitar in 1983 at his first public concerts of the eighties. By the mid-eighties, he was seen with an Abe Rivera custom solid-body. This luxurious carved guitar was made of exotic woods and inlayed with pearl. The Rivera solid body became Pat's main instrument throughout the late eighties and the nineties. It is seen on the album covers of *Return* (1987), *The Maker* (1994), and *Nightwings* (1996).

After toying with a new black Gibson Les Paul Custom and experimenting with a Parker Fly guitar (heard on *Stone Blue*) in the nineties, Pat moved to Gibson and designed a signature model in conjunction with the Gibson Custom Shop. This guitar was issued in 1998 and came in two versions: Custom and Standard. The P.M. Custom has a thin semi-solid mahogany body with a highly figured maple top, gold-plated hardware, ebony fingerboard without markers, and a straight string-pull headstock. The Standard has the same dimensions with plainer wood under a painted top and nickel-plated hardware. Pat played both models, most often a Custom in cherry sunburst and a black Standard, for about ten years.

Currently Pat plays and endorses a Benedetto Pat Martino signature model. This guitar has a thin 14½-inch chambered mahogany body, carved maple top, two Benedetto A-6 humbucking pickups, ebony fingerboard, and black hardware.

In the early days of his career, Pat used Fender and Ampeg amplifiers. Studio shots from the sixties picture him plugging his L5 into an Ampeg combo amp. He has also expressed a fondness for Fender Twin Reverb amps for live and studio playing prior to the nineties. Pat also occasionally used Acoustic 134 amps with four 10-inch speakers in the seventies. He beefed up his rig with high-power 300-watt Crown DC300 power amps and a rack system during his Joyous Lake touring. At that time, he also used various preamps and effects processors, such as a Roland Be-Ba fuzz tone and an Electro-Harmonix Dr. Q envelope follower. The former is heard on "Line Games," the latter on "M'Wandishi"—both on *Joyous Lake*.

Upon his long-awaited return to public performing in the early eighties, Pat briefly endorsed and played Polytone amplifiers, though he generally preferred Roland JC-120 amps by decade's end. With 1994's *Interchange*, Pat began recording direct (into the board) as a regular practice. He relied on rented Fender and Roland amps while touring. Currently, Pat uses an Acoustic Image Clarus amplifier, both on the road and in the studio as a preamp. In concert, he employs the appropriate speaker cabinets. These range from rented Fender and Marshall cabinets to larger stadium systems. When recording, Pat plugs his P.M. guitars into the Clarus and then routes the signal to the board via the amp's direct output. These days, he frequently adds reverb and occasional light echo with a Lexicon rack-mounted unit during live performance.

Pat is notorious for using extra-heavy strings and extra-heavy picks. These are vital components of his big, robust sound. In the past, Pat has used flat-wound and semi-polished strings, beginning with a .016 high E string. A typical Martino set would be (from high to low) .016, .018, .026, .036, .046, and .058. These days, he uses an extra-heavy, custom-gauged flatwound set made by GHS. Currently, the GHS Custom Shop markets a slightly lighter flatwound Pat Martino set, gauged .015–.052. Over the years, Pat experimented with a variety of picks made from different materials. He has used super-heavy picks made of celluloid, wood, metal, stone, and plastic. I have one of his ebony picks of the seventies in my collection, and, believe me, it is *heavy!*

Courtesy Pat Martino

LICKS

FIG. 1: HARD BOP

Here's a classic line from Pat's vintage hard bop years. This long winding phrase is played over a fast swing groove in cut time and contains several key ingredients. Prime among these are the chromatically tinged descent in measures 1 and 2, interval leaps, skips, and arpeggios in measures 3 and 4, and a trademark minor-mode ending pattern in measure 5. Note the deliberate accents. These impart a staccato punctuation to the phrase, which is vital to its rhythmic impact. This line is in G minor and based on the G Dorian mode, but with Pat's *minorizing* perspective, it can also be used over C7 and Em7♭5, as heard on many Martino recordings. That's the beauty and malleability of his conception.

FIG. 1.

FIG. 2: BOSSA NOVA BURNER

The second Martino phrase is played with a moderate bossa nova feel and is a telling example of his approach to the time-honored ii–V–I progression (Dm7–G7–Cmaj7, in this case). It is also a definitive demonstration of his double-timing approach. In this passage, the sixteenth note gets the beat, and the melody line spells out three of his favorite devices. The first is the rising chromatically embellished D minor idea in measures 1 and 2. This is followed in the middle of measure 2 (beats 2–4) by an unmistakable *dominant seventh substitution*: A♭ melodic minor (the ascending form only) played over a G7 chord. This procedure generates a *fully altered scale*, which automatically colors the melody with raised 9ths and 5ths (B♭ and E♭, respectively) and a ♭9th (A♭). The resolution to C major in measure 3 contains a third Martino motif made of rising arpeggios and a bebop-based chromatic line, which fills in and decorates the C hexatonic scale.

FIG. 2.

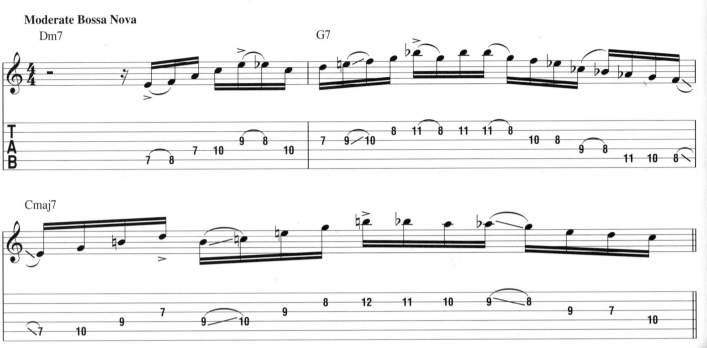

FIG. 3: FIERY FUSION

Pat is a master of combining traditional jazz sounds with post-modern atonal and intervallic gestures. This phrase is a fusion line in F minor and can be played over Fm7 or Bb7. This abstract melody contains all twelve tones of the chromatic scale or, put another way, a twelve-tone row, and flaunts several diverse ideas. The first is the rising melody in measure 1. This is made from the F minor pentatonic scale. The next section in measures 2 and 3 involves *perfect 4th* interval patterns.

The first of these is a sequence of seventh chord arpeggios in 4th intervals: Fm7–Cm7–Bb7. The second is made exclusively of 4th intervals (known as *quartal* harmony) and wide interval jumps. Both are favorite figures. The uncategorizable arpeggios in measure 3 (beats 2 and 3) present another famed Martino-ism. The descent in measures 3–5 is a typical "outside" sequential line that poses Eb minor, Bb major, and E+ sounds in a descending cycle over F minor.

FIG. 3.

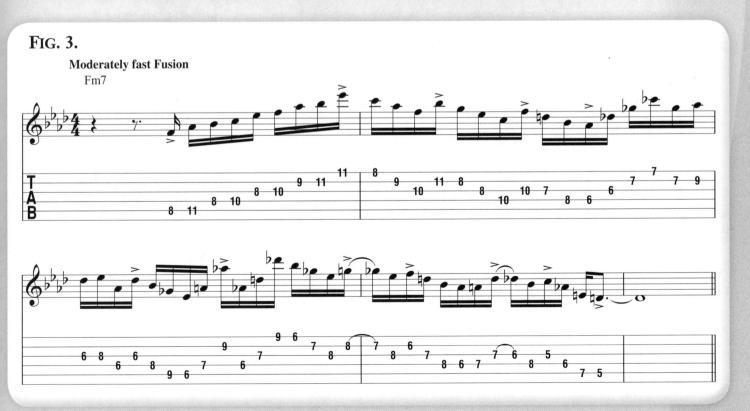

PAT METHENY

© Photofest

At age eighteen, he met future employer Gary Burton, who recommended him for a teaching post at the famed Berklee College of Music in Boston. At twenty, he began an important period with Gary Burton's group on the ECM jazz label. At twenty-one, he made his debut record *Bright Size Life* (1975) on ECM. The rest, as the cliché has it, is history.

To say Metheny plays jazz guitar for a new generation is an understatement. While he is quick to cite Jim Hall as the "father" of the style he and a number of his contemporaries chose, he is equally influential in the current circle. The vanguard of the new breed, Metheny is unapologetically eclectic and versatile. He has been since he started his recording and performing career, veering off into tangents loosely described as fusion, new age, minimalism, electronica, post-bop, free jazz, and world music. It's been a lifelong quest for expression with Metheny to present that multi-faceted vision in a cohesive but unrestrained presentation.

*P*at Metheny is one of the biggest stars in jazz. If that notion comes off as oxymoronic, consider the facts. Metheny has made thirty-four albums, selling over 20 million units worldwide. He has earned seventeen Grammy awards. He has been nominated for thirty-three Grammies—across genres in twelve categories, winning in ten of them (the only one ever to achieve this). And he has struck gold with three albums.

Metheny is the leading guitarist in contemporary jazz, routinely filling large halls and stadiums in all corners of the globe without compromising his music. He is also a transcendent performer comfortable with a wide range of cohorts, from Michael Brecker, Jaco Pastorius, Herbie Hancock, Joshua Redman, and Chick Corea to Paul Simon, Joni Mitchell, Enrique Morente, Jerry Goldsmith, and Bruce Hornsby.

It would appear Metheny was destined for guitar greatness. He picked up the guitar at age thirteen. By sixteen, he was a local legend in his native Kansas City region and won a *Downbeat* scholarship. He duly impressed master jazz guitarist Attila Zoller, who invited him to New York. Metheny attended the University of Miami as a teenager and was teaching advanced students there by the time he was seventeen.

To the listener, there are many Methenys. There's the one in the early ECM period, whose work was characterized by dreamy impressionistic atmospheres. There's the one shaping the tighter, arranged output of various Pat Metheny Group projects. There's another, the master improviser, involved in spirited collaborations with Ornette Coleman (*Song X*), Michael Brecker (*Time Is of the Essence*), Brad Mehldau (*Metheny Mehldau*) and others. And then there's the conceptualist, whose narrative guides the musical journeys in *As Falls Wichita*, *So Falls Wichita Falls*, *Secret Story*, and *Imaginary Day*. As if to underscore the point, his 2011 album *What It's All About* (Nonesuch) revealed yet another aspect of the Metheny mosaic. After nearly forty years of recording under his name, this all-acoustic solo collection was the first to be issued without a single Metheny original. Instead, the program found the guitarist exploring new riches in classics written by the Beatles, Paul Simon, Paul Williams, Carly Simon, Burt Bacharach, Henry Mancini, and others. Heck, there's even a Metheny reading of "Pipeline" for solo acoustic. In any case, one common denominator pervades the diverse environments of the last four decades: they are all enlivened by Metheny's imaginative and colorful guitar playing.

INFLUENCES

Pat Matheny was raised in a musical family. His grandfather, father, and older brother Mike all played trumpet. Metheny learned to read and write music at an early age from his brother. Early listening included jazz artists Miles Davis, John Coltrane, and Ornette Coleman. During junior high school years, Metheny "fooled around" with tunes like "Louie, Louie" and "Little Latin Lupe Lu." Largely self-taught on guitar, he learned jazz tunes like "Solar" and practiced eight hours a day while in high school. Metheny later studied theory at the University of Miami.

Metheny's jazz influences include guitarists Jim Hall, Wes Montgomery, Joe Pass, Grant Green, Joe Diorio, Jimmy Raney, and Kenny Burrell. Metheny cites Montgomery's *Smokin' at the Half Note* as particularly important. He also claims other jazz instrumentalists as influences: vibraphonist Gary Burton, pianists Keith Jarrett, Chick Corea, and McCoy Tyner, bassist Steve Swallow, and avant-garde free jazz saxophonist Ornette Coleman.

Metheny is an admirer of numerous pop and rock music artists, including The Beatles, James Taylor (after whom he named the song "James" on *Offramp*), Bruce Hornsby, Cheap Trick, and Joni Mitchell (with whom he performed on her *Shadows and Light* 1980 live tour). Metheny is also a fan of Buckethead's music.

STYLE

Pat Metheny boasts one of the most individual and unique guitar styles in jazz. Like his forebears, Wes Montgomery, Django Reinhardt, and Charlie Christian, he is immediately recognizable and distinct from his contemporaries. And like those predecessors, he founded a school of playing that is widely copied and/or alluded to by today's younger musicians.

Metheny's playing conveys a modern post-bop jazz conception. Asymmetric phrasing, angular lines, modernistic interval leaps, extensive chromaticism, looping ostinato figures, unpredictable textural shifts, rhythmical elasticity, and unusual across-the-barline passages mark his single-note playing. Metheny's personal phrasing choices shape the flowing nature of his improvised lines. He favors a linear approach filled with slides, slurs, and legato flurries, expanded by inserted double stops and partial chord textures. Unlike most guitarists in the fusion camp, Metheny remains closer in tone and feeling to his lyrical heroes Hall and Montgomery.

He adheres to the bebop genre's traditional clean arch-top sound with heavier flatwound strings. He rarely bends strings and generally eschews the overdriven timbres of rock-oriented fusionists.

Metheny is an accomplished chord player with an approach that is as wide ranging as his solo improv style. He is an inventive and supportive accompanist behind Michael Brecker or Joshua Redman. In his own groups, Metheny varies his ensemble work on acoustic and electric guitar from Latin/Brazilian chord figures, strummed patterns, and plucked/fingerstyle arpeggiations reminiscent of folk and country to dissonant modernistic sonorities in more harmonically complex compositions. A noteworthy chordal example is the elegant Nashville-tuned main rhythm figure that propels "Phase Dance."

Original compositions figure prominently in the Metheny equation. That's one reason his quicksilver style eludes his most ardent disciples. His compositions are well-conceived vehicles for *his* unconventional

playing. Solos like "Third Wind" on 1987's *Still Life (Talking)* or "Bright Size Life" (from his 1975 debut album) drive that point home unerringly. Metheny has asserted that early on his personal style didn't ideally suit typical song vehicles favored by traditional jazz guitarists—so he composed music that would. Most consider his playing within this environment as definitive. However, he is capable of functioning effectively within a more standard context—but in his own way—as heard in standard tunes like "All the Things You Are" and "Solar" on 1990's straight-ahead jazz album *Question and Answer*.

Metheny's compositions reflect sonic globalism. It's an eclectic musical view wherein Brazilian rhythms, sounds of the American heartland (which, at times, lend a familiar folk/country tinge), Asian modality, New Age minimalism, and electronically generated techno soundscapes merge with post-bop jazz harmony and melodic freedom, ethereal acoustic colors, and jazz-rock fusion tangents. Many of his recordings are distinguished by wordless Latin-influenced vocalizing (as on *Still Life*), similar to Milton Nascimento, which became a fixture in his repertory. As regards to electronics and techno sounds, Metheny was a pioneer of the guitar synthesizer, using the instrument regularly on record and in concert. This is another identifier of his arranging and style.

Though generally associated with a soft, clean guitar sound, traditional acoustic colors, or synth guitar timbres, Metheny occasionally adopts an edgy distortion for jazz-rock fusion lines—as in "Fear and Trembling" on 2007's *Metheny Meldhau Quartet* album. Unlike most jazz guitarists, Metheny uses a number of alternate tunings, including Nashville high-strung tuning ("Phase Dance," "Sueno Con Mexico," "Country Poem" and "New Chautauqua"), D tuning and various 12-string tunings, like (from high to low) F–F, G–C, F–B♭, E♭–A♭, C–F, and B♭–E♭, the signature tuning heard on "San Lorenzo" (*Pat Metheny Group*).

ESSENTIAL LISTENING

Pat Metheny's definitive work is sprawling, spread out amongst numerous albums of the last four decades. For fans of his ECM period, his debut *Bright Size Life*, *Pat Metheny Group*, and *Offramp* are recommended. *Still Life (Talking)* is an example of Metheny's globalism, reconciling his Brazilian influence with his Missouri roots. Fans of live Metheny are directed to *The Road to You* and *Travels*. Listeners interested in the straight-ahead modern jazz side of Metheny are advised to explore *Question and Answer* and *Trio 99→00* as well

as his collaborations with Brad Mehldau and sideman dates with Michael Brecker and Joshua Redman. Those with a penchant for the exotic should check out *Song X* and *Zero Tolerance for Silence*.

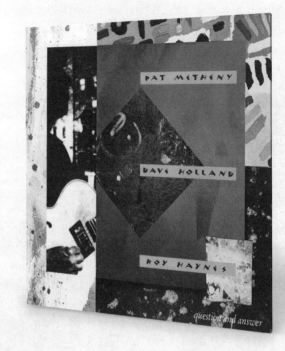

ESSENTIAL VIEWING

Pat Metheny can be seen in concert on a number of well-recorded DVDs. Recommended are the Pat Metheny Group offerings *The Way Up (Live)*, *Speaking of Now (Live)*, *Imaginary Day (Live)* (all on Eagle Rock Entertainment), and *We Live Here (Live in Japan)* (Image Entertainment). Also worth searching for is *Dejohnette-Hancock-Holland-Metheny* (Geneon-Pioneer). This 1990 concert finds Metheny in very fast company indeed with three of the most influential jazz artists of the modern age.

Metheny is well represented online. There are numerous clips of live performances worldwide tracing his youthful beginnings to his ascension and pre-eminence as a fully developed artist.

SOUND

Pat Metheny generally favors a clean, fat tone a la Wes Montgomery and Jim Hall. He sets his tone control low (almost off) for a darker sound and boosts the signal in the mid range on his amp, which allows the tone to cut through the mix without high-end sharpness.

Metheny played a blond 1958 Gibson ES-175N archtop guitar with a single pickup for most of his career. This modified instrument has binding on the headstock and, at one time, had two pickups (in an L5 layout) and a synthesizer interface. When it was last seen it had been changed to a single neck-pickup configuration with holes for the switch and controls crudely filled and the cavity for the bridge pickup open. Metheny replaced its one-time broken strap button with a plastic toothbrush handle, which still graces the guitar.

Currently Metheny plays Ibanez signature models. Ibanez markets two Metheny models. Both are laminated-maple arch-tops with neck-body joints at the seventeenth fret. The PM-120 has two pickups, ebony fingerboard with abalone/pearl block inlays, three controls (two volumes, master tone), and an uncommon double-cutaway body, which looks like a cross between an ES-175 and Howard Roberts' "black guitar." The P35 has a more traditional design with a single Venetian cutaway shape, five-piece maple/bubinga neck, rosewood fingerboard with abalone block inlays, a single pickup, and two controls. In 1990, Metheny played an earlier version of the PM with different specs: pickup placement like an ES-175, headstock with no inlay, and an ebony tailpiece. Metheny also has a Sadowsky solid-body nylon-string electric guitar, a Fender Telecaster, and a Coral electric sitar in his arsenal.

Metheny has a number of acoustic guitars made by Canadian luthier Linda Manzer. The most unusual is a triple-neck forty-two-string "Pikasso" guitar with a six-string neck and two unfretted 12-string drone necks plus additional sympathetic strings. The most recent use of the Pikasso was on *Metheny Mehldau Quartet* in Metheny's impressionistic composition "The Sound of Water." It is also heard on albums like *Quartet, Imaginary Day, Jim Hall & Pat Metheny, Trio→Live*, and the *Speaking of Now Live* and *Imaginary Day* DVDs. Manzer has made other acoustic guitars for Metheny, including a standard six-string, a mini guitar (heard on "Letter from Home"), an acoustic sitar guitar, a 12-string, and a baritone guitar in modified Nashville tuning used for the recording of *One Quiet Night*. Metheny also plays Ovation and Guild Mark 2 nylon-string acoustics, a Guild D40C cutaway dreadnaught, Guild F-212C cutaway 12-string, a GEWA harp guitar ("Oasis" on *Watercolors*), and Fylde and Ibanez acoustic 12-strings.

During his seventies stint with Gary Burton's group Metheny used an electric 12-string, often in creative new tunings (like 4ths and 5ths instead of octaves), to color the band's sound. His instrument of choice then was either a Guild Starfire-12 or a Fender Coronado. He later used Ibanez and Epiphone Casino-style electric 12-strings. On Metheny recordings, the odd-tuned 12-string is heard on "Sirabhorn" (*Bright Size Life*) and "San Lorenzo" (*Pat Metheny Group* and *Travels*).

For years, Metheny used a Roland GR-300 Guitar Synthesizer. He debuted his application of the guitar synth in 1982 on *Offramp*. Unlike other guitar synth users, Metheny gravitates to a small number of sounds. He treats each of the synthesized timbres as a separate instrument and plays each as an instrument instead of incidental color. One of the patches that he used often was incorporated into Roland's JV-80 "Vintage Synth" expansion card titled "Pat's GR-300."

© Jan Persson CTSIMAGES

Through most of his performing career (1974-1994) Metheny used a solid-state Acoustic 134 amplifier with four 10-inch JBL speakers, prized for its mellow mid-range tone and loud clean volume. He used Peavey and later Yamaha G-100 2x12 combos as alternative amps. In recent years, he switched for reasons of reliability and portability to a Digitech 2101 GSP guitar preamp. In the studio, particularly when recording live with a jazz band, Metheny often runs his guitar into a direct box (feeding an isolated amp) and plays in a separate room with loud monitors instead of headphones.

Metheny often uses digital delays to produce an enlarged dimensional sound, likened to a chorus effect. He prefers the "natural" chorus created by studio-quality delay units to stomp boxes. For years, he has used the Lexicon Prime-Time rack-mount delay for this purpose. The output of his Digitech preamp or Acoustic 134 was connected to two Lexicon delays. One is set at 14 ms (left side) and the other at 26 ms (right side). Each has a slight pitch bend controlled by the unit's VCO sine wave. This creates the "chorused" sound. The processed signal is sent to Yamaha power amps and 15-inch EV speakers on stage. Metheny uses three discrete sources: two processed signals and a straight signal. Live, he prefers to hear his center unprocessed amp tone flanked by distant delayed sounds from spread right/left speakers. Additionally, his straight guitar sound is processed with a slight delay set at 450–500 ms to add length to his notes.

Metheny strings his electric guitar with a D'Addario Jazz Light Chromes flatwound string set (gauged .011–.050). D'Addario makes a special set of "Pat Metheny Deadwound" strings for him because he prefers strings that sound old for the characteristic "thump"—an essential part of his sound. He uses thin D'Addario picks and attacks strings with the round end, holding the pick upside down.

LICKS
FIG. 1: PAT'S SAMBA

This complex single-note phrase is a definitive Pat Metheny line played over a brisk samba groove. It contains a number of idiomatic moves and substitutions. Played in relentless sixteenth notes over an F7sus4 chord (or E♭/F, an eleventh chord) it is a study in the sorts of movement—melodically and harmonically—found in countless solos in his repertory. Notable are the abundant legato passages (slides, pull-offs, and hammer-ons), quick position changes, and the many "cells" and small nuclear figures used throughout. The latter are generally arranged in four-note groups and here fall into several categories: pure chromatic lines (ascending and descending) plus a skip, 3rd intervals moved chromatically (measure 2), and pentatonic patterns (measure 3). Often, Metheny links cells to create longer two-beat or greater figures, as in measure 1 (beat 4) to measure 2 (beat 1) and measure 2 (beats 3 and 4). He manipulates these patterns freely in his melodic flow to generate brief excursions into remote tonalities—i.e., "playing outside"—a fixture of his jazz improv style. In the course of this shifting phrase, his melodies over F7 suggest visits to C7, G♭, A♭, G, Gm, A♭m, Am, E♭m, E♭, and Cm.

FIG. 1.

Fast Jazz Rock Samba

F7sus4

FIG. 2: PAT'S DISSONANT BLUES

This bristling Pat Metheny passage takes place over a 12-bar blues in A and begins in bar 8 over the VI chord (F#7). Like many post-bop jazz artists playing over the blues form (Chick Corea in "Matrix" comes to mind), Metheny approaches the chord progression freely and embellishes the solo with considerable dissonance and chromaticism. In the past, he has described his conception as "angular" and "semi atonal," and he might have been thinking of flights like this. Throughout, he plays numerous trademark chromatic lines and melodic/harmonic substitutions replete with slurs, clearly stretching the blues tonality beyond traditional jazz or even the most harmonically active bebop. This is a departure—more like the avant-garde "free jazz" of his idol Ornette Coleman applied to guitar. In measures 5–9, Metheny sets up a series of wide-interval arpeggios, which is the apotheosis of angularity. He plays ear-catching arpeggios built on 5th intervals. They occur first as part of a chromatically descending sequence (measure 5–6) and then are developed in a longer phrase, which ascends in 4ths and combines 5ths and a chromatic tone (measures 6–9).

FIG. 2.

FIG. 3: PAT'S PASTORAL SIDE

Pat Metheny has a folksy pastoral side that complements his modern jazz proclivities and emerges in tunes that allude to his heartland roots. This catchy chord figure is a case in point. Here, he tunes his guitar to high-strung "Nashville tuning" (strings 1 and 2 are normal; the other four tuned an octave higher and replaced with much lighter gauges) for a unique timbre. The pattern is deceptively simple with three iterations of the basic riff, first played over D major

and then verbatim over Bm7, its relative minor. This is answered and offset by a mildly dissonant statement of the figure in B♭maj7♯11, connoting the Lydian mode (of F major) as its harmonic source. Such subtle harmonic digression is typical of Metheny's command and thoughtful use of modal jazz mixed with simpler, almost pop, elements. The blend is organic in his music and one example of what makes his compositions so accessible yet fresh and unique.

FIG. 3.

Nashville tuning

Moderately

*D/Bm7

*Played over D major 1st time, Bm7 2nd time.

B♭maj7♯11

WES MONTGOMERY

© Photofest

sound reverberates across the entire musical spectrum—in the heaviest hard rock and the lightest New Age settings. It is equally at home in commercial jingles, smooth jazz, syrupy "elevator music," and virtually all forms of contemporary pop music.

INFLUENCES

Wes Montgomery was raised in a musical family. His brothers, bassist Monk (an early pioneer of electric bass) and pianist Buddy, were role models in his formative years. The three later performed and recorded together as the Mastersounds in the mid fifties. As a youth, Wes dabbled on the four-string tenor guitar, a gift from Monk, but described his efforts as "not really playing." Nonetheless, he would certainly have become familiar with the basics of fingering, coordination, touch, etc.

Wes has cited proto-bop guitarist Charlie Christian as his primary influence—particularly the masterpiece "Solo Flight." A late bloomer, Wes picked up the guitar at age 19 and taught himself by copying Christian's solos and riffs. A year later, he was gigging regularly, playing Christian solos at the local 440 Club in Indianapolis. Wes also acknowledged the influence of Django Reinhardt to a lesser degree and George Henry, a little-known regional guitarist from Chicago. He later listened to Barney Kessel, Jimmy Raney, and Tal Farlow, the leading players of the fifties. Like most jazz guitarists, various wind players such as Charlie Parker, Clifford Brown, Dizzy Gillespie, Miles Davis, and John Coltrane also affected Wes's single-note style and harmonic concepts.

Wes was the quintessential "ear player." He did not read music or study the theoretical side of music but absorbed and reinterpreted everything he heard around him in his immediate environment. As he came of age, these settings provided contact with players like vibist Lionel Hampton, trumpeter Fats Navarro, bassist Charlie Mingus, and pianist Milt Buckner. Wes also cited singers like Nat "King" Cole, Frank Sinatra, and Tony Bennett as influential.

Jazz guitar music—and all other music for that matter—wouldn't be the same without John Leslie "Wes" Montgomery. Wes was the avatar and guiding force behind the second great epoch of electric jazz guitar. If the first began with the innovations of Charlie Christian in the late thirties, then the next revolution belongs to Wes. Like the shock waves caused by Christian's solo flights, Montgomery's contributions resound through music history. He embodied and redefined the art of modern jazz guitar. After Wes burst onto the scene in 1959, all jazz guitarists were regarded as pre-Montgomery or post-Montgomery.

From Wes Montgomery, it is possible to draw a lineage and timeline that includes most subsequent jazz guitarists: George Benson, Pat Martino, Henry Johnson, Emily Remler, Lee Ritenour, and Pat Metheny to name a handful, as well as the most esteemed rock and blues players like Jimi Hendrix, Robbie Krieger, Carlos Santana, Larry Carlton, Eric Johnson, and Stevie Ray Vaughan. Ubiquitous today, the Wes Montgomery

STYLE

Wes Montgomery was the pre-eminent hard bop guitarist… and more. As a leading exponent of the genre, he was solidly rooted in blues and fluent in the language of bebop. Montgomery's single-note playing and harmonic conception reflect the modernism and sophistication of traditional bebop merged with the soulful blues edge and grittiness of hard bop. Wes applied the advanced harmonic concepts of chord substitution, altered chord dissonance, and extended modal melodies to his repertory and tempered these exotic elements with funky double stops and blues licks. Moreover, he had an uncanny rhythmic sense and inherent swing feel that lent a natural, organic quality to his improvisations.

A true musical pioneer, Wes did not confine himself to straight-ahead jazz. He explored various musical tangents throughout his career, experimenting with pop songs, rock grooves, Latin and Afro-Cuban rhythms, R&B and funk, and varied orchestral settings.

Octave playing is a prime identifier of the Montgomery guitar style. This approach involves the use of parallel octaves to render melodies that are normally found as single-note lines. At this, Wes is the uncontested champion of all time. Another identifier is Montgomery's astonishing facility with block chords. The ease and grace with which he played pianistic chord-melody passages at breakneck tempos struck many listeners, including seasoned players, as "impossible." Underlying it all is an ever-present infectious swing feel. Wes never sacrificed feel for complexity or technical concerns.

Montgomery had a great regard for large-scale form in his improvisations. His improvisational strategy often followed a three-tier approach in which he progressed from single notes to octaves and finally block chords, each of which is represented in the three licks of this chapter's music.

His physical picking technique is unique in the annals of guitar lore. Early on, he ditched the plectrum in favor of plucking notes and strumming chords exclusively with his thumb. When plucking single notes, Wes rested the fingers of his right hand on the upper bout face, necessitating the pearl inlays on custom guitars. This manner of attack resulted in not only a thicker, warmer sound but also an extremely personal voice on the instrument and earned the reverential nickname of "The Thumb" from his peers and fans. Most of Wes's single-note melodies, even those taken at double-time or fast tempo, were articulated with downstrokes, though film clips readily available today reveal he occasionally used alternate picking. Because most of his lines were done with down strokes, Wes generally slurred and slid between positions with his left hand to accommodate the articulation and connect phrases.

ESSENTIAL LISTENING

Practically everything Wes Montgomery recorded must be considered essential listening. At the top of the heap is *Smokin' at the Half Note* (Verve), an influential live/studio album that inspired a generation of musicians, including Pat Metheny. Recorded at the height of Wes's dominance at the famed New York City venue, it is further distinguished by the sympathetic backing of pianist Wynton Kelly and the Miles Davis rhythm section (from *Kind of Blue*).

Wes's debut record as a leader *The Wes Montgomery Trio* is an uncontested jazz classic, as is the follow-up effort *The Incredible Jazz Guitar of Wes Montgomery* and subsequent releases *So Much Guitar, Boss Guitar,* and *Full House* (all on Riverside). Also highly recommended is the definitive 12-disc box set *Wes Montgomery: The Complete Riverside Recordings*. This sprawling collection gathers every track recorded for the label from 1959–1963, which was his most straight-ahead jazz period.

Impressions: The Verve Jazz Sides is a serviceable 2-disc set that contains most of Wes's jazz tracks recorded during the Verve years of 1964–1966, including bonus live pieces from the important Half Note dates. Serious Wes Montgomery fans are directed to *Wes Montgomery—Movin': The Complete Verve Recordings*, a 5-disc set that collects all of Wes's work for the company, including his two albums with Jimmy Smith and the overdubbed live tracks released as *Willow Weep for Me*.

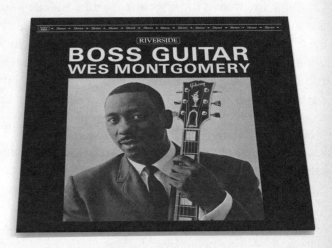

© K Abe CTSIMAGES

Sound

Wes made the Gibson L5CES his trademark instrument, and as a result, it is closely associated with the sound of modern jazz guitar. The L5 has been the gold standard in jazz guitar, in its amplified and acoustic forms, for over eighty years. It's a deluxe arch-top electric with a carved spruce top, 17-inch body, and a single cutaway shape. Wes used at least six different electric L5CES's on his definitive recordings from 1960 to 1968. The majority of these were double-pickup production models. When playing standard double-pickup production line L5s, Wes favored the neck pickup for its warmer tone.

Wes used a sunburst version with two Alnico pickups in the late fifties, seen often in photos from live club performances in Indianapolis (like those taken at the Essex House in 1959) and, curiously, a Gibson ad from 1964. He switched to humbucking models in the early sixties. Wes had a sunburst (cover of *The Very Best of Wes Montgomery*, Verve) and blond model (cover of *Full House*), both with Venetian cutaways. Wes played an early sixties L5 with a Florentine cutaway and sunburst finish on the 1960 *Full House* live album. It is also seen on the cover of Wes's first album for Verve, *Movin' Wes* (1964), and the reissue *Easy Groove* (Pacific Jazz/Liberty Records).

Essential Viewing

Wes Montgomery performances on film languished in obscurity for years. Vestapol videos obtained some footage from his 1965 British TV concerts for the BBC and added them sporadically to the *Legends of Jazz Guitar* series on video in the nineties. They followed up with a more definitive must-see volume *Wes Montgomery: Belgium 1965*. More recently, these and other British, Dutch, and Belgian appearances were compiled in one disc of the 2007 *Jazz Icons 2* and released as the *Wes Montgomery: Live in '65* volume of the DVD set.

Wes Montgomery is well represented online. Much of the European footage from the aforementioned releases is now digitalized and viewable as single songs. Snippets of NPR's *Just Coolin'* documentary on Wes is also available. Other lesser known but equally compelling European clips have surfaced. Among the essential new video is "Blue Monk" (Hamburg, 1965, with Johnny Griffin), "A Cool Glass of Wine," and other rehearsal takes from Hamburg, Germany.

Two of Wes's L5s were unique custom-made sunburst models built around 1965. These were basically Gibson L5C acoustic models with a Venetian cutaway and fitted with a single neck-position humbucking pickup. One of his custom L5s (the one seen most in current videos) had a heart-shaped pearl inlay on the upper bout. The other had a reversed humbucking pickup (turned 180 degrees so that the polepieces faced the bridge side) and his name and a diamond inlaid on the body cutaway bout near the pickguard.

On his 1959 debut recording session, Wes borrowed Kenny Burrell's L7C with a Charlie Christian bar pickup. Prior to 1959, Wes employed various less-expensive Gibson arch-tops, such as an ES125D with two P-90 pickups. He played the latter on a 1958 recording session with David Baker. Montgomery strung his guitars with heavy-gauge (low to high: .058 through .014) Gibson HiFi flatwound strings.

Wes amplified his guitars during his groundbreaking Riverside period with various late fifties and early sixties Fender tube combo amps. These included tweed, white

Tolex, and blackface types. Legend has it that famed engineer Rudy Van Gelder kept an old Fender Deluxe amp around just for Wes in his New Jersey recording studio. Wes also used an Ampeg combo amp in mid-sixties Verve recording sessions with Creed Taylor. In the mid-sixties, Montgomery switched to solid-state Standel Custom amps with a 15-inch speaker for most of his live playing. Specifically, Wes used the Custom 15 combo model equipped with dual channel tone controls, a contour control, reverb, tremolo, and a JBL D130 15-inch speaker. He alternated between Standel transistor and Fender tube amps for the remainder of his career.

A forward thinker, Wes occasionally experimented with sounds and instruments atypical of the jazz genre. In search of a deeper guitar tone to contrast the flute, he played a six-string bass for "Tune Up," "Body and Soul," and "Sandu" on *Movin' Along* (Riverside, 1960). He also experimented with combining miked amplifier and direct signals on "So Do It" on *Movin' Along*. A more extreme version of this studio technique accounted for the chorus-effect processing heard in "Heartstrings" on *The Montgomery Brothers: Groove Yard* (Riverside. 1961). Wes used an electronic tremolo effect on "Oh, You Crazy Moon" on *Willow Weep for Me* (Verve, 1965) and "Portrait of Jenny" on *Smokin' at the Half Note* (Verve, 1965) to add depth and dimension to the balladic statements.

LICKS
FIG. 1: CLASSIC WES BOP

This bopping phrase is a perfect example of Wes Montgomery's *linear* single-note style and horn-like conception. When playing single-note lines, he often employed a horizontal approach, climbing up and down the fingerboard in a linear manner, and alluded to the blowing phraseology of jazz wind players.

Three important Montgomery components are found in this excerpt. The ascending decorated-arpeggio figure, as in measure 1, is a fixture of Wes's style. Note the use of E and C♯ to color the line. The syncopated rhythmic pattern in measure 2 is another characteristic element. The quick descending run with its telltale hammer-ons, pull-offs, and slides in measure 3 completes the phrase. Interestingly, Wes never used his pinky (fourth finger) for executing slippery passages like this one. Instead, he favored an index-middle-ring fingering, which has more in common with rural blues and rock guitarists than most jazz guitar players.

This lick occurs in D minor and has a modal sound typical of hard bop jazz in the sixties. Never one to be pigeonholed, Wes also played this type of melody over Fmaj7 chords in standard tunes and over G7 chords, as in a blues in G.

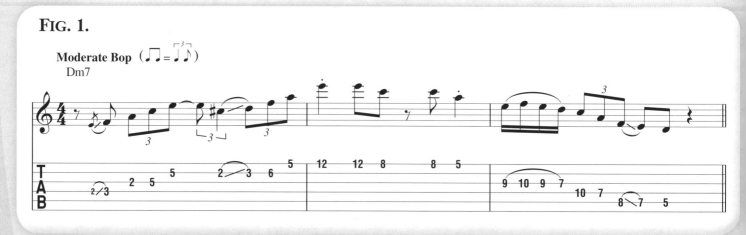

FIG. 1.

Moderate Bop

Dm7

FIG. 2: DEFINITIVE WES OCTAVE LICK

Wes Montgomery's use of octaves is arguably the most identifiable feature of his style. He incorporated octaves in both thematic playing and improvisation. This lick exemplifies his parallel-octave soloing approach. For octaves, Wes invariably used a locked-hand technique and two fingered shapes, each with a deadened string separating the fretted notes. Only the fingered two-note shape is sounded; all other notes are muted with the fret hand. This not only keeps it clean but also adds the requisite thickness and texture to the sound.

This lick is in D minor and contains two familiar Montgomery elements. The first is the rising arpeggio line embellished with slurs (half step below the principal notes) in measure 1. This "leading tone" or targeting effect is endemic to Wes's style and was used with single notes and chords as well. The second is the melodic sequence begun on beat 3 of measure 1, which is imitated twice in measure 2. This section exploits a typical syncopated rhythmic motif often found in Wes's lines. The imitative procedure results in a thematic, very musical quality, which is a cornerstone of his style.

FIG. 2.

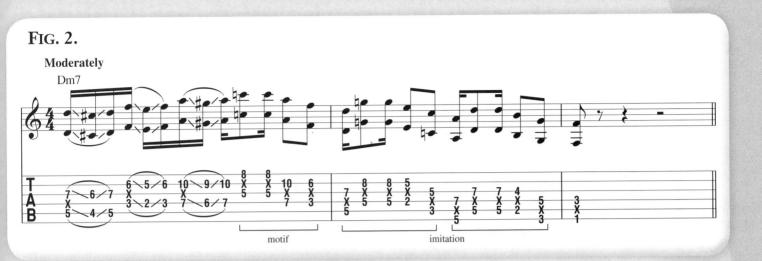

FIG. 3: SWINGING BLOCK CHORD LICK

Wes Montgomery is credited with making the leap of applying "piano thinking" to the guitar. This lick depicts the sort of improvised chord-melody phrase that astounded listeners when Wes first appeared on the scene. The first two measures feature a typical ii–V pattern in F, while measures 3 and 4 contain a favorite Wes turnaround figure. Note the signature use of *diminished chords* throughout the phrase in measures 1, 3, and 4. Wes applied diminished chords to progres-sions as both passing chords (check out measure 1) or as *chord substitutions*. In the latter case, diminished chords replace the dominant seventh chords D7 and C7 in measures 3 and 4 and create an altered chord sound characteristic of modern jazz harmony. The half-step moves in measure 2 produce a trademark Montgomery harmonic gesture. Wes used this sort of lick anywhere a ii–V–I chord change is found, including a blues.

FIG. 3.

OSCAR MOORE

© CTSIMAGES

Metronome poll every year from 1945–1948. He also received the coveted *Esquire* silver and gold awards in these years.

Moore left the Nat Cole Trio in 1947 when the leader opted for simpler pop vocal songs and lush string arrangements over the drummerless jazz trio he had established in the forties. In the ensuing years, Moore relocated to Los Angeles and recorded all too infrequently. During this period, he is best remembered for an R&B stint from 1947–1954 with his brother guitarist Johnny Moore in the Three Blazers and his jazz work in a quartet with pianist Carl Perkins in 1954–1955.

Initially overshadowed by the appearance of Charlie Christian in the late thirties, Moore was recognized as a harmonically advanced and highly accomplished player in the following decade. As such, he is an important "missing link" in the evolution of the electric guitar during the swing era, through the subsequent rise of bebop and birth of modern jazz. Moore's innovations fill the gap in the crucial period beginning with the death of Christian in 1942 and the emergence of new players like Barney Kessel, Johnny Smith, and Tal Farlow in the late forties and early fifties, though he was not part of that particular stream. In fact, in many ways his rhythmic, bop, and blues-inflected lines presage more modern stylists like Grant Green and Wes Montgomery. He is a true unsung hero of jazz guitar deserving of greater recognition.

Though his name may not draw knowing nods from the listeners of today, Oscar Moore's guitar licks are among the most memorable in Americana. Moore is perhaps best known for his impeccable contributions to Nat "King" Cole's version of "The Christmas Song (Chestnuts)"—a tune that's among the most standard of great American standards and a staple of the holiday season. The momentous track, recorded in 1946 by the original King Cole Trio, represents a high water mark in the productive career of the famed bandleader and was one of a select handful of pop hits in the era to feature beautiful jazz-tinged post-Charlie Christian guitar playing.

Oscar Moore's decade-long tenure with Nat Cole's group began in 1937. During that period, he also recorded with notable jazz artists like Art Tatum, Lionel Hampton, the Capitol Jazzmen, and Lester Young. By the mid forties, Moore was the music's newest star. He was rated Number One Guitarist in the prestigious *Down Beat* Reader's Poll and the

INFLUENCES

Oscar Moore was drawn to music at an early age. Born on Christmas day, 1912, in Austin, Texas, he was raised in Phoenix, Arizona, the son of a blacksmith and brass bandleader. Moore was essentially self-taught on the guitar, though he received some brief informal tutelage from a traveling worker named Carl Gomez. In later years, he absorbed the styles of jazz guitarists Charlie Christian and Django Reinhardt and cited classical guitarists Andres Segovia and Vicente Gomez as other significant influences.

STYLE

Barney Kessel once said that Oscar Moore practically created the role of the jazz guitarist in small combos. In the years between the swing era, with its emphasis on large horn-dominated ensembles, and the modern jazz era of the fifties, with its various quartets and quintets, Moore was the consummate guitar pioneer. His work with the Nat Cole Trio established the template in piano-guitar-bass ensembles. Moore's innovations and conception informed the approach of subsequent similar trios, including Oscar Peterson's trio with Herb Ellis and Ray Brown and Tal Farlow's 1950's trio with Eddie Costa and Vinnie Burke.

Oscar Moore is most readily recognized by his mellow single-note style, a snippet of which was, and is, heard by millions in his "Christmas Song" break. Like his predecessor and colleague Charlie Christian, Moore was an *electric guitarist*—one of the first of note in history. Accordingly, he favored lines that reflected a horn-like conception and conveyed a strong sense of swing. Moore's broad musical vocabulary encompassed classic blues licks and rhythmic swing-era melodies in addition to bebop and modern jazz elements. A masterful improviser, he exploited long strings of eighth notes as well as elegant melodic lines and shorter punctuating figures regularly in his solos. Moore incorporated slurs and legato phrasing abundantly into his playing to reinforce the guitar-horn impression, and would occasionally exaggerate these for more colorful glissando effects, as did Django Reinhardt and Les Paul in this period. He freely added earthy blues-based string bends and finger vibrato (as could be executed with the heavy-gauge strings of the day) to his more soulful phrases.

Moore also boasted a rich harmonic lexicon quite different from the simpler, less dissonant chord structures of the swing era's rhythm-guitar players. Unlike the triad-based players that preceded him, Moore employed bebop-inspired extended and altered chords and pianistic sonorities, sometimes voiced as knuckle-busting tone clusters. He was also fond of using parallel 3rds to harmonize melody lines, particularly as an alternate texture to single notes and fuller chords or in connecting phrases. The technique of moving from one texture to another ad lib in improvisation is an identifier of his style.

ESSENTIAL LISTENING

Nat King Cole: The Complete Capitol Trio Recordings (Mosaic) is a definitive set containing all of the Nat Cole Trio material from 1943–1949 as well as radio transcriptions. *Hit That Jive Jack: The Earliest*

Recordings (Decca) is a worthwhile collection of Cole Trio tracks from 1940–1941. Moore is featured on a number of important cuts in *The Best of the Nat "King" Cole Trio: The Instrumental Classics* (Capitol Jazz). *The Oscar Moore Quartet with Carl Perkins* (VSOP Tampa/Skylark Records) is a superb re-issue of Moore's straight-ahead jazz sessions of 1954.

ESSENTIAL VIEWING

Oscar Moore is seen prominently online in numerous vintage clips of the Nat "King" Cole Trio. Among the offerings are "Better to Be by Yourself," "I'm a Shy Guy," and "Solid Potato Salad," plus a number of lip-synced movie performances.

SOUND

Oscar Moore played non-cutaway arch-top acoustic guitars with a custom retro-fitted bar pickup for most of his career. His main instrument was a luxurious late-thirties or early-forties blond Gibson L-5 with a 17-inch body and a "Charlie Christian" bar pickup in the neck position. This guitar was seen in numerous performances and photo sessions with Nat "King" Cole's trio. It was featured in a 1947 Gibson ad campaign that capitalized on the success of the Cole Trio. During the late forties, as a result of his fame with the trio, the "Charlie Christian pickup" was dubbed the *"Oscar Moore pickup"* in Gibson's literature.

Earlier, Moore briefly played a blond 1940 Gibson ES-300—basically an electrified L-7, equipped with a *long diagonal pickup*. This was Gibson's 17-inch electric production model and was designed to optimize the amplified guitar's acoustic response by covering a larger 6¾-inch long diagonal space under the strings.

The longer pickup, striking in appearance, called for four M55 Alnico magnets and was mounted diagonally under the bass strings at the end of the fingerboard to the treble strings at the bridge.

Moore also played a top-of-the-line blond Epiphone Emperor acoustic arch-top guitar. This instrument, essentially the Epiphone equivalent of high-end Gibson arch-tops, was seen in a photo from a 1939 NBC radio broadcast. The cover shot of *The Oscar Moore Quartet* (re-issued CD) shows Moore playing a blond pre-1936 L-5 acoustic with a smaller body and a dot-inlaid fingerboard.

Moore most likely plugged his Gibson electrics into small Gibson amps, which was the typical amplified sound of the era. This would have included the EH models in the late thirties and early forties, the BR models in the mid-to-late forties, and the GA models in the fifties.

LICKS

FIG. 1: FREE-TIME EXCURSION

The first lick occurs over a ii–V–I progression in D♭ and contains several distinctive facets of the Oscar Moore style. The *parallel 3rds* in measure 1 are used to harmonize the E♭m7 (ii) chord and exploit an insistent D leading tone to the pattern. The A♭9 and A♭13♭9 *extended* and *altered chords* in measure 2 are indicative of the modern jazz sonorities Moore regularly used, as is the Dmaj7 in measure 3 employed as a *tritone substitution* for A♭7. The decorative fills in measures 3 and 4 are staples of Moore's playing. Note the slurred mordent lick in measure 3 and the use of an exotic A minor arpeggio and melody over A♭7 in measure 4. The former was a favorite ornament in Grant Green's approach, while the latter is a cliché of the hard bop language. This lick is played in free time over a slow ballad tempo.

FIG. 1.

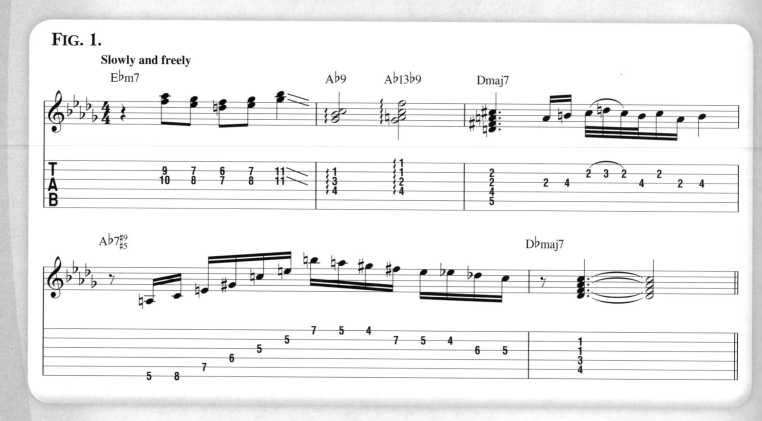

FIG. 2: SWINGIN' BLUES

This swinging phrase is played over a loping blues groove in B♭. The melody is typical of the kind of line Moore used in the opening measures of a 12-bar blues progression. Note the use of the take-off pickup lick, which begins the phrase, as well as the C♯–D approach tone pattern and legato three-note mordent figure in measure 1. The chromatic passing tones in measure 2 are slurred in Moore's characteristic horn-like fashion. The two-note interval jump (C to F) in measure 3 is a familiar swing jazz punctuation, while the arpeggio in measure 4 is an extension of B♭7, producing a modal thirteenth chord sound that is clearly ahead of its time.

FIG. 2.

FIG. 3: RHYTHM CHANGES

The third lick is played at a brisk swing tempo over the first three measures of a "Rhythm Changes" progression in A. This phrase poses various blues sounds over major-key chords—a proven tactic in many forms of modern music. Note the prominent use of the ♭3rd blue note, C♮, throughout. The quick rake-picked backward sweep in measure 1 (the first full measure) is a classic "smear" articulation device favored by countless players. Here, the sweep-picked figure implies an Am6 arpeggio played against the A major tonality for a nice bluesy but sophisticated effect. Moore's blue-toned melodic bent is maintained through the end of the phrase with greater emphasis on the F♯ and C notes in the riff-like figures of measures 2 and 3.

FIG. 3.

JOE PASS

© Ray Avery CTSIMAGES

*I*f Joe Pass had not been sidelined with drug addiction, he surely would have taken part in the great jazz guitar wave of the fifties. During that golden age, when players like Barney Kessel, Johnny Smith, Kenny Burrell, Jimmy Raney, Tal Farlow, Jim Hall, Herb Ellis, Howard Roberts, and Wes Montgomery came to prominence, he would have been one of the genre's leading innovators. As it was, fate had different plans for Pass. While learning the art and craft of bebop in New York City, he fell prey to the same habit of the milieu that plagued modern jazz musicians like Charlie Parker, Miles Davis, and John Coltrane. After knocking around, in and out of prison, for over ten years with heroin addiction, Joe entered Synanon in 1960. What followed is one of jazz guitar's greatest success stories.

Joe first gained public recognition with his guitar playing as part of the house band on 1961's *Sounds of Synanon*. His debut album, *Catch Me* (1963), and its landmark sequel, *For Django* (1964), established Pass's credentials in no uncertain terms. By 1965, he was in demand as one of most sought-after jazz sidemen of the era, backing artists such as George Shearing, "Groove" Holmes, Gerald Wilson, Benny Goodman, and Les McCann. At decade's end, Joe had released a string of albums on the Pacific Jazz label (these are finally available on CD in a

must-have Mosaic Records' collection) and was a local legend in Los AngeLes's jazz scene—Lee Ritenour once referred to him as "the president of bebop" on the West Coast, a notion shared by many up and coming guitarists of the day.

In 1972, Joe broke new ground with his *Virtuoso* album. The promise made by his Pacific Jazz sides was fulfilled on *Virtuoso*. This record featured Joe playing unaccompanied, improvised jazz guitar for an entire program of twelve songs. A set that sounds as fresh and impressive today, *Virtuoso* elevated standards in the music overnight. From this point on, virtuoso became Joe's handle. He reigned supreme in the solo guitar genre and did so until his untimely death in 1994. In retrospect, Joe Pass is one of the most important musicians of the twentieth century and remains the quintessential complete jazz guitarist.

INFLUENCES

Tales from the Joe Pass mythos have it that Gene Autry, the Singing Cowboy, inspired a nine-year old Joseph Anthony Passalaqua to pick up the guitar and become one of the world's greatest musicians—an idealized and romantic picture, but hardly accurate. Joe debunked that story years ago. Truth be told, Joe himself didn't recall exactly what prompted him to start playing… he just did. When he did, he took part in the neighborhood music scene in Johnstown, New Jersey—just hanging out with other guitarists, learning Italian singalong songs of the day, and listening. Lots of listening.

For about a year and a half, Joe took formal guitar lessons with a local multi-instrumental player. He learned to read music, worked through some Nick Lucas method books, and studied some simple guitar techniques from the *Carcassi Classical Guitar Method*. At this age, he practiced approximately six hours a day under the watchful eye and strict scrutiny of his father. By age twelve, Joe was an accomplished improviser and was playing professionally at local dances with older musicians. In this period, he became aware of jazz players like saxophonist Ben Webster and trumpeter Roy Eldridge.

In the forties, Joe was lured to the modern jazz sounds emanating from New York City. There he became conversant in the new language of bebop and jammed with many of its leading performers. Joe cited Dizzy Gillespie, Charlie Parker, Art Tatum, and Coleman Hawkins as influential in this phase of his development. In later years, he was also influenced by the piano style of Oscar Peterson. Joe Pass has named only three guitarists as having an influence on his playing: Charlie Christian, Django Reinhardt, and Wes Montgomery.

STYLE

Joe Pass has been likened, rightfully, to the great wind (sax and trumpet) and keyboard players of jazz. In a pure musical sense, his single-note style has much in common with instrumentalists of the classic bebop and hard bop schools. Hardly one for labels, Joe has always referred to himself as an improvising musician who happens to play and express himself through the guitar. Nonetheless, his agile single-note lines contain many of the melodies and phrases one associates with giants like Charlie Parker, John Coltrane, Dizzy Gillespie, Clifford Brown, and Sonny Rollins. It is primarily out of this framework that he operated. His execution and technique were hornlike and on par with his wealth of ideas and immense vocabulary, allowing single-note improvisations to flow like a saxophonist's stream of consciousness.

Joe also had a tougher funky aspect to his playing that incorporated bluesy string bends, double stops and partial chords, mutated swing licks, and rhythmically-charged R&B-inspired riffs. This side of his musical personality surfaced early on in solos with hard bop players like "Groove" Holmes and Les McCann and on blues and rock-oriented numbers like "Ode to Billie Joe" on 1970's *Intercontinental*.

Over the years, Joe developed a highly advanced harmonic approach that rivals most pianists' playing. He was particularly adept at improvising unaccompanied chord-melody solos. These mini-masterpieces are brilliantly showcased on the *Virtuoso* recordings and many other solo albums. In this setting, Joe was truly in a league of his own. Harnessing a variety of finger-picked, hybrid-picked, and flat-picked articulations and a patented mixture of ad lib chord passages, spontaneous counterpoint, and fleet bebop lines, he has reinterpreted—that is, virtually re-written at will—many of the greatest standard songs of history.

ESSENTIAL LISTENING

For Django (BGO Records, import), *Virtuoso* (Pablo), *Portraits of Duke Ellington* (Pablo), and *Intercontinental* (BASF) are jazz guitar essentials. *The Best of Joe Pass* (Pacific Jazz) is a serviceable single-disc overview of his early years. Also recommended are *The Complete Pacific Jazz Joe Pass Quartet Sessions* (Mosaic Records 5-disc collection), the Pablo compilation *Guitar Virtuoso*, and the dynamic pairing of Joe Pass and Oscar Peterson on *Oscar Peterson Et Joe Pass a Salle Pleyel (Live)* (Pablo). The aforementioned classic *For Django* is a high-water mark in jazz guitar and is contained, including previously unheard alternate takes of "Rosetta" and "Limehouse Blues" and the un-issued "Georgia on my Mind," in the Mosaic set.

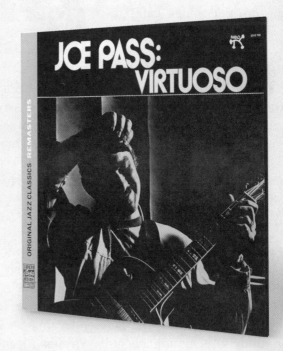

ESSENTIAL VIEWING

Norman Granz's Jazz in Montreux: Joe Pass '75 (Eagle Rock Entertainment), *The Genius of Joe Pass* (Vestapol), and *Joe Pass in Concert: Brecon Jazz Festival, 1991* (Vestapol) are more than illuminating. These releases are invaluable audio-visual documents of Joe's style and highly recommended. Regarding illumination, Joe lent his wisdom and experience to instructional videos as well. Among these are *Joe Pass: Jazz Lines* (Warner Bros), *Joe Pass: The Blue Side of Jazz*, and *Solo Jazz Guitar* (both on Hot Licks). *An Evening with Joe Pass* (Warner Bros) splits the difference between guitar instruction and concert performance.

Joe Pass can be seen and heard in a number of video clips online, many from the aforementioned Vestapol releases. Among the must-see highlights are varied group performances: trios on "All the Things You Are" and "Have You Met Miss Jones," "Soft Winds" (with the Oscar Peterson quartet), "Donna Lee" (with the Clark Terry Sextet), and several duets on standards with Ella Fitzgerald, demonstrating Joe's skills as an accompanist.

Online solo outings include "Joe's Blues," "You Are the Sunshine of My Life," "The Very Thought of You," a spontaneous untitled blues from the 1975 Montreux Jazz Festival, "Ain't Misbehavin'"/"Prelude to a Kiss" (from Norman Granz's *Improvisation* documentary), and clips from his 1985 appearance on *The Guitar Show*. Also notable are the documentary clips made during the recording of Pass's 1993 recording with Roy Clark, *A Meeting of Masters: Roy Clark and Joe Pass Play Hank Williams*. These feature performance segments and short but telling interviews from his final session.

© Jan Persson CTSIMAGES

SOUND

Many a guitarist has been surprised to learn that Joe Pass played Fender solid-body guitars on his earliest jazz recordings. Normally associated with surf and rock 'n' roll performers, the Fender Jazzmaster and Jaguar models seem unlikely foils for his advanced bebop style. The old axiom: "It's the pilot, not the plane" comes to mind. Joe's Fender guitar sound is heard on recordings like 1961's *Sounds of Synanon*, 1962's *Something Special* ("Groove" Holmes), and 1963's *Catch Me*, his first album as a leader. Joe also employed a Fender Bass VI six-string bass guitar for a couple of tracks on the latter date—for example, his solo on "Mood Indigo."

Joe played these atypical jazz axes until a kind and generous soul laid a Gibson ES175D on him in 1963. This guitar was an arch-top electric-acoustic with two humbucking pickups, a sunburst finish, and a 16-inch laminated body. The 175 became Joe's workhorse instrument for most of his career and can be heard on such classic recordings as 1964's *For Django* and

1973's *Jazz Concord* (with Herb Ellis). In the seventies and eighties, Joe dabbled sporadically with a few other arch-top guitars, including a custom-made James D'Aquisto arch-top acoustic with a thinner body and a floating pickup, and an Ibanez JP20 signature model. He later lent his name to a line of Epiphone Joe Pass signature guitars in the nineties.

In 1992, Joe took delivery of a custom-made Gibson ES175. According to jazz guitarist John Pisano, Joe's longtime friend and frequent musical collaborator, this instrument has a thinner body (2¾ inches in depth), a single humbucking pickup, a sunburst finish, gold-plated hardware, and an ebony fingerboard. John also mentioned that this is the guitar heard on Joe's final recordings, including his last, *A Meeting of the Masters: Roy Clark & Joe Pass Play Hank Williams*.

Like most jazz guitarists, Joe used the neck pickup on his 175D almost exclusively and adjusted the tone control to produce a warm bassy sound. Joe strung his guitars with a custom medium-heavy gauge set: .013, .017, .024., .032, .042, .052. He used various brands in the mixed set: Thomastik-Infeld flatwound strings for the low E and A, GHS round-wound Boomers for the D and G, and Thomastik-Infeld or D'Aquisto for the B and high E. Joe had an unusual habit of breaking or biting his picks in half to a smaller size, which he felt was more comfortable. These were originally smaller tear-drop shaped picks. After Joe broke them, he played with the pointed end.

In the sixties, Joe usually performed and recorded with various Fender tube amplifiers. He played several combo and piggyback models including a Twin Reverb and a white Tolex Bandmaster. The latter was seen and heard, mated to a Fender Jaguar, in a telling 1962 TV performance included on the *Genius of Joe Pass* video. By the early seventies, Joe switched to Polytone solid-state amps and became one of the company's leading endorsees. He generally favored the 102 model with two 8-inch speakers and one 12-inch speaker. Joe began using the Polytone Mini-Brute II with a single 12-inch speaker in the eighties; he plugged directly into the amp and did not use effects.

LICKS
FIG. 1: FORWARD PASS

This characteristic single-note Joe Pass bebop lick is typical of the jazz horn vocabulary applied to guitar. Phrases like this turn up regularly in Joe's improvisations. He generally used this type of line over chord changes. Note the outlining of various chord sounds in the phrase as it moves through the changes. The melody in measures 3–5 is particularly telling. The ascending pattern in measures 1 and 2 is a paraphrase of a classic bebop sax lick and is one of Joe's favorite melodies. It is played with an up-tempo swing feel.

FIG. 1.

FIG. 2: MODAL PASSAGE

This lick depicts the modal side of Joe Pass. In the early sixties, modal tunes like "So What" and "Milestones" became prevalent in modern jazz, presenting a serious alternative to the faster-moving chord changes of bebop. Typically, seasoned players of the genre use a variety of "inside" and "outside" scale sounds to color and elaborate on the slow-moving tonal areas of modal jazz. Such is the case in this phrase. It is played over a static D minor chord and contains two favorite Pass melodies often played as substitutes. The first, in measures 2 and 3, exploits a symmetrical diminished scale pattern that was often employed by bop trumpeter Dizzy Gillespie. The second is a descending whole tone scale pattern, also symmetrical, in measures 4 and 5. Note that both patterns sound peripherally close to D minor but weave in and out of the basic tonality with ear-catching passing notes.

FIG. 2.

FIG. 3: PASS THE PIANO, PLEASE

You might call this lick an example of Joe's "lap piano" style. Play this one with your fingers or with pick and fingers—what Joe has called "ad lib style." This three-measure phrase is depictive of the sort of spontaneous chord-melody work heard on the *Virtuoso* sessions. The basic chordal motion is C major to C7 and finally to D7. Through this progression, Joe makes a number of interesting musical detours. Note the use of a broken-chord chain of ii–V patterns in measures 1 and 2. This figure establishes a bass note-chord-bass note motif that sounds like an homage to jazz stride piano style. The chord cycle is then effectively contrasted by a florid single-note bebop melody in measure 3. This lick is a thumbnail sketch of the textures and tangents Joe pursued in his solo chord-melody style.

FIG. 3.

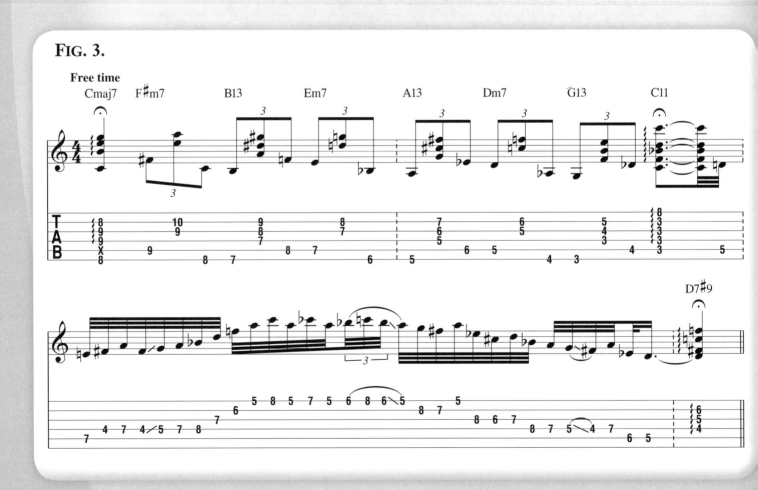

LES PAUL

Beyond his innovations in the recording and guitar manufacturing realms, Les was a gifted guitarist with an immediately recognizable style and irrepressible personality on the instrument. In the mid thirties, he was a transcendent jazz player who performed and recorded with Art Tatum, Louis Armstrong, Eddie South, and many other major jazz artists. Subsequently, his playing affected generations of future musicians. As far back as the early thirties, Les made history on his groundbreaking coast-to-coast radio programs. There, he introduced the electric guitar to a pre-Charlie Christian audience as Les Paul, the jazzman and as his alter ego, Rhubarb Red, a flashy country picker. Since then, Les's work has been embedded in the very core of the American music tradition. His forties and fifties pop records with Bing Crosby, the Andrews Sisters, and finally Mary Ford catapulted the electric guitar to new heights, greater public attention and led inexorably to the guitar-dominated culture of today.

*L*es Paul's impact on music is incalculable. One can scarcely imagine what the modern world might have been like without him. A true genius and renaissance man, Les is one of those rare towering figures of the genre who truly made a difference and whose contributions are manifold. He was an indefatigable inventor whose pioneering experiments with multi-track recording led to the technology we all routinely enjoy. Similarly, Les's tinkering with solid-body guitar design engendered the Les Paul line of Gibson guitars, which remain an industry standard and have been heard in virtually every type of music played on the planet. That's no hyperbole—even venerated classical guitarist John Williams picked up a Les Paul when he recorded with the electric guitar.

Jazz guitarists George Benson, Stanley Jordan, Al Di Meola, Wes Montgomery, and Pat Martino have openly acknowledged Les's influence on them as have rock musicians like Jeff Beck, Jimmy Page, Steve Howe, James Burton, Link Wray, Peter Frampton, Steve Miller, and Mike Bloomfield, among others. Suffice it to say that Les Paul is the grandfather of every electric guitarist to have picked a note since the thirties. He is a genuine international treasure and is worthy of enthronement in the hierarchy of music history. Les remained active as a performer and personality until the final hours of his long and productive life. Though he recently passed on at the venerable age of 94, Les Paul, the avatar of the electric guitar and contemporary music, will never be forgotten.

INFLUENCES

Born Lester William Polfuss, Les Paul was drawn to music early in life. The instrument that first caught his ear was the harmonica, which he played at age nine. Les is self-taught on the guitar and assembled his style from an array of disparate sources. He was inspired by Gene Autry at age eleven and listened to country and western music via the Grand Ole Opry. He picked up some basics from the Sears Roebuck *E-Z Method for Guitar*, which came with his first guitar.

Jazz and swing musicians, particularly pianist Art Tatum and trumpeter Roy Eldridge, also heavily influenced Les. His guitar influences include Eddie Lang, the leading jazz player of the twenties, chord giant George Van Eps, and gypsy virtuoso Django Reinhardt. Django's flamboyant runs, dazzling technique, and bombastic colorful acoustic effects had a profound impact on Les's developing style. Additionally, Les has also cited the guitarist with the Three Keys, who used a capo and a thumbpick, as a seminal influence.

STYLE

Les Paul had many sides to his musical persona. No matter which hat Les was wearing, what immediately endeared the listener were his humor, grace, and inventiveness. Speedy, fluid, and hard-swinging runs, as well as tasteful legato melodies, characterize his single-note playing. Les was the guitar's first texturalist, producing unpredictable and varied passages decorated with rapidly fluttered trills, exaggerated slurs and slides, tremolo-picked lines, palm muting, artificial harmonics, raked arpeggio figures, and jazz chords. He frequently added blues-inspired licks (with string bends and double stops) and used driving rock-like repeated figures to build toward a musical climax in his phrases. Live and on record, Les was the consummate showman. His solos were replete with tongue-in-cheek showboating and crowd-pleasing antics.

© Photofest

Much of Les's style on his popular hit records was tied to his multi-tracking and electronic wizardry with the guitar. In the twenties, Les first jabbed a phonograph needle into his acoustic guitar in an attempt to amplify it. Since then, his pursuit of the electronic side of the electric guitar has been part and parcel of his approach and opened a previously unimagined sonic universe for the rest of us. With his ingenious sound-on-sound technology, signal processing, and overdubbing techniques, Les could transform his instrument into an orchestra, choir, horn section, or rock band (as on "The System"). He was the first guitarist to routinely use now-common electronic effects like echo and delay, phase shifting, fuzz, volume swells, and to experiment with close miking, variable tape speed, and electronic doubling and harmonizing.

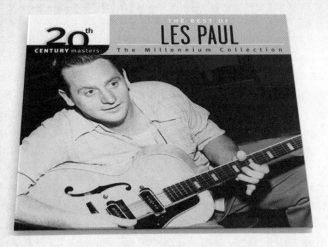

ESSENTIAL LISTENING

Les Paul with Mary Ford: The Best of the Capitol Masters (Capitol) is a twenty-song set covering Les's most influential tracks during his Capitol period. *The Complete Decca Trios—Plus (1936–1947)* (MCA) is a varied collection of his early work showing Les to be at home with jazz, pop, and Hawaiian music. *Masters of the Guitar-Together: Chet Atkins/Les Paul* (RCA Special Products) is a compilation of the leading cuts from the Chester and Lester albums, revealing his comfort with country, swing, and jazz formats.

ESSENTIAL VIEWING

Les Paul: Chasing Sound (Koch Vision, 2007) is a recent DVD documentary featuring Les's personal reminiscences and plenty of footage of Les Paul performing with his trio as well as his duets with Chet Atkins, Keith Richards, and Merle Haggard and many artist testimonials, including those from B.B. King, Tony Bennett, Jeff Beck, and many others. *Les Paul: Live in New York* (Questar, 2010) documents the final Iridium club performance to be officially taped. Guests include Steve Miller and Jose Feliciano. Also worth searching for are Jeff Beck's tribute *Rock and Roll Party: Honoring Les Paul* (Eagle Rock Entertainment, 2011) and *The Wizard of Waukesha* (out of print, 1975), an earlier documentary video.

Les Paul is well represented online. There are numerous clips from past and current videos as well as rare jams with Chet Atkins, Brian May, and Jeff Beck, club performances of his trio, and an entertaining live demo of the Paulverizer. Also enthralling are the vintage black & white clips from his early years. These include a signature trio performance of "Dark Eyes" and a number of excerpts from the Les Paul/Mary Ford TV show of the fifties.

SOUND

Les Paul's sound is the sound of music technology on the move. In 1927, Les acquired a low-budget Sears guitar and almost immediately thereafter got his first professional guitar—a Gibson L-5 acoustic arch-top. The L-5 remained one of his primary instruments until the advent of Gibson's Les Paul line in 1952.

In the early thirties, as "Rhubarb Red" on Chicago's WJJD and with his own jazz group on WIND, Les played an L-5 with a retrofitted pickup. In 1934, he commissioned the Larson Brothers of Chicago to build him a custom hollow-body arch-top guitar with a ½-inch maple top and no F-holes to minimize vibrations. Les equipped this instrument with two pickups, creating what is probably the world's first dual-pickup electric guitar.

Les also used a modified Epiphone arch-top with two pickups in the late thirties and the forties. This guitar, easily identified by its six block-inlay fingerboard, natural finish, and two modified Charlie Christian-style pickups, was his main instrument in the first hit-making phase of the Les Paul-Mary Ford duo. The famed "Log" of 1941 was Les's experimental solid-body; it was essentially a plank with acoustic wings and two pickups built in the Epiphone factory. This instrument predated the advent of commercial solid-body electric guitars by nearly a decade and was used on many important Les Paul-Mary Ford hit records in the forties. During this period, Les alternated between the Log and his modified Epiphone in the studio. A radical departure from the norm was his use of an aluminum guitar on "Lover," "Caravan," and "Brazil."

Since the early fifties, Les has played various prototypes of Gibson's Les Paul line. He used gold-tops and black Custom models in the fifties for classic tracks like "Tiger Rag," "Meet Mr. Callaghan," "I'm a Fool to Care," and "Vaya Con Dios." For decades, Les has preferred the Les Paul Recording model guitar, which was first marketed in the seventies. He played a modified prototype of the production guitar. This instrument was equipped with a low-impedance pickup system and an internal steel bar for improved sustain. Les usually mounted a vibrato bar on his guitars. His personal guitar was fitted with a Bigsby, but he has also been seen with a Gibson Vibrola bar (on his Les Paul SG Custom) and what appears to be a hand-made vibrato tailpiece (as on the Log).

In the thirties and forties, Les plugged into various Gibson amps. He was seen with the EH-150 and EH-185 models in the studio. In his liner notes for *The Best of the Capitol Masters*, Les mentioned using a vintage Fender Twin amp (the tweed model made before the Twin Reverb) on "Lover" and "Caravan." From his earliest days, he used altered Gibson pickups or has built his own. Les's personal guitar was fitted with a "Paulverizer"—an onboard remote control box for a tape recorder. This control, mounted on the guitar at the tailpiece, enabled Les to reproduce many of his studio effects live in concert.

LICKS

FIG. 1: LES'S BOOGIE BLUES

This rollicking phrase combines several Les Paul signature licks against a partial chorus of up-tempo blues. Many of these sounds were absorbed into the early rock 'n' roll and rockabilly styles. The phrase begins with a solid groove riff involving unisons on adjacent strings—also a favorite motif of T-Bone Walker and Charlie Christian. In measures 3 and 4, we find a classic Les Paul-ism: rapidly fluttered trills played with a minimum of picking. Note the use of a familiar swing jazz melody at the heart of the trill figures. The phrase is completed with bent double stops and a swing-inspired sixth chord strummed figure. The double stops are bluesy *tritone dyads*, which have become a staple of the later rock genres. Les would frequently insert such ear-catching and iconoclastic material into old chestnuts like "In the Good Old Summertime" and "Tiger Rag." A touch of fast slap-back echo (one repeat) and gobs of reverb add the final garnish to this trademark Les Paul line.

FIG. 2: LES'S MINOR MAGIC

This slippery phrase is played over a fast swing groove in D minor and presents several unmistakable Les Paul traits, often copied but rarely equaled. The long scalar sequence played in measures 1 and 2 is a prime identifier of Les's style. This lick is grouped as triplets and is moved down the first string in a connected, almost sitarish, manner. Patterns like this became standard in the rock guitar approach of the sixties and seventies—but remember, you heard it here first. Les was playing these kinds of licks as far back as 1944. Similarly, the shredding pull-off flurries in measures 3–5 are also staples of Les's repertory and have inspired players like Jeff Beck, Chet Atkins, Jimmy Page, and Cliff Gallup, among many others. The lick ends with a quirky figure consisting of an open D string and a whining released string bend doctored with fast vibrato. Les tends to shake these notes vigorously with his vibrato bar for an exaggerated wobbly effect.

FIG. 2.

FIG. 3: LESTER LEAPS

This characteristic phrase is filled with barn-burning, high-energy licks played over a fast polka groove in G. The passage runs the gamut of the entire fretboard and contains several classic Les Paul maneuvers. The first is the rising triplet line in measures 1 and 2. This pattern is a staple of Les's repertory and is often used to approach a dramatic high note in his lines—in this case, to pose a musical question. Les plays these sorts of licks both as slurred and legato flurries and as quick alternate-picked groups as in this example. The answer is heard in the blistering triplet riffs of measures 3 and 4. This section is lightly palm muted and articulated with tremolo picking. The phrase ends with a slurred ascent into a favorite raked arpeggio figure and a swing-oriented 6th-interval line. Add a light slap-back echo to color this lick for a wetter Paul-verizing effect.

FIG. 3.

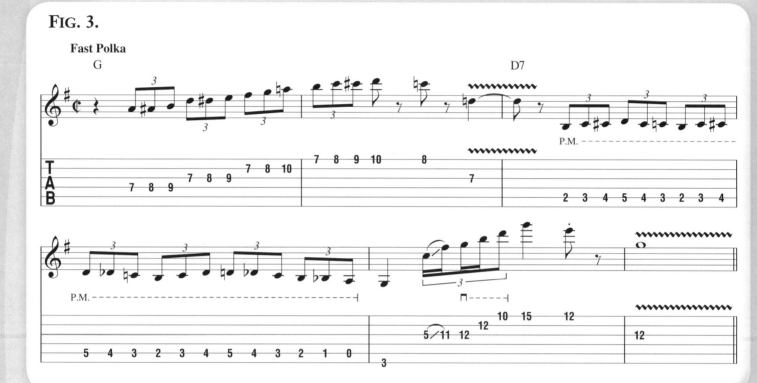

© CTSIMAGES

JIMMY RANEY

Jimmy Raney began playing professionally in bands when he was thirteen. This was during World War II at a time when most musicians were fighting overseas. The vacuum allowed Raney to secure pro union jobs at a precocious age and to work in prestigious local venues like Churchill Downs—not that he couldn't have gotten there on his own. He honed his approach on the bandstand as a teenager and soon moved into gigs with name bands.

In 1944, Hayden Causey recommended Raney as a replacement in Jerry Wald's New York-based group, which featured pianist Al Haig in the lineup. Haig introduced Raney to the new music percolating underground called bebop. Through Haig, he learned of Charlie Parker, Dizzy Gillespie, and Thelonius Monk. Prior to that revelation Raney was influenced, like most of his contemporaries, by music from the swing era and guitarists Oscar Moore, George Barnes, Django Reinhardt, and Charlie Christian.

The great migration of regional musicians from the American South and Southwest to the national mainstream in the forties and fifties was not limited to blues and rock 'n' roll. We openly acknowledge artists like Muddy Waters, Howlin' Wolf, T-Bone Walker, B.B. King, Bo Diddley, Elvis Presley, Carl Perkins, Buddy Holly, Eddie Cochran, and Roy Orbison, but what about the great innovators of jazz guitar?

Jazz guitar, a distinct sub-genre of the ever-evolving American art form, has had its share of important players from south of the Mason-Dixon Line. Consider the origins of the era's leading innovators: Charlie Christian (Oklahoma City), Barney Kessel (Muskogee, Oklahoma), Oscar Moore (Austin, Texas), Johnny Smith (Birmingham, Alabama), and Herb Ellis (Farmersville, Texas). So, what's the point? Is it something in the water? Or is it the possibility that great innovation often requires a secluded regional incubation chamber? That may always remain a mystery. What isn't a mystery is the ascension and lasting impact of Kentuckian Jimmy Raney, one of the most influential and important of the post-Charlie Christian guitarists.

Raney got his real start as a professional jazz artist when he moved to Chicago in 1946 to work with players like Lou Levy, Cy Touff, and Sonny Stitt (then with Dizzy Gillespie's band) when he was in town. There, he blossomed as a modern bebop guitarist and caught the attention of famed bandleader Woody Herman. In 1948, at age twenty-one, Raney played with Herman's "Four Brothers" group, which included sax giants Stan Getz, Zoot Sims, Serge Chaloff, and Al Cohn. Trumpeters Shorty Rogers and Ernie Royal were also in the Herman band. In this milieu, Raney absorbed ideas and approaches from these early bebop masters and built the foundations of his jazz style.

When Raney took up official residence in New York City in 1949, he roomed in a "musician's building" with upcoming guitarists Tal Farlow and Sal Salvador—two kindred spirits in the incipient modern jazz movement who were similarly pursuing the acquisition of the bebop language on the instrument. Sharing ideas and musical solutions and friendship with players of like mind led to his greater progress in both aesthetic and professional realms.

In 1951, Raney participated in the famed Storyville quintet concerts under Stan Getz's leadership (with Al Haig on piano) and contributed an important original composition, "Parker 51," to the repertory. The Storyville tracks constitute a high water mark in his career, document his evolution as a bebop guitarist, and remain essential listening. In 1953, Raney replaced Tal Farlow in the Red Norvo Trio and toured extensively in America and Europe. In 1954, he backed singer Billie Holiday and subsequently won the coveted "Best Jazz Guitarist" critics polls in *Downbeat*.

Raney made his first albums as a leader in 1954. The *Jimmy Raney Visits Paris* (volumes 1 and 2) sessions are among his most definitive, as are the 1954–1955 tracks released as *Jimmy Raney-A*. The latter group included famed pianist Hall Overton. In 1956, Raney teamed up with trombonist Bob Brookmeyer for the *Jimmy Raney* album and in 1957 recorded an atypical duet-plus-horns and rhythm section outing with Kenny Burrell named *Two Guitars*. Raney remained active on the New York scene through the fifties, adding Broadway show stints to his impressive jazz credentials. He returned home to Louisville and enjoyed a self-imposed retirement from the pro life in the sixties and early seventies.

Reemerging in the mid-seventies, Raney released a string of fine albums that found him in top form and often in the company of his guitar-playing son Doug Raney, who is blessed with a similar sound. Landmark recordings of his later period include *Live in Tokyo* (1976), *Raney* (1981), *The Master* (1983), *Wisteria* (1986), and *But Beautiful* (1990). Touring and recording for numerous jazz labels, Raney remained active until his death in 1995.

INFLUENCES

Jimmy Raney was born and raised in Louisville, Kentucky—a hotbed of country and western and hillbilly music in the thirties and forties. He picked up the guitar from his mother's side of the family and began playing at age ten. At that point, he learned a few basic chords and some simple pop and country tunes. Raney was trained formally as a youth, beginning his studies at eleven with local teacher A.J. Giancolla and the Gibson guitar method.

He later studied with noted jazz guitarist Hayden Causey. At this stage, Raney learned to read music and to play improvised solos and variations on pop tunes, gravitating to the mainstream swing jazz style. As with most jazz guitarists of his era, Charlie Christian was an important early role model. Raney also admired Oscar Moore, George Barnes, and Django Reinhardt. In the mid forties, Raney was introduced to bebop, the revolutionary art music of modern jazz, and began to incorporate sounds from alto saxophonist Charlie Parker and trumpeter Dizzy Gillespie into his guitar playing.

In the late fifties, Raney took composition lessons with Hall Overton, a pianist and teacher at Julliard who was versed in classical and jazz. In this period, he studied theory and compositional techniques and wrote pieces for piano, string quartet, and various orchestral settings as well as guitar and string trio. Several of Raney's compositions of this genre reveal a strong Bela Bartok influence.

STYLE

Jimmy Raney is a pivotal guitar player in early bebop. He is generally grouped in a powerful triumvirate of jazz guitar innovators of the early fifties, including Barney Kessel and Tal Farlow. These three players, as well as Chuck Wayne and Sal Salvador, are deemed to be the first prominent guitarists to move from the older Charlie Christian swing-based style to bebop and modern jazz.

Raney's single-note style contains many of the prominent attributes and gestures of bebop. With its challenging harmonies, complex melodies, exotic chord substitutions, and unusual rhythms, bebop became a fascination for Raney early on and ultimately a career path. In the forties, Raney began actively emulating and reinterpreting the genre's uncommon sax and trumpet melodies on the guitar. His assimilation of the bebop language, with its long, intricate melody lines, necessitated a strong command of the fingerboard and unique phrasing.

His guitar approach includes characteristic horn-based extended and altered chord arpeggio outlines, chromatic tones, and angular interval leaps. Moreover, Raney cultivated an even wind-inspired legato sound—quite different from the heavy pick attack of many contemporaries—distinguished by his familiar slurred articulation found in numerous lines and melodies. The bop conception and phraseology remains a cornerstone of modern jazz guitar, and Raney was one of its earliest and most significant practitioners.

Raney's pioneering jazz style and sound influenced legions of players to follow, including the great Wes Montgomery. In fact, the components of his approach were well summarized by Wes—the most potent voice in the second-generation hard bop guitar style and an admirer of Raney—"Jimmy Raney is the opposite of Tal Farlow. They have the same ideas, the same changes, the same type runs, the same kind of feeling, but Jimmy Raney is so smooth and he does it without a mistake. He has a real soft touch—it's the touch he's got."

Many listeners concur. Raney's cool-toned sound is still considered one of the warmest and most beautiful guitar timbres in jazz. That, along with his subtle but persuasive sense of swing, fluid linear approach, and gift for melody, is an unmistakable identifier of his style.

ESSENTIAL LISTENING

Jimmy Raney's earliest albums are indispensable classics of evolving bop guitar. Highly recommended are *Jimmy Raney-A* (Prestige), *Jimmy Raney Visits Paris* (Volumes 1 and 2) (Original Vogue Masters, distributed by BMG), *Jimmy Raney featuring Bob Brookmeyer* (Verve), and *Two Guitars: Kenny Burrell/ Jimmy Raney* (Prestige). Also essential is *Stan Getz at Storyville—Vol.1 & 2* (Roulette Jazz), which combines all the live performances that first brought Raney to the public ear.

Essential later Raney works include *Live in Tokyo* (Xanadu. 1976), *The Master* (Criss Cross), *The Influence* (Prevue), and *Raney* (1981) (Criss Cross), a quartet session with his son Doug.

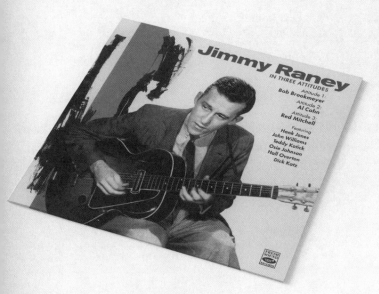

ESSENTIAL VIEWING

Jimmy Raney is featured on the DVD concert set *Guitar Masters Live in Germany 1973 & 1980* (Ais) with fellow jazz guitarists Jim Hall and Attila Zoller. He is also seen in numerous telling clips online. Among the offerings are informal live performances of "Billie's Bounce" and "Out of Nowhere," segments from Raney's 1987 TV appearance on *The Guitar Show* (including a chord-melody outing on "Autumn in New York"), and some instructive moments from a 1993 guitar workshop at the University of Louisville, in which he addresses chords, scales, timing, sight reading, and other topics.

SOUND

Jimmy Raney played a variety of instruments in his career. In the earliest pro days, he used a low-budget Gibson arch-top fitted with a floating DeArmond pickup. He plugged this into a "little square Gibson" (most likely the workhorse EH-150 model). Raney later played a Gibson ES-150 equipped with a stock Charlie Christian bar pickup. This instrument, made in 1939 or 1940, is pictured on most of his fifties album covers.

When Raney returned to professional life, he was seen using a natural-finish Gibson L-7 acoustic arch-top. This guitar was heavily customized with retro-fitted P-90 single-coil pickups and a unique two-knob/ single switch control circuit. Raney used this unusual instrument in the late seventies and later a couple of stock Gibson ES-175s (sunburst and blonde models). In his final years, Raney played an unusual blonde Hofner Attila Zoller model (designed by the noted German jazz guitarist) with a single floating neck pickup and body-mounted controls. He is seen with this instrument in numerous video clips online.

Raney alternated between standard medium-gauge round-wound and flat-wound strings as well as nylon tape-wound strings throughout his career. He preferred a conventional medium-gauge pick.

LICKS

FIG. 1: ZIGZAGGING BEBOP

Jimmy Raney burst upon the scene with his playing in the Stan Getz lineup. Among the sessions that raised the guitarists' bar was the live recording at Storyville of 1951. This phrase is from that set and presents Raney's improvisations over a charging bebop tune. The tempo is fast, and Raney's phrasing is clearly taken from the saxophone camp. In fact, Raney was one of the first to successfully transfer sax conception to guitar. This line is a case in point. The quick zigzagging melody follows the modified B♭ "Rhythm Changes" of the tune and includes an interesting navigation of the tricky turnaround in measures 6–7. Check out the outlining of the unusual progression: B♭–D♭7–G♭7–F7. Here, Raney mixes chromaticism with angular interval jumps and closes with a bopping blues lick.

FIG. 1.

FIG. 2: II–V–I SAX-STYLE

This characteristic line is also from the legendary Storyville concert. Inspired by Raney's improvisations on "Cherokee" changes, this section takes place over a ii–V–I progression in B major. Note the sax phrasing implicit in the legato approach to the melody. Also noteworthy is Raney's abundant chromaticism, found as straight passing tones in measure 1, as bop encircling patterns to B in measures 2–4, and an important functional leading tone to D♯ in measures 3–5. The C double-sharp leading tone in both cases pushes to D♯ and a trademark arpeggio melody.

FIG. 2.

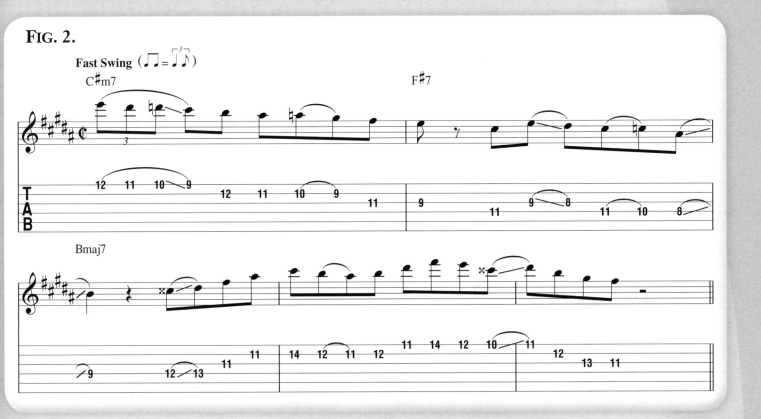

FIG. 3: EXTENDED ARPEGGIOS AND CHROMATICISM

This lengthy zigzagging phrase is definitive and reflects Raney's playing after his "comeback" in the late-seventies. Among the notable points are his use of an extended arpeggio (C13) in measure 1 and the seamless connection to a diminished scale line in measure 2 over A7. Measures 3 and 4 present two of Raney's extended chord arpeggios on D7 and G7, respectively. Note the building of each idea on the 3rd of the chord: F♯ for D7♭9 and B for G7♭9. Note also the use of a portion of the diminished scale to inflect each chord with its flatted 9th—E♭ and A♭, respectively. Raney exploits a riff-like idea based on the diminished scale in measures 4–5. The bopping line in measures 6–8 is a horn-based ii–V–i pattern in D minor. And check out the trademark blend of chromatic passing tones, arpeggio patterns (A7 in measure 7 and Dm7 in 8), and diatonic stepwise melody—bebop deluxe.

FIG. 3.

DJANGO REINHARDT

© CTSIMAGES

and composed almost a hundred pieces. Django and his Quintet of the Hot Club of France (QHCF), featuring violinist Stephane Grappelli, were legendary in Paris from their 1934 debut, and Django's reputation and mythos quickly spread throughout Europe. He made his first recordings that year for Odeon, but the company rejected them because they were "too modern." However, the quintet persevered and within a year was regarded by the public as France's answer to American "hot jazz"—at the time, an unimaginable accolade. Within a year, Django rose in stature from an unknown gypsy guitarist to a world-class jazzman, suitable to share soloing duties with Coleman Hawkins, the world's leading saxophonist. Following the date, Hawkins sang Django's praises to visiting jazz musicians, further stoking the fires of "le jazz hot."

Django's QHCF began recording its most definitive music in 1936 under a new contract with Pathe-Marconi. In 1937, the group took up residency at the Big Apple, the top nightclub in Paris. That year, Django also recorded the first of his solo guitar pieces, "Improvisation" and "Parfum," and was recruited by Swing Records—Europe's first specialty jazz label—to play alongside Coleman Hawkins and the All-Star Jam Band. The results are genuine classics of the period. By late 1937, Django's fame had spread to Britain, and his subsequent 1938 English concert tour proved an enormous success. While in London, the quintet recorded for Decca, yielding the haunting Gypsy jazz classic "Nocturne." In 1939, Django recorded with members of Duke Ellington's band. These tracks remain pinnacles of the swing era and have been described by famed musicologist Gunther Schuller as "all-time gems" and "among the finest achievements in jazz."

Django's ascension and prolific output continued through WWII and the dark period of Nazi occupation in France. In the Nazi view, Gypsies were, like Jews, racially inferior and subject to extermination. More than half a million Gypsies died in German camps of this period. However, Django had attained superstar status throughout Europe by 1941, and his popularity protected him and even afforded him limited travel privileges. Indeed, it is postulated that

Django Reinhardt is a towering figure in guitar lore and music history. He was the first European jazz performer to be honored and admired by American contemporaries and arguably has remained Europe's most important and recognizable jazz artist. In the thirties, Django founded a distinctive form of music, a style of improvisation, and an ensemble sound that thrives to the present day. His legacy is tremendous and far-reaching, inspiring musicians, writers, filmmakers, and artists of all stripes.

Jean-Baptiste (Django) Reinhardt was born in Liberchies, Belgium, in 1910. He was a Gypsy: a member of the Manouche branch, who entered Europe through the Balkans and Hungary and whose lineage is traced to the ancient Indian sub-continent. His family traveled throughout France and Belgium, leaving Germany after the Franco-Prussian War of 1870. Django was born and bred in a bohemian culture of wandering musicians and artisans; that ethos and freedom shaped his expression, temperament, and output during his lifetime.

Django's output was remarkable, especially considering his infirmity, restless nature, and the upheaval of World War II. He made about a thousand records in his lifetime

Django's presence was tolerated, perhaps necessary, to promote the appearance of normalcy and quell public insurgencies. In this period, Django formed a second QHCF, with clarinetist Hubert Rostaing replacing his long-time partner Grappelli.

When Paris was liberated in 1944, it became a Mecca for American soldiers and officers, most of them jazz fans that sought out Django. Fred Astaire was in that group. Django's performances and recordings quenched the thirst for "le jazz hot" and began another period of ascension. He recorded with members of Glenn Miller's band in 1945 and made a series of auspicious guest appearances on AFN (American Forces Network) radio. In 1946, Django was invited to America as a special guest star with Duke Ellington's orchestra and toured New York, Chicago, Detroit, Pittsburgh, St. Louis, Kansas City, and other major venues. He also played two concerts under his own name at the famed Carnegie Hall in NYC.

By the late forties, Django gradually outgrew the confines of strict Gypsy Jazz and the original QHCF sound. He began playing electric guitar and updated his approach with modern jazz elements. He also favored a more modern combo sound with a bass-drums-piano rhythm section. In 1950, Django withdrew from full-time performance and recording into semi-retirement to paint, fish, play billiards, compose, and lead a simpler life. He died from a stroke on March 15, 1953 at the age of 43.

"Djangology" is the title of a classic Reinhardt composition connoting the study of all things Django. It is also the name of countless compilations and single album re-issues over the last several decades. In the mythos of Gypsy jazz, it has come to mean something greater and transcendent; it has grown to define a distinct form of music and manner of performance. Though Django was gone, he was not forgotten. He was honored in the famed Modern Jazz Quartet composition and recording of 1953 and in Joe Pass's 1964 homage *For Django*.

In recent years, Djangology has enjoyed a revival. Django's music has been rediscovered by a new generation. Players like Birelli Lagrene, Howard Alden, Stephane Wrembel, and John Jorgenson have catapulted the sounds back into the global music mix. In pop culture, Djangology continues to exert its musical spell at numerous Gypsy jazz tributes and festivals worldwide and on the screen with feature films such as Martin Scorsese's *New York, New York* (1977) and Woody Allen's *Sweet and Lowdown* (1999).

INFLUENCES

Django Reinhardt was raised in the Gypsy environment in France and Belgium where virtually every occasion was accompanied by music. He received a used banjo guitar (guitar neck with banjo body) at age twelve. Completely self-taught, he learned by listening and watching musicians in the camp and at a neighborhood café, picking tunes out by ear.

Django began playing professionally at twelve in dancehalls with popular accordionist Guerino. His early repertory was comprised of European cabaret and dance music. He played tunes like "Dinah" and "Sheik of Araby" at fledgling performances, and they remained staples. He later recorded these pieces with his QHCF. In his youth, Django listened to and was affected by local French jazz and novelty bands in Paris as well as nationalist European composers Edvard Grieg, Maurice Ravel, and Claude Debussy. These influences later surfaced, respectively, in "Fantaisie," "Bolero De Django," and "Nympheas."

Django was familiar with classic American jazz of the twenties as well as earlier New Orleans, Dixieland, and Traditional styles, and musicians like saxophonist Sidney Bechet and pianist Bix Beiderbecke. American jazz artists, such as guitarist Eddie Lang, violinist Joe Venuti, composer/bandleader Duke Ellington, and particularly trumpeter Louis Armstrong, were among his favorites. The latter is alluded to in "My Sweet" and "Swing 42."

Bebop, the new more complex jazz of the late forties, inspired Django's playing and composing in his later years. His electric work reveals the influence of Charlie Christian as well as Charlie Parker and Dizzy Gillespie, particularly on tracks like "What Is This Thing Called Love?" from the 1950 Rome sessions.

STYLE

Django Reinhardt mastered conventional guitar techniques by the time he was a young teenager. He developed his signature style when he relearned the instrument after a catastrophic accident. A fire badly burned and disfigured his left hand in 1928. The event forced Django to create unique fingerings where he could make music with his thumb, two fingers, and two barely-useable fused digits. And what music! His style influenced generations of guitarists to follow: Les Paul, Johnny Smith, Chet Atkins, Joe Pass, Jeff Beck, Willie Nelson, Julian Bream, Al Di Meola, Birelli Lagrene, John Jorgeson, and the legions of players in the current Gypsy jazz revival.

Django played Gypsy jazz: a form of improvised music with a distinct European flavor and tinges of classic American jazz and swing. Gypsy jazz was originally played on acoustic instruments in a string band—generally a quartet consisting of two rhythm guitars, an upright bass, and a lead guitar. Many modern Gypsy jazz groups amplify their string instruments but preserve the acoustic timbre established by Django. The ensemble was often enlarged with a violin (as in Django's most famous quintet) or less frequently a wind instrument. At the heart of Gypsy jazz was the "La Pompe" rhythm style. A Polka-style groove popular in Europe, it provided the music's pulse, forward motion, and percussion, replacing drums, and is similar to the quarter-note" boom-chick" accompaniment of bluegrass.

Django was a flamboyant performer in the tradition of Gypsy entertainers. His guitar style has rightfully been described as virtuosic, belying his physical handicap. Django's music is emotional and dramatic,

distinguished by his fiery technique and his combination of dark, minor-mode pieces and the chromatically tinged Gypsy style with upbeat swing jazz.

After his accident, Django played runs and melodies largely with his index and middle fingers. He formed chords with two or three fingers and his thumb. He didn't use barre chords. Django rarely played simple triadic voicings, preferring enriched seventh, sixth, ninth, 6/9, diminished, augmented, and various altered chords, such as dominant sevenths with flatted 9ths.

Django rarely played scales in solos. He favored chord-outlining arpeggios of two-octaves or greater. His fast intricate runs were essentially arpeggios decorated with chromatic neighbor tones, passing tones, and enclosures. Django cultivated a *linear* approach with quick lateral shifts along the fingerboard. The long lines in "Django's Tiger" are telling examples. He also played diminished runs and arpeggios (often as substitutes for dominant seventh chords) and aug-

mented chord dissonances ("Diminushing"). Django applied the 6th tone to major and minor-mode melodies, as was the practice of swing-era jazz. On rare occasion and generally for coloristic purposes, Django used the harmonic minor scale as a source for exotic gypsy sounds. In later years, Django added bebop elements to his playing when he began favoring the electric guitar.

Django was a colorful soloist, using contrasts in textures to add depth to his guitar improvisations. He was a pioneer of octaves. His first recording of "Dinah" in 1934 featured a lengthy eight-measure octave passage in the bridge of his solo, presaging the style Wes Montgomery codified in the fifties. Django also included partial chords and double stop textures in his solos.

Django exploited many modern guitar effects. He used exaggerated trills, long descending and ascending glissando figures—often on a single string (a la Les Paul and Jeff Beck)—legato patterns, repeated licks, string bends, rapid vibrato, harmonics, palm-muted sounds, and ghost notes. His articulation was idiosyncratic and varied depending on the execution of his ideas. He used sweep picking for arpeggio figures, economy picking patterns (for example, three down strokes and an upstroke in "Rythme Futur," B section), and lengthy tremolo-picked phrases. Django generally used a plectrum but occasionally played fingerstyle, as in the balladic "Tears."

Among his most renowned compositions are "Djangology," "Nuages," "Minor Swing," "Belleville," "Dinette," "Fleur d' Ennui" (A Gypsy jazz tango), "Blues Clair" (12-bar blues in C with extended solos), "Swing Guitar," "Melodie au Crepuscule," "Manoir de Mas Reves (Django's Castle)," "Stompin' at Decca," "Micro" (an "I Got Rhythm" contrafact), "Blues Minor" (a favorite 12-bar blues in A minor, recorded four times), "Cavalerie," and "Swing 42." Django also created dazzling performances on popular songs, jazz standards, 12-bar blues, and oldies of the day such as "Honeysuckle Rose," "Tiger Rag," "Ain't Misbehavin,'" "Swanee River," "Rose Room," "Sweet Georgia Brown," "I Found a New Baby," "Limehouse Blues," "Dinah," and "It Don't Mean a Thing."

Django recorded several solo guitar compositions. The most famous are his "Improvisations," with evocative subtitles like "Echoes of Spain" (No.4). "Naguine" (written for his wife) is an improvisation based on a blues in G major. These compositions liberally mixed gypsy, blues, classical music, and jazz allusions and were open-ended excursions showcasing his single-note and chord-melody guitar skills.

Essential Listening

Django Reinhardt's music remains essential in jazz and guitar history. His recordings from the mid-thirties to the late forties are definitive. They find him leading the Quintette du Hot Club de France or similar string-band groups, often with violinist Stephane Grappelli or the occasional guest jazz horn players.

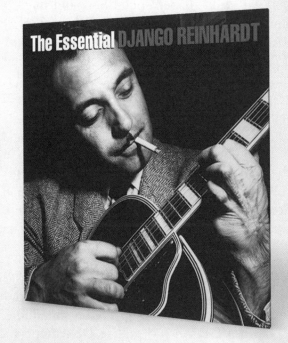

Jazz Masters 38: Django Reinhardt (Verve) is a serviceable single-disc overview. Deeper explorations are available in the ten-disc box set *Django Reinhardt* (Membran Music). The Mosaic Records box set *The Complete Django Reinhardt and Quintet of the Hot Club of France: Swing/HMV Sessions 1936–1948* is a triumph and highly recommended. It is a large, collectible package with six discs and a lavish book of photos, biographic essays, session notes, discography, and historical information.

Serious Django fans are also directed to his later electric guitar work. Worthy collections include *Django in Rome 1949/1950* (a four-CD box set re-mastered by Ted Kendall) (JSP) and *Django Reinhardt: The Rome Sessions* (79 Jazz Time).

Essential Viewing

Video clips of Django Reinhardt are understandably scarce. A few essential filmed snippets have surfaced online: *Django Reinhardt—Cortometraje Documental* (from a 2003 documentary), *Django in the Netherlands*, *Django Reinhardt in Train (1945)*, *Django Reinhardt Clip 1945*, *Django Reinhardt 30/05/1946*, *Django Reinhardt—Life Documentary*, *Django Reinhardt Video Quintette du Hot Club de France*, and *Django Reinhardt—Nuages Documentary* contain several clips of Django performing.

SOUND

Django Reinhardt played a particular acoustic steel-string guitar for most of his life. The Selmer-made acoustic guitar, designed by Mario Maccaferi in the thirties, was his instrument of choice and is closely associated with him. Django played several versions: the early *Orchestre* 1932 model (later called the *Jazz* model) with a D-shaped sound hole and fingerboard extension, the *Modele Jazz* 1936 with an oval sound hole and a standard 21-fret fingerboard, and the *Modele Django* of 1939. All had flat single-cutaway bodies, Spruce top, a wide moustache wooden bridge, three-piece walnut neck, slotted headstock, and an ornamented mandolin-style tailpiece. Django's personal favorite was the No.503 *Modele Django* from 1939. In 1964, Naguine donated this guitar to Cite de la Musique, Paris, where it is on display. Django also played later forties Selmer versions with a flat headstock and maple neck and body. He was also seen with non-cutaway Gibson L-5 and Gretsch Synchromatic arch-tops in the forties.

Django experimented with electric guitars in the mid forties. He amplified his Selmer with a Stimer magnetic surface-mounted pickup in the soundhole. He also played a Gibson L-5 with a DeArmond pickup and an Epiphone "Electar" amp. "Folie A Amphon" (1947) was recorded on an electric guitar. Having left his Selmer at home, Django played an electric guitar during his US tour of 1946–1947. He was seen using a late-forties Gibson ES-300 with a single P-90 pickup.

Django played an electric guitar for the famed Rome recordings of 1949–1950. By 1951, he used his amplified Selmer almost exclusively.

LICKS

FIG. 1: ZIGZAGGING SWING

This long zigzagging line is found in countless variations in numerous Django Reinhardt solos. At the core of the phrase is the sleek opening passage that splits the difference between modern jazz improvisation and classical violin etudes. The brisk ascending melody in measure 1 (the first full measure) is a sequence in sixteenth notes arranged in four-note groups that outline a C major arpeggio with neighbor notes and enclosure patterns. Note the chromatic tones F♯ and D♯ to maintain thematic continuity in the section. A favorite lick, it has remained a staple in the jazz genre since the thirties and was also played by saxophonist Cannonball Adderley and pianist Oscar Peterson in addition to a slew of bebop guitarists like Joe Pass and Howard Roberts. The chromaticized run in measure 2 moves the melody momentarily from C major to A♭m6. The minor sixth arpeggio is characteristic of Django's style and of the swing jazz vernacular in general. Here, the A♭m6 arpeggio leads to a typical cadence of E♭9 to D9. Django often decorated the ninth-chord sonority with a 13th extension, as in this case the C note over E♭9, which leads seamlessly into D9 a half step lower.

FIG. 1.

FIG. 2: DJANGO'S ARPEGGIOS

Django was known to make extensive use of two-octave arpeggio melodies in his improvised solos. This phrase is a case in point. The first two chords of the progression, A7 and Cm6 in measures 1 and 2, are expressed as quick ascending arpeggios replete with color tones. Note the same ending note (B♮) in both of the opening arpeggio lines. Django often executed these types of melodies with a fingering that suited his linear style and his penchant for down-stroke sweep picking. The final piece of the phrase over Gmaj7 exploits descending chromatic motion down a single string (the first string)—a familiar Django Reinhardt device.

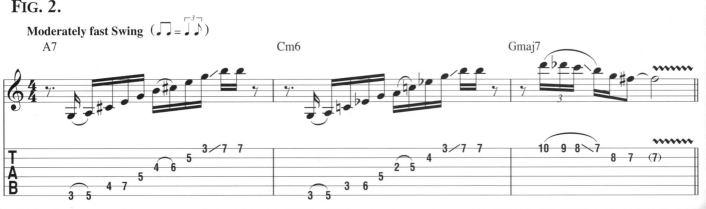

FIG. 3: DJANGO'S OCTAVES

Django was an early pioneer of parallel octave playing. This signature line from the mid-thirties presents his take on the sound and reveals a technique that is similar to what Wes Montgomery perfected and codified in the fifties and sixties. Note the strummed attack, muted string (marked with Xs), and locked parallel shapes employed in measures 1–2 to define an ascending melody over the F chord. In measures 3–5, there are hints of the bebop language creeping into Reinhardt's single-note swing style. The melody is typically arpeggio-based in measure 3, outlining a C9 chord, but exploits more modern elements in measure 4: a chromatic approach into the 7th (B♭), angular wide-interval jumps and an F/C extension (Fmaj7 arpeggio played over C7). The final string bend is a fixture of Reinhardt's improvisation style and alludes to his affinity for blues.

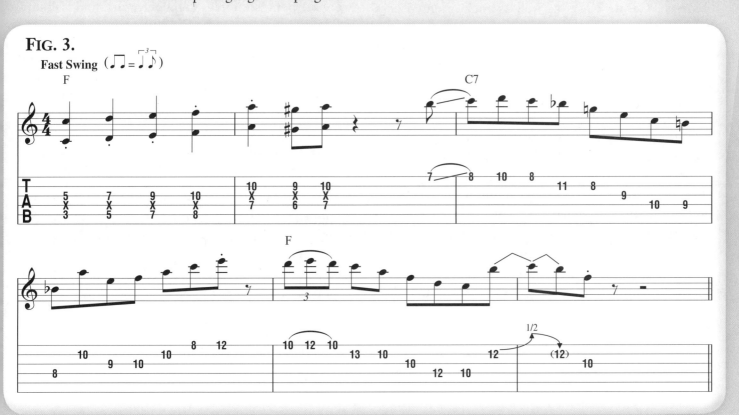

LEE RITENOUR

© Jan Persson CTSIMAGES

An emblematic figure of the era, "Captain Fingers," as he's known by his appreciative cohorts, has been called the industry's most sought-after session man. A composer, arranger, and performer, Rit had played on hundreds of prestigious recording sessions by the mid seventies and was in the upper echelon of the triple-scale pantheon before his twenty-seventh birthday.

A partial list of Lee Ritenour's illustrious clients by 1978 ran a wide range of genres and included Ray Charles, Aretha Franklin, Steely Dan, Henry Mancini, Natalie Cole, Barbra Streisand, George Benson, Herbie Hancock, Earl Klugh, John Denver, Quincy Jones, Sonny Rollins, Joe Henderson, Art Garfunkel, Diana Ross, Cher, Kenny Loggins, Stanley Turrentine, Sergio Mendes, Kris Kristofferson, George Duke, Gato Barbieri, Seals & Crofts, Blue Mitchell, and Sparks. Rit's contributions in film scores for *Saturday Night Fever*, *Grease*, *Roots*, and *Three Days of the Condor* were further testimonies to his versatility and visibility.

The golden age of the L.A. studio scene begun in the sixties reached an apex by the mid seventies. Guitar-driven acts like the Beach Boys, the Monkees, and Elvis Presley set the stage, routinely employing the talents of various, often jazz-schooled, session pickers for hire on hit records and movie scores. Players like Howard Roberts, Barney Kessel, Tommy Tedesco, Carole Kaye, as well as rock-oriented aces Glen Campbell and James Burton, epitomized the first wave. They were the revered specialists of the era, called in to perform tailor-made idiomatic licks on demand for pop dates or to read and interpret daunting modern scores.

In short order, a new star was born: the studio guitar virtuoso. It was inevitable. Too big to be contained in the faceless, nameless milieu of the sixties session world, the new breed of player exploded out of the jazz, rock, and pop circles in which they operated and into the mainstream. Guitarists on Top 10 records, TV underscore, and motion picture themes began to attract and garner greater public awareness—particularly with the musically astute listeners of the seventies. The movement made L.A.-bred working stiffs into marketable personalities with their own record deals, fan bases, and international tours. It was in this rarefied atmosphere that many music hounds first got wind of Lee Ritenour.

Since the golden age of the L.A. studio scene, Lee Ritenour has ascended to and remained at the top level of jazz-pop fusion artists, selling out concerts worldwide and releasing one ambitious recording after another. His output in what was once an uncategorizable genre set the tone and approach and informed the aesthetics employed by countless musicians in the smooth jazz movement of the 1990s and 2000s.

In the early nineties, Ritenour reestablished his straight-ahead jazz credentials with *Stolen Moments* (1990), a set containing originals, standards, and pieces by Oliver Nelson and Miles Davis, and *Wes Bound* (1993), a tribute to Wes Montgomery. He also appraised his seventies roots in the Larry Carlton collaboration. Rit's contemporary efforts continue to push the envelope, but he will always be fondly remembered and recognized for his musical hegemony in an era gone but not forgotten.

Influences

Lee Ritenour was drawn to music from an early age. Intrigued with the guitar at age six, he began studying at eight. By ten, he could read music and had worked with several teachers. Ritenour was absorbing a wide variety of sounds by his pre-teen years. Particular favorites included jazz guitarists Wes Montgomery, Howard Roberts, Larry Coryell, Gabor Szabo, Kenny Burrell, and Charlie Christian in addition to jazz saxophonist John Coltrane, blues guitarist B.B. King, and rock acts like the Beatles, the Jimi Hendrix Experience, and Cream.

Rit was influenced to enter studio work through contact with famed arranger-guitarist Jack Marshall, jazz and recording artist Howard Roberts, and session-man/educator Duke Miller. In his teenage years, he studied jazz informally with Howard Roberts and Joe Pass and pursued harmony and theory in depth with Miller. This training was augmented by private lessons with famed classical guitarist Christopher Parkening and exposure to Brazilian music and guitarist Oscar Neves during a gig with Sergio Mendes.

Style

Lee Ritenour's style of the studio era merged traditional bebop, jazz-rock fusion, R&B, pop, and world beat. Too early to be categorized as instrumental R&B or "smooth jazz," and quite unlike its predecessors, the repertory was affectionately dubbed "TV jazz" (a reference to the jazz-rock genre in Hollywood), the more pejorative "fuzak" (a mélange of fusion and Muzak elevator music), or the sufficiently inaccurate "happy jazz." Much of it was jazz-oriented, as befits Rit's roots and tastes and the lengthy improvisations and exotic harmony, but transcended the label by the infusion of funk, rock, blues, pop, classical, and electronic elements into his compositions and arrangements. As such, he was one of the era's most visible crossover artists and remains so to the present.

Eclectic and competent in a wide variety of styles, Rit is renowned for his balance of taste and technical prowess. In the studio, he was one of those rare musicians who could serve up a hit making hook and burn with jazz-rock freedom and intensity with equal aplomb. In the heyday of his seventies studio career, Rit was fond of "grease," regularly exploiting effects devices like tape echo, phasing, flanging, and wah-wah. However, these "toys" never interfered with or supplanted his ability to deliver pure, unadorned guitar statements.

As an improviser and guitar soloist, Rit has an uncanny command of many diverse approaches and techniques.

That's one reason his licks graced records by artists as diverse as Ray Charles, Debby Boone, Sonny Rollins, Sergio Mendes, and the Bee Gees. Rit's rock playing can be gutsy, blues-based, and pentatonic or filled with bopping jazz-inflected runs, highly technical passages, and sophisticated rhythms. Rit often applies modern jazz extensions, superimpositions, bebop and modal lines, and side-slipping atonality into his improvisations over a static vamp or pedal point.

Rit's straight-ahead jazz playing, often rendered on the genre's traditional electric arch-top, is convincing and well conceived. He often states melodies in octaves, as on his cover of the Beatles's "A Day in the Life," in a manner and timbre (articulating with the thumb) typical of his idol, Wes Montgomery. Moreover, Rit frequently adds acoustic guitar pieces and interludes performed on nylon-string with accomplished, authentic classical and/or Brazilian technique, to his already impressive repertory.

Rit was often recruited as an expert rhythm guitar player. His style in this regard was as broad as his solo pallet, running the gamut from funk rhythms and rock grooves to jazz comping, pop hooks, and arpeggiated classical parts. One of his specialties was the coloristic muted guitar lick, frequently processed with trade-mark slow phasing or wah-wah, which acted as a percussive ostinato in arrangements. Rit also exploited tremolo picked and slurred double stops treated with echo delays.

Essential Listening

Captain Fingers (1977, Epic) and *The Captain's Journey* (1978, Elektra) are the definitive Lee Ritenour albums of the L.A. Studio era. Several essential tracks from his early records are currently available on a compilation, *The Best of Lee Ritenour* (Epic). Also recommended are Lee's more recent jazz releases—*Stolen Moments* (1990, GRP) and *Wes Bound* (1992, GRP)—as well as a long-awaited collaboration with fellow studio star Larry Carlton, *Larry & Lee* (1995, GRP).

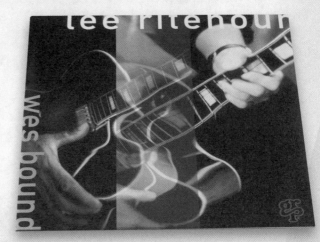

ESSENTIAL VIEWING

Illuminating and entertaining, Lee Ritenour's early instructional video is worth searching for. Recorded in Japan and released in the U.S. by Star Licks, it sheds light on Rit's many musical philosophies and strategies.

Rit is well represented online in a wealth of telling video clips. Vintage highlights from the golden age of L.A. jazz-rock fusion include "Rio Funk," "Sugarloaf Express," and a classic avant-garde performance from his Friendship band (with Alex Acuna and Ernie Watts) at the Montreux Jazz Festival. Also worth searching for are "Four on Six" with George Benson (both on jazz boxes) at a 1997 Wes Montgomery tribute, "Stolen Moments" with Brian Bromberg (1990), "It's On" with George Duke and Marcus Miller (Ramsey Lewis' *Legends of Jazz*), "What a Fool Believes" with Michael McDonald (1992), and a low-fi but nonetheless compelling live performance of "Room 335" with Larry Carlton on their world tour (Japan, 1995).

SOUND

At the height of his studio career, Lee Ritenour was closely associated with the workhorse guitar of the age: the thin-line, semi-hollow Gibson ES-335. He was initially seen with a seventies walnut model (as in the 1974 Monterey Jazz Guitar Summit) but by 1976 found his primary guitar voice in the vintage 1960 cherry-red dot-neck model he plays to the present day.

Rit's alternate instrument was a sunburst 1949 Gibson L-5C (with a floating Johnny Smith pickup) he used for arch-top jazz sounds. For consistency, both guitars were strung with Ernie Ball regular slinky stings. Currently, the Gibson custom shop produces a limited edition Lee Ritenour L-5 model in its signature series. This guitar is based on Rit's single-cutaway acoustic L-5 arch-top and includes refinements like a thinner body (2 5/8 inches), a floating BJB pickup, and a fine-tuning fingers tailpiece.

As a busy and eclectic studio guitarist, Lee had assembled a large arsenal of instruments by 1978. The highlights of his working collection included a blonde 360/12 Rickenbacker electric 12-string, several Ibanez solid bodies and semi-solids (he was an early Ibanez endorser and R&D guy), a sunburst Gibson Les Paul Standard, a blonde Les Paul Deluxe, a two-tone sunburst fifties Fender Stratocaster, and an Ovation electric classical. His acoustic lineup featured a nylon string, a National resonator, a sunburst Guild steel six-string, a blonde Guild 12-string, and a Martin six-string.

Rit's amplifiers of the seventies reflected the period's varied studio needs. He used modified, all-tube Fender combo amps (usually a Deluxe Reverb or a Princeton), Music Man hybrid combos (preferring the 210-65 model), and Yamaha solid-state amps. He currently uses Mesa-Boogie Road King amplifiers with Boogie Dual 12 speakers as well as Fender '65 Twin Reverb reissues and an Alessandro custom tube amp and cabinet.

© Rob Shanahan

Like most accomplished studio guitarists of the era, Rit was adept at effects use, often coloring his rhythm parts and licks with all manners of grease. A favorite and subtle processor was the onboard Dan Armstrong Orange Squeezer compressor box usually seen plugged into the face of his 335. The Mutron Bi-Phase became a signature Rit effects sound heard on numerous film scores and pop records like "Deacon Blues" (Steely Dan). He also regularly exploited the Roland Boss CE-1 Chorus Ensemble (heard throughout *The Captain's Journey*), a Maestro Echoplex tape delay, a Sho-Bud volume pedal, and a Crybaby wah-wah pedal.

Rit was one of the first guitarists to utilize the legendary effects rack and pedalboard setups of the L.A. studios. In 1978, his standard rig (built by Chris Foreman, designer and engineer at Altec Lansing) employed a buffer amp to minimize signal loss and housed a Maestro Echoplex, Mutron Bi-Phase, Oberheim Voltage Controlled filter, MXR Flanger, Mutron Octave Divider, MXR Phase 90, MXR Filter,

Roland Bee-Baa fuzz box, a Vox wah-wah pedal, and a Goodrich volume pedal.

A work in progress, Rit's current pedalboard houses a Rodenberg Gas Distortion Pedal, Rodenberg 808 Distortion Pedal, Fulltone Wah-Wah Pedal, Fulltone Choral-flange Pedal, Xotic Effects BB Preamp, Radial Tone Bone amp switcher, and Aphex Punch Factory.

LICKS
FIG. 1: RIT'S FUNK JAZZ FUSION

This challenging phrase finds the Captain navigating jazz-rock fusion waters. Check out the mix of sophisticated polychords, extended voicings, and a blistering intervallic melody that defies tonal classification. This line is predominately comprised of fast sixteenth notes and exploits wide leaps and chromaticism, as befits the jazz/fusion bag. The melody seems to be grounded in C7 at the outset yet travels seamlessly to E♭ minor via the G diminished scale.

FIG. 1.

FIG. 2: RIT'S BLUES FUSION

Rit was one of the most exciting jazz-rock soloists in the L.A. studio world. This phrase is a case in point. The opening idea is a solid blues-based melody, which poses a G minor sound over the C11 funk vamp—a sound also favored by his idols Wes Montgomery and John Coltrane. The passages in measures 3 and 4 exploit a rhythmically charged line distinguished by repeated notes and strong accenting. The closing sequence is a favorite lick outlining B♭ and F major triads and chromatic approach tones, which cadences in C minor at the conclusion. All in all, it's a typically multifaceted Ritenour line.

FIG. 2.

FIG. 3: RIT'S BEBOP FUSION

This excerpt comes off like a collision of hard bop, atonal jazz, and modern rock. The first passage in measures 1 and 2 is a modified horn-like bebop line with characteristic chromatic passing tones and interval contours. The second section in measure 3 finds Rit venturing into a remote tonality of B minor over a C11 funk vamp. This is akin to the *side slipping* technique of avant-garde jazz players like John Coltrane and McCoy Tyner. Note the move from B minor to C minor implicit in the melody, which acts like a large leading tone. The final licks are straight out of the Jeff Beck playbook. Here, Rit milks a series of synth-like fusion riffs (a la Jan Hammer) replete with idiomatic string bends and repeated sixteenth-note groups.

FIG. 3.

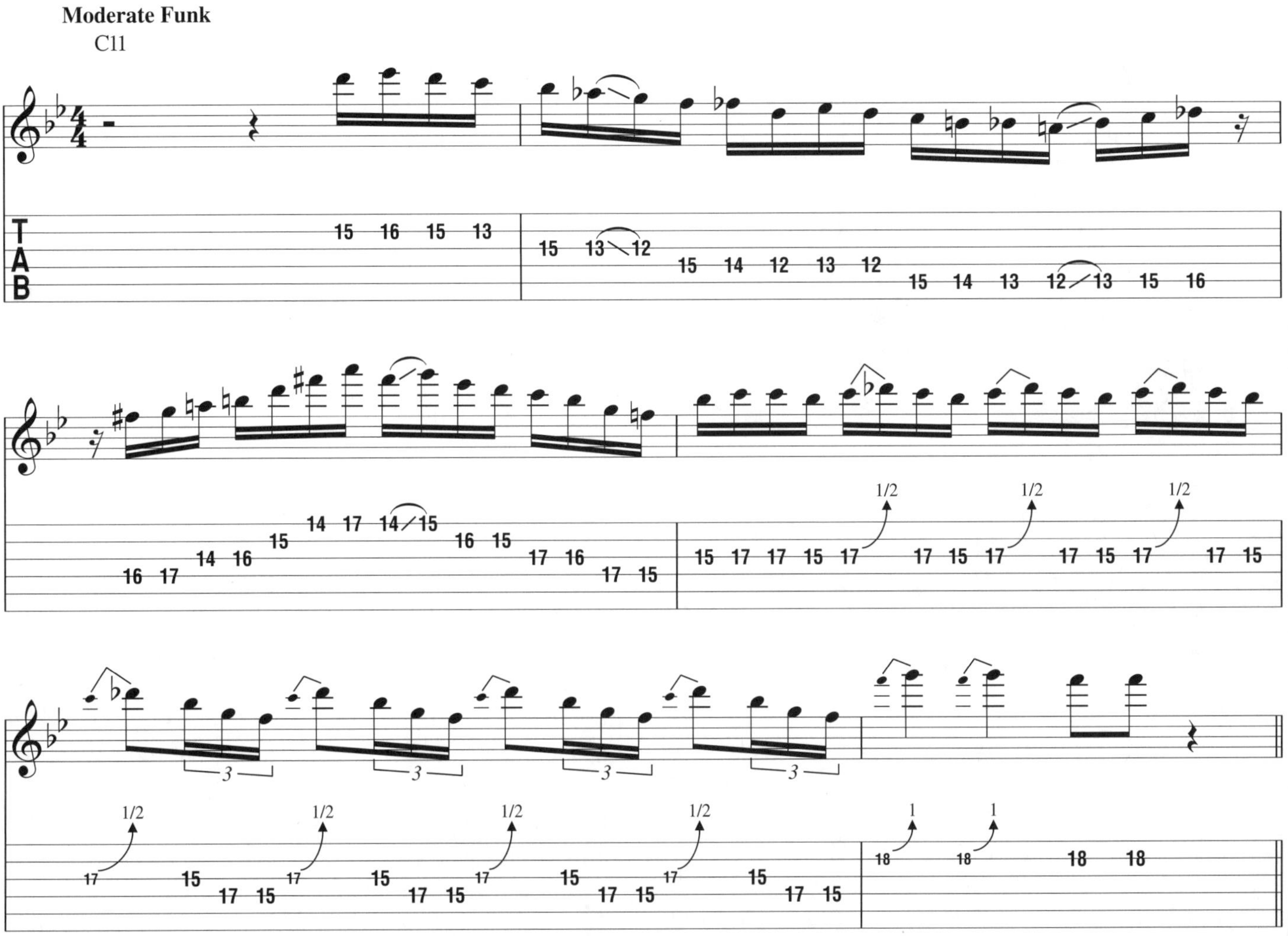

HOWARD ROBERTS

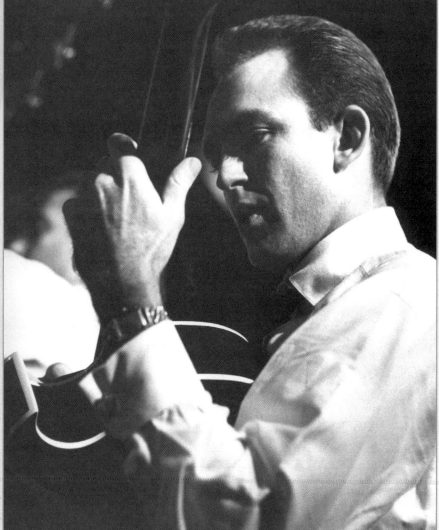

© Ray Avery CTS·IMAGES

Along the way, HR designed and lent his name to no less than a half dozen Howard Roberts guitar models marketed by Epiphone and Gibson, created and marketed the first line of boutique guitar amps (*Benson Electronics*), founded Playback Music, and wrote and self-published the first definitive modern guitar tutorials in the seventies (*The Howard Roberts Guitar Book* is one), produced the massive reference work *Guitar Compendium*, developed a color-coded beginner's guitar method *(Praxis)*, and anticipated the rise of computer-based interactive guitar learning systems a decade and half before they were the norm. And those are just the tip of the iceberg.

Stories about HR—the man and the myth—abound in guitar lore. He was a consummate music student his whole life. He mastered the guitar at an early age, turned pro at fifteen, and began building his multi-faceted musical style with the blues and jazz— enhanced by a fascination with the Schillinger system of composition. The story goes that he swept up after hours to attend a Schillinger class in his native Phoenix area. When HR moved to Los Angeles in 1950, he arrived with only a guitar, an amp, and one suit for gigs. While paying his dues on the club and tour circuit, he patched that suit a number of times—once with staples! He lived on milk and cookies and slept on friends' couches—and even in friends' cars—while making the rounds in L.A.

*M*ost great jazz performers are lucky to enjoy one successful run in the music business; guitarist Howard Roberts had three. One: HR was one of the movers and shakers in the fifties West Coast jazz scene. Along with Barney Kessel, Herb Ellis, and Jim Hall, he epitomized the blend of post-bop and cool-jazz guitar styles that was brewing in and around Los Angeles and was one of the most distinctive soloists of the genre. Two: HR was an in-demand, highly sought-after, triple-scale, first-call (you pick the adjective), studio guitar player of the sixties. His expertise and creativity on challenging sessions, which would turn an ordinary mortal's hair white, were legendary. And three: HR the guitarist-educator-philosopher founded the now-famous MI (Musicians Institute) in the seventies. This institution grew out of his mythic guitar seminars, evolved into GIT, and has grown into one of the leading vocational schools in the world.

HR met and befriended Barney Kessel and was eventually introduced to Jack Marshall, who became a mentor, employer, collaborator, and lifelong friend. Marshall helped him secure some fruitful gigs, got him involved in studio work, and was instrumental in facilitating his record deal with Capitol. A milestone of the period was HR's jazz guitar flourishes in Marshall's score to the western series *The Deputy* (starring Henry Fonda). Every week, the TV audience of the late fifties was treated to HR's sublime jazz guitar playing, though he was not yet a known commodity.

Through Barney Kessel, HR received a contract with Verve Records in the fifties and released a handful of jazz albums that remain cult classics of the genre to this day. In this period, HR also expanded his studio credits to include contributions to countless now-classic TV shows. *Peter Gunn*, *Twilight Zone*, *The Munsters*, *Dragnet*, *The Dick Van Dyke Show*, *Batman*, *Gidget*, *Love American Style*, *Bonanza*, *Have Gun Will Travel*, *The Jetsons*, *Get Smart*, and *Mission Impossible* are just a handful of successful weekly programs that featured HR as a soloist. Tip of the iceberg, again.

HR was also heard on enumerable film scores and rock tracks of the fifties, sixties, and seventies. Accompanying those sessions are the mythic HR studio stories. One of the most-told tales recounts Howard shaking the rainwater out of his nylon-string acoustic before nailing the complicated intro—perfectly—to *The Sandpiper* ("The Shadow of Your Smile") with a full studio orchestra looking on in disbelief.

Another tells of how a studio guitarist sitting in the second chair woke HR from his catnap just before the red light went on. He proceeded to sight-read the daunting written score—which had more black on the page than white—while half asleep. And fellow studio legend Carol Kaye recalls how HR could groove like a dedicated rocker on a Jan and Dean surf song one moment and deliver an astonishing authentic jazz solo the next.

There are many more such tales in the HR studio saga as there are HR-propelled Top 20 hit records by Elvis Presley, Ricky Nelson, Eddie Cochran, Peggy Lee, Robert Mitchum, Lou Rawls, Bobby Darin, Pat Boone, Dean Martin, and Larry Williams. Evidently, HR even got to the Beatles. In the midst of Beatlemania, they covered William's "Bad Boy" complete with stinging bluesy guitar licks. HR returned the favor with his jazz-rock interpretation of "A Hard Day's Night" in 1964.

In the early sixties, HR developed a musical form that crossed over into rock and pop territory while maintaining its jazz roots. This indescribable and utterly unique approach is heard on many of his Capitol albums. In these grooves, HR cultivated and perfected a singular jazz style informed by contemporary rock, blues, pop, and R&B that stuck to a commercial format with tight, radio-friendly arrangements and brief but ear-catching guitar excursions.

Some of those guitar excursions caught the ear of Steely Dan/Doobie Brother guitarist Jeff "Skunk" Baxter, who extolled praises for HR and *HR Is a Dirty Guitar Player* during several interviews in the rock and pop magazines of the seventies. But that's hardly an anomaly. The list of players HR has influenced is legion encompassing many divergent stylists; among them are rockers Duane Eddy (the King of Twang), Frank Beecher (Bill Haley's Comets), Terry Kath (of Chicago), Jerry Miller (of Moby Grape), and Harvey Mandel (Butterfield Blues Band), as well as session giants Lee Ritenour, Tim May, Mitch Holder, and Steve Khan, and jazz players Howard Alden, Jimmy Bruno, Jerry Hahn, and Ron Eschete. By the way, HR was a favorite of Wes Montgomery. And there's more. A Howard Roberts guitar has been seen in the hands of Rush's Alex Lifeson, Ted Nugent, and Robby Robertson of the Band. The HR legacy runs deep and wide, indeed.

INFLUENCES

HR's earliest influences include the country music he heard in his household and environs. When he started playing at age eight, he played by ear and also learned some basics from informal beginner lessons. His first important teacher was Horace Hatchett, who introduced HR to jazz guitarists Django Reinhardt, George Van Eps, and Barney Kessel. The Van Eps chord-melody influence is heard prominently on "Winchester Cathedral" (*Jaunty Jolly*), while the Kessel stamp is perceptible on HR's fifties Verve recordings. Django's affect was less prominent but surfaced in the gypsy-style quasi-classical sequences he sometimes worked into improvisations.

HR picked up additional blues and jazz influences when he was about fifteen and already playing in the black clubs in the Phoenix area. He remembers being around Miles Davis and Bud Powell as they passed through town on tours.

HR was also influenced by classical music. He studied the Joseph Schillinger system of composition—a mathematical approach—from composer Fabian Andre while in Phoenix and later, inspired by Jack Marshall in Hollywood, learned classical guitar. HR also studied composition and arranging with L.A. teacher Albert Harris.

HR updated his style and list of influences as he evolved musically. By the late sixties, he cited rock guitarists Jeff Beck, Jerry Garcia, Joe Walsh, and George Harrison as personal favorites.

STYLE

Pickers of all persuasions have marveled at the loose, soulful blues-funk quality of HR's guitar playing. This primary aspect is complemented by technically adept and complex neo-bebop lines, spiraling intervallic passages, eccentric but mellifluous phrasing and feel, and beautiful harmonically rich chord-melody phrases. These ingredients have been part and parcel of his style since the early days. A noteworthy attribute of HR's approach is his ability to assume the mood of the particular piece he is playing. To this end, style, technique, and vocabulary are fluid and transitory concerns in his conception.

HR's personal style maintained a forward trajectory after his debut. He was initially touted as a bebop guitarist with an ear for modernism. Two strikingly different albums sum up his approach in the fifties. The eclectic *Mr. Roberts Plays Guitar* (1957) featured HR's jazz guitar with a string quartet, while *Good Pickin's* (1959) is a bop-oriented straight-ahead date. The latter has been reissued in CD and serves as a splendid example of HR's fifties bop style.

In the Capitol years, HR seemed to revel in a new period of discovery and innovation. Perhaps it was the shorter succinct arrangements that prompted him to say a lot in a smaller space. Maybe it was the cross-pollination from all the varied styles he encountered and assimilated in the session world, or maybe it was just a measure of his own natural evolution as a player. During this period, HR redefined countless jazz standards and show tunes like "Autumn Leaves," "Misty," and "Chim Chim Cher-ee" and included them in eclectic programs that featured his uncommon take on pop hits, such as "A Hard Day's Night" and "Winchester Cathedral." In any case, HR's style of the early sixties veered off into unprecedented tangents and presaged the fusion sounds of the coming decade.

At the end of the sixties, HR incorporated elements of the acid rock movement into his playing. This included amp distortion, exaggerated string bending, feedback, and sound effects, which he even injected into standards like "Shiny Stockings." Check out the Magic Band live version for illumination as well as adventurous albums such as *Antelope Freeway* (1971) and *Equinox Express Elevator* (1972).

ESSENTIAL LISTENING

Color Him Funky and *HR Is a Dirty Guitar Player* remain the definitive Howard Roberts recordings of the Capitol period. These were recently available as a two-disc set, *Dirty 'N' Funky* (Guitarchives), and now through a Euphoria collection. Also essential are *Something's Cookin'* and *Jaunty-Jolly*; again currently re-issued by Euphoria. *Good Pickin's* (re-issued as a Verve/PolyGram import) is also highly recommended, as are the two HR live sets from V.S.O.P. Records, *The Magic Band: Live at Donte's* (#94) and *The Magic Band II* (#102).

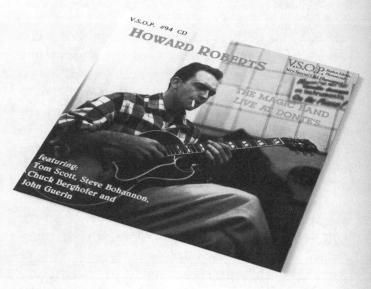

ESSENTIAL VIEWING

Video clips of HR performing are surprisingly scarce, considering that there were video cameras at his GIT facility and that he played there with faculty members and guest artists. The Roberts Music Institute provided one such rare gift to the guitar-playing world in 2009. This clip, recorded at his school, features HR in action playing an extended version of the classic standard "Star Eyes" with a jazz quartet.

SOUND

HR has been involved with the design of his personal instruments since the early days. Arguably the most personal was the one-of-a-kind, heavily altered "Black Guitar" he assembled in the early sixties—heard prominently on recordings through the seventies. This instrument was originally owned by Herb Ellis and was a thirties Gibson ES-150 (the "Charlie Christian" model). Among the many modifications performed were the replacement of the neck and fingerboard, the reshaping of the neck, the upgraded P-90 neck pickup, the thinner body, new binding throughout, the black lacquer finish, and a unique double-cutaway shape

(Venetian cutaway on the treble upper bout, a notch cutaway on the bass upper bout). Interestingly, a variant of this design has appeared recently in the form of the Ibanez Pat Metheny model. Prior to the Black Guitar, HR played a single-pickup Gibson ES-175 with a P-90 pickup (now owned by Jim Hall) in the fifties as well as a slightly modified Gibson L-10.

In the mid-sixties, HR collaborated with Epiphone to create the first of a series of signature model guitars. The most notable feature of these instruments was the oval soundhole, instead of the common f-holes of most arch-top electrics. Available in Standard and Custom models, the guitar had a carved L4-C body (like a more solid ES-175), a long-scale fingerboard, and a single floating mini-humbucker mounted at the end of the fingerboard (like the Gibson Johnny Smith). HR's original Custom prototype made in 1964 had a built-in pickup, and that was one reason it was his favorite Epi HR guitar. Unfortunately, it was stolen three months later and was replaced by the production model, which he didn't like as much. HR used the Black Guitar and at least two different Epi Customs on recordings throughout the sixties and early seventies. The Epi HR's were discontinued in 1969.

Gibson and HR resurrected his namesake guitar as a production model in the mid-seventies. The Gibson Howard Roberts Custom was introduced in 1973, and in 1976, the HR product line was expanded with the addition of the fancier Gibson Howard Roberts Artist. These HR guitars stayed in the catalog until 1982 when they were replaced by the Gibson Howard Roberts Fusion model. The Fusion is a semi-solid guitar with a structure like the ES-335 but with a smaller, single-cutaway body, two humbuckers, and a stop tailpiece (replaced in 1990 with a fingers-style trapeze tailpiece). The HR Fusion became a favorite axe of rock players Alex Lifeson and Ted Nugent. A testament to his vision and staying power, it remained in production as the Howard Roberts Fusion III.

As a busy studio pro, HR maintained a large case filled with the standard tools of his trade. Over the years, his arsenal included a Les Paul, Telecaster, ES-335, ES-175, Stratocaster, six-string bass, Martin flat-top acoustic, 12-string electric, 12-string acoustic, nylon-string acoustic, mandolin, banjo, ukulele, a Fender Pro amp for alternate twangy sounds, and full gamut of sound processors.

HR played Gibson GA-50 combo amps in the fifties. That was the basis of his early jazz sound with the P-90-equipped ES-175. As his need for more power, flexibility, and volume increased, HR collaborated with Ron Benson to design and ultimately market the

Courtesy Patty Roberts/Wolf Marshall

first line of boutique amps in the sixties. These began as one-offs, built in Benson's garage at first, but rapidly gained favor with a number of studio and jazz players in the mid-sixties, prompting a more professional production method. HR's aim was to duplicate the sound of his Gibson GA-50 jazz amp and the lightweight Gibson Falcon studio amp with better specs, modern features, and more wattage. The Benson HR model also had reverb, a built-in distortion effect, and JBL speakers. HR's earliest Benson sound is heard via the small prototype used on the *Color Him Funky* album of 1963. By the late sixties, he was using a larger, more sophisticated combo model. HR's Benson amp tone became an industry standard, and his imagineering and marketing strategies set the stage for future boutique amp lines like Mesa-Boogie, Dumble, and Soldano.

LICKS

FIG. 1: ZIGZAGGING BEBOP

HR's jazz improvisation is always enthralling, diverse, and musically exciting. This telling phrase contains a potpourri of classic ingredients. Prime among these is the zigzagging *neighbor-note* pattern in measure 1. Here, HR outlines the C major chord with lower neighbor tones, which is a favorite device. Another is found in measure 4, where HR expounds on a common melodic theme that springs from classical etudes, was a favorite of Django's, and rose to become a cliché in hard bop. A noteworthy bebop mannerism occurs in measure 3. Check out the A minor–Ab minor move that functions as a substitute for an *altered dominant* chord (G7 altered).

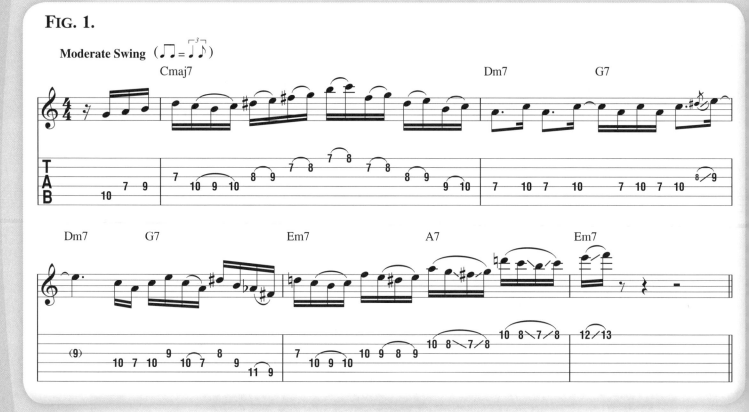

FIG. 1.

FIG. 2: CHORD-MELODY INTRO

HR's intros were musical gems. They were as compelling as his cadenzas and often functioned as effective mini-compositions or preludes. This phrase illustrates his chord-melody style applied to an extemporaneous ethnic-tinged intro to a well-known standard. Note the signature alternation of single-note and chordal textures. This is a textbook excerpt, juxtaposing arpeggio and scalar runs with moody, introspective chord colors. Note the fast opening run in E minor, which cadences on a ringing Am9 chord replete with jangly open strings. Similar textures are found in the Emb6 chord in measure 5 and the droning A minor figure in measures 6–7. HR adds characteristic sophisticated

extensions and alterations in the section via an F#°7 chord over D7 (producing a D7b9 sound) in measure 3 and his famed "Peter Gunn" chord (Gadd9/B) in measure 4. Interestingly, Eric Johnson borrowed this distinctive voicing for his main riff in "East Wes." HR closes the brooding minor-mode intro with a rapid scalar run reminiscent of flamenco guitar expanded with his sitarish sequences in measure 8. Note the use of mixed modes. HR uses a combination of the Aeolian mode and harmonic minor scale and inserts a G# tone for melodic flow in measure 9 to achieve the exotic Spanish effect.

FIG. 2.

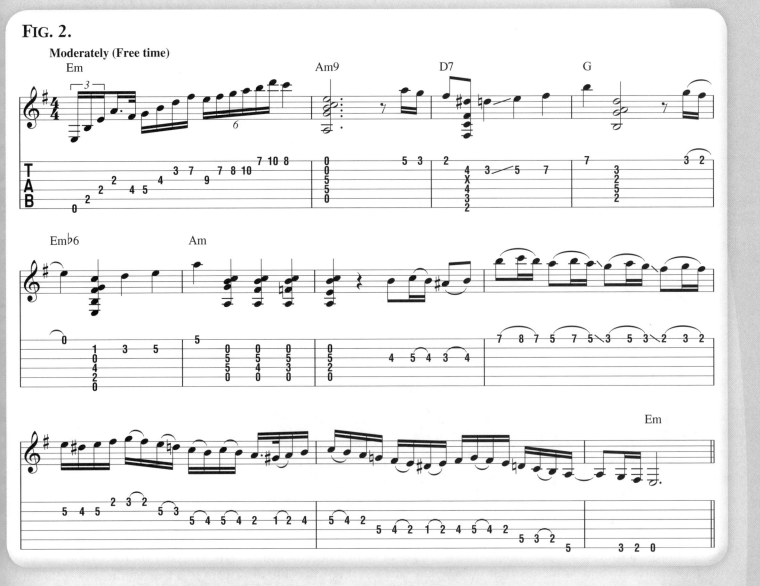

FIG. 3: SWINGING CHORD-MELODY LICK

HR's chord-melody work is depicted in this definitive phrase. This one is truly emblematic, weaving together triad figures, single-note melody, and arpeggiation for a characteristic result. In a generation teeming with sterling and distinctive chord-melody stylists (Johnny Smith, Kenny Burrell, Barney Kessel, Jim Hall, Wes Montgomery, et al), HR was unique in his interpretation of the erstwhile George Van Eps pick-style lead/rhythm approach. It has been rightfully said that he was the only one to make this vintage 1930's approach swing in the modern era, and this passage makes a convincing argument. And who else but HR could turn a hippie-era novelty tune into a colorful and unpredictable jazz vehicle?

FIG. 3.

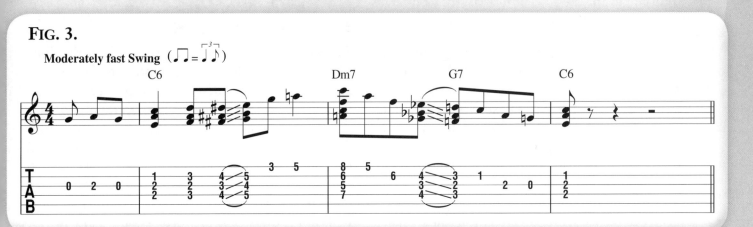

JOHNNY SMITH

© CTSIMAGES

*J*ohnny Smith is one of the most remarkable guitarists to come to prominence after Charlie Christian and Django Reinhardt made their marks on the scene. Equally at home with a jazz combo or a studio orchestra, as a bandleader or an unaccompanied soloist, in a duet with a vocalist or a pop record session, he is one of a small handful of jazz artists whose work garnered great public recognition at the very beginning of his career. Following his initial breakthrough, Smith rose in prominence to become one of the world's most visible and admired guitarists with a series of definitive albums on the Roost label. By the time he went into semi-retirement in 1957 and moved to Colorado, Johnny Smith had attained legendary status.

In addition to receiving the accolades of the jazz world, Smith's 1952 hit recording of "Moonlight in Vermont" (with Stan Getz) went on to become one of the best-selling instrumental singles of all time. Moreover, Smith is the composer of another well-known instrumental, "Walk, Don't Run," which has become a rock 'n' roll garage-band standard and part of musical Americana. Recorded by Smith in its original form in 1954, the intriguing, classically-tinged jazz piece was subsequently covered by his buddy Chet Atkins and was ultimately made into a mega-hit by The Ventures. Such is the transcendent musicianship of the man and the range of his influence.

For many, Johnny Smith is the personification of the "cool jazz" scene. His understated virtuosity, cool-toned guitar sound, and individualistic albums like the experimental *Flower Drum Song* (which combined a cello with a jazz trio) and *The New Johnny Smith Quartet* furthered this impression. However, taken in the totality of his work, these uncommon settings prove Johnny to be an eclectic artist who simply defies classification within the rigid strictures of jazz.

To hear Johnny Smith tell it, he doesn't belong in the annals of jazz guitar. Be that as it may, this self-effacing master is one of the most appreciated players in the genre. Just ask modern virtuosos John Scofield, Larry Carlton, John McLaughlin, George Benson, Larry Coryell, Jimmy Bruno, or Pat Martino. These players and many others hold Smith up as a defining role model in jazz guitar, but the maestro himself isn't so sure. He reserves the "jazz label" for pickers like Joe Pass, Wes Montgomery, and Tal Farlow and considers his own style to be something else—something different and divergent. The semantics wars notwithstanding, the name Johnny Smith is synonymous with guitar excellence. For decades, he has been revered by legions of savvy musicians for his precision, technique, advanced harmonic sense, and the sheer beauty of his guitar tone.

INFLUENCES

The eclectic Smith approach is based on the colorful mosaic of his diverse music interests. He has cited Spanish classical guitarist Andres Segovia and Belgian/French Gypsy jazz innovator Django Reinhardt as his primary influences. A self-taught musician, Smith developed his formidable technique as a youth playing along with Chesterfield Supper Club Band on the radio. Also a factor in his background is the early hillbilly/country music he pursued as a member of the Fenton Brothers—his first professional band, in 1939.

History has it that Smith picked up the instrument at age five, initially inspired by his father, a five-string banjo player, and grew to be accomplished on the trumpet, violin, and viola as well as the guitar. He is also a master arranger and was a highly sought-after studio musician in the fifties.

In 1982, Johnny claimed George Van Eps as his all-time favorite guitarist but also cited Carl Kress as important for his chord playing. He also named Chuck Wayne, Jimmy Raney, Joe Pass, Wes Montgomery, George Benson, Pat Martino, Jim Hall, and Harry Leahey as single-line players he enjoyed.

STYLE

Johnny Smith is one of the original virtuosos of the electric guitar. For decades, he has been acknowledged as a consummate master of the plectrum style. This aspect of his musicianship was exhibited early on in his fifties output of the Roost years. From the sweeping three-octave runs of "Moonlight in Vermont," "Tea for Two," and "Easy Living," to the lightning-fast articulate solos that distinguish "Tabu," "Jaguar," "I'll Remember April," "Un Poco Loco," "Samba," "'S Wonderful," "Tickle Toe," "Three Little Words," and "Time After Time," Smith's complex but listenable single-note improvisations are legendary in the annals of guitar lore—jazz or otherwise.

Exacting precision and technical prowess have long been hallmarks of the Johnny Smith style, however these factors have always been held in check by his sense of taste and clarity. Whether interpreting an up-tempo bebop line, digging into a straight-ahead swing groove, delivering a lilting jazz waltz, or rendering a gentle rubato ballad, Smith is an authoritative and powerful soloist with an immediately recognizable sound and unflagging chops. In addition to Smith's considerable skills as a jazz soloist and a technician, he is a fine blues player, as demonstrated on "Blues Backstage," "Fitz," "Bag's Groove," "Blue Lights," and particularly evocative moments in "Satin Doll" and "Sentimental Journey." What does it all mean? Barney Kessel once summed it up neatly with the telling observation: "No one in the world plays the guitar better."

Johnny Smith is one of the most distinctive chord stylists in any genre. His lush pianistic sonorities and intricate block chord playing are musical signatures and quite different from other guitarists of the era. Imagine the jazz voicings of pianists Art Tatum and

George Shearing combined with the impressionistic piano colors of Claude Debussy, realized and interpreted on an electric guitar, and you have an inkling of how Smith transformed the instrument. In this regard, he has always been in a class of his own.

Exemplary chord-melody moments in Smith's Roost catalog include "Moonlight in Vermont," "Yesterdays," "When I Fall in Love," "I Didn't Know What Time It Was," "You Don't Know What Love Is," "Vilia," "I Remember Clifford," "My Romance," and "The Lady Is a Tramp." An early reading of "Autumn Leaves" finds Smith creating a flamenco-inspired mood with dazzling arabesques, double-timed passagework, and classically influenced chords on acoustic guitar. And the uncommon chiming harmonics in the theme of "It Never Entered My Mind" make the track worth the price of admission alone.

In retrospect, an incongruous Roost record like *The Man with the Blue Guitar* seems an obvious expression of Smith's broader musical pallet. This 1962 recording found him in a solo guitar context for an entire album spinning his plectrum magic with a diverse set of standards, classical, and folk pieces. Here, his beautiful tone, touch, and technique on the instrument are directed at popular show tunes by Rodgers and Hart, Gershwin, and others, modern works by Debussy, Scriabin, and Ravel, and novel adaptations of old folk songs like "Shenandoah" and "Black is the Color."

Further evidence of Smith's eclectic nature was flaunted on his *Phase 2* album (Verve) of the sixties. This "jazz" recording featured the maestro's take on atypical pop tunes like "Exodus," "Don't Sleep in the Subway," "This Guy's in Love," "Sunny," and the Doors' "Light My Fire."

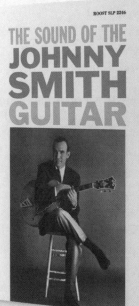

ESSENTIAL LISTENING

The Roost years exemplify the definitive Johnny Smith sound and style. The Mosaic eight-disc box set *The Complete Johnny Smith Small Group Sessions* is the gold standard and holy grail and contains all the important recordings from 1952–1964. For those interested in a single-disc sampler, *The Johnny Smith Quintet: Moonlight in Vermont* (Roulette Jazz, reissued by Blue Note) remains a serviceable introduction. Other worthy Roost reissues include sessions from 1954 packaged as *Walk, Don't Run* (Blue Note), *The Sound of the Johnny Smith Guitar* (Roulette Jazz/EMI), which combines two quartet albums from 1960 on a single disc, and *Johnny Smith and His New Quartet* (Fresh Sound Records, Spanish import).

Also highly recommended and worth searching for are the two Verve era recordings of 1967: *Johnny Smith* and *Johnny Smith's Kaleidoscope*, both Polygram imports. The former is packaged as an Elite Edition with several bonus tracks, booklet, and additional liner notes.

ESSENTIAL VIEWING

Videos of Johnny Smith are understandably rare but well worth the search. Online Johnny can be seen playing "What Are You Doing the Rest of Your Life" on his D'Angelico at a 1984 festival with an all-star jazz group in Mobile, Alabama. Another informal clip from the same period finds Johnny with his blonde Gibson in a duet with Mundell Lowe on "Seven Come Eleven."

SOUND

Johnny Smith has had four high-profile electric arch-top guitars named after him over the last few decades. Though he consistently favored a D'Angelico throughout his career, he lent his moniker to an early top-of-the-line Guild guitar in 1956, the Johnny Smith Award model: a single-cutaway acoustic arch-top fitted with a floating neck-mounted DeArmond Model 100 pickup. This eventually became the Artist Award model in 1960.

For his Roost recordings, Johnny used three different amplified arch-top guitars, all made by the legendary John D'Angelico of New York City. His original was a 21-fret model, which was lost to a fire in the fifties. Another was borrowed from fellow jazz guitarist John Collins (with Nat King Cole's group). Smith's second custom D'Angelico New Yorker became his main guitar. It had a smaller 17-inch Excel-size body, like a Gibson L-5, instead of the standard larger 18-inch body. Johnny's custom New Yorker had a sunburst finish and a 20-fret fingerboard with 25-inch scale length. Smith had the instrument fitted with a suspended "Loutone" pickup (essentially an improved DeArmond-style unit) attached near the fingerboard.

In 1960, Smith developed the famed Johnny Smith guitar in collaboration with Gibson. The Gibson Smith guitar, based in large part on his D'Angelico, has remained an industry standard and was one of the earliest, and certainly most renowned, amplified acoustic arch-tops to feature a neck-mounted floating pickup. The guitar employed a mini-humbucker, now commonly referred to as the "Johnny Smith pickup," and had a single volume control and output jack mounted on the pickguard. No electronics or hardware were actually built into the guitar. Interestingly, this essentially acoustic amplified instrument was used by Stevie Ray Vaughan ("Stang's Swang") and George Benson ("Breezin'") on some of their most famous recordings.

A second more elaborate version of the Gibson Smith guitar (the JS-D, Johnny Smith Double), with two suspended mini-humbucking pickups and separate tone and volume controls on the pickguard, was issued in 1963 and became the most expensive model in the company's jazz artist line. When seen with a Gibson JS guitar, Smith preferred the single-pickup style. While the Johnny Smith guitar was an impressive and popular instrument and remained in the Gibson catalog until 1989, Smith continued to play his D'Angelico into the seventies and eighties. In the late seventies, he replaced his original Gibson Johnny Smith with a blonde Gibson JS model equipped with a finger-style adjustable tailpiece instead of the earlier L-5 type.

In the nineties, Johnny endorsed a Heritage Johnny Smith model with a single suspended pickup, a hand-carved 17-inch body, and a finger-style adjustable tailpiece. He finally came full circle after Fender acquired Guild and the talents of famed luthier Bob Benedetto. The ill-fated 1956 guitar was revived, redesigned to suit Smith's discriminating specifications, built by Benedetto, and reissued as the new improved Johnny Smith Award in 2004. This luxurious instrument was the most recent flagship model of the Guild arch-top line. It featured a single Benedetto S6 floating mini-humbucker, a carved German Spruce top, European maple back and sides, a five-piece American maple neck, gold hardware, and the Guild harp tailpiece.

In the fifties, Johnny played his D'Angelico through the unusual Ampeg "Fountain of Sound" JS-20 amplifier, which he designed, used, and endorsed in the fifties. This unique piece of gear sat on four legs, pointed its 15-inch speaker upward at the ceiling, and, for all intents and purposes, more closely resembled a Danish-modern coffee table than a guitar amp. Smith's original idea was to cut down on feedback, allow the guitar to be better heard by the band members, and save the audience from high volume levels. While with the NBC orchestra, he also collaborated with Ampeg to produce a hi-fi guitar amp with flat frequency response.

In later years, Smith used an Emrad combo model, which also bore his name: the J.S. II. This was a solid-state amp, designed for a perfectly flat frequency response like his earlier Ampeg tube model and was equipped with a 15-inch JBL speaker—his personal preference. He was seen using this small combo amp during his performances and workshops of the early seventies. In 1984, at the jazz festival he played his D'Angelico through a Fender Twin Reverb amp.

In the early sixties, Johnny used Black Diamond No. 100 strings. He modified his round-wound strings by polishing them with a glass until they were as smooth as flat-wounds. Gibson later marketed a Johnny Smith string set. The gauges were fairly heavy (.013–.056) and had a flat-wound low E string in an otherwise round-wound set. Johnny used a heavier .058 flat-wound low E string on his personal guitar. Johnny used "stubbies," small heavy-gauge picks made by Ernie Ball.

LICKS
FIG. 1: CHORD-MELODY STYLE

Johnny Smith's chord-melody approach is one of his most outstanding and envied musical traits. This example presents a typical phrase in his famed chord-melody style. Here, he voices the chords pianistically, often using "clusters"—forms that exploit 2nd intervals and necessitate wide stretches on the guitar. Caveat: Ease into these fingerings! Stretch gradually and don't hold the stretch for too long, as you could hurt your hand. That said, the sound is gorgeous due to the cluster sonorities and sustained legato phrasing. Let the chords ring to full duration for the definitive Smith effect. The move in measure 4 (B♭7) features a particularly intriguing and challenging technique. Keep the F note on string 5 fingered as you slide the upper chords up chromatically—if you can, that is.

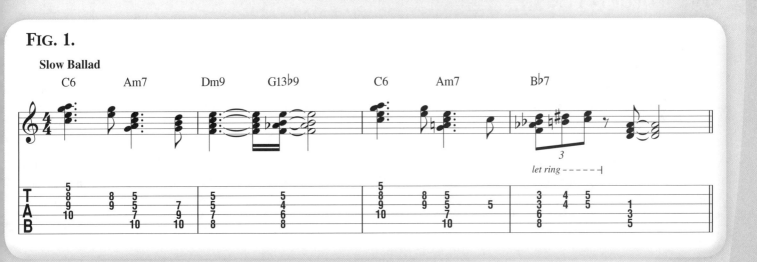

FIG. 1.
Slow Ballad

FIG. 2: BURNIN' SWING

High velocity cool jazz is the name of the game in this definitive Johnny Smith phrase—cool and yet hot, that's a viable descriptor for a lot of Smith's improvisations. This passage begins with a favorite technical line employing quick triplet rhythms and two of his signature melodic devices. Note the two-octave minor arpeggio pattern that combines A7 and pure D minor sounds. The pattern is answered by an ascending, uncategorizable melody. You could say, correctly, that it is based on a guitar fingering more than a scale or tonal center. That's how we get the G♯ and C♯ in the line and the E unisons in the transition from string 3 to 2. Smith completes the statement with a swinging lick in the upper register. Note the use of syncopated rhythm and diatonic scale sequencing in this section; the emblematic use of the D harmonic minor scale over the Em7♭5–A7 progression is also noteworthy.

FIG. 2.

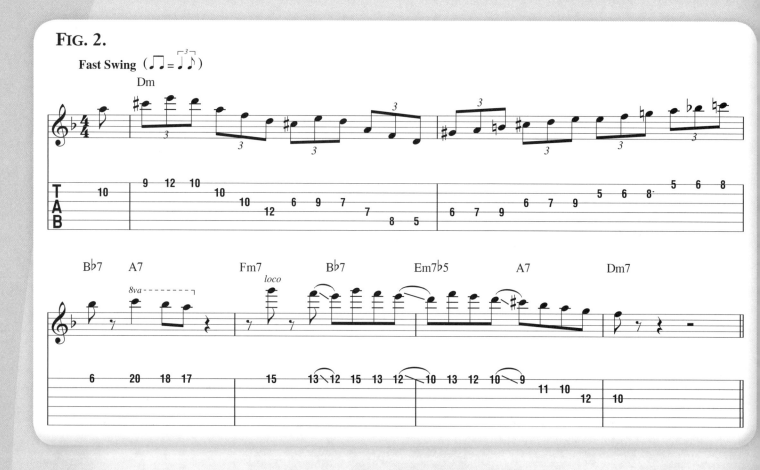

FIG. 3: DROP D TUNING

Johnny Smith was one of the first modern jazz guitarists to exploit drop D tuning. He used this tuning to facilitate pianistically voiced chords on the guitar—specifically the root-5th-10th spread on the lowest three adjacent strings. The Drop D sound is depicted in this signature phrase. At the heart of the passage is a characteristic pattern that exploits a number of colorful elements: the open tuning, natural harmonics, open strings, and interesting partial chords, voiced as dyads. Smith sets up a repetitious hypnotic pattern with these materials—harmonic, dyad, and open string—in measure 1 and then continues the figures with unfolding variations in measures 2–7. Note the clever voice leading contained in the progression and the beautiful textural effects developed with this simple germ of an idea. The phrase closes with a favorite "orchestral" voicing of a G major chord. Check out the atypical intervallic spread, G–D–B–G, and the smart use of the open tuning to make the voicing practical on the guitar. And that's just a small part of Johnny's genius.

FIG. 3.

Drop D tuning:
(low to high) D-A-D-G-B-E

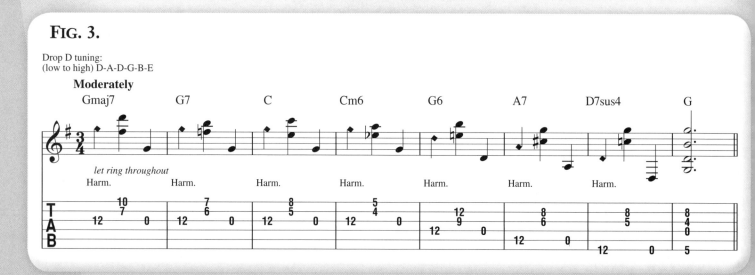

MIKE STERN

© Jan Persson CTSIMAGES

*I*n the supernova that is jazz-rock, Mike Stern holds a stellar place. If the center of the jazz-rock universe is the big bang begun with trumpeter Miles Davis, then all his disciples and devotees are important stars in the resultant galaxies. With Davis's expanding universe came a constellation of ambitious innovators, a new art form, and an enduring legacy. At its genesis are John McLaughlin, Chick Corea, Joe Zawinul, Herbie Hancock, Wayne Shorter, and Tony Williams. Their bands—Mahavishnu Orchestra, Return to Forever, Weather Report, Head Hunters, and Lifetime—are extensions of Miles Davis's foray into fusion and, along with Davis's ensembles, absolutely defined the term *jazz-rock* in the early seventies. And their bands underscored the significance of Miles Davis and his far-reaching, all-embracing, and kaleidoscopic vision in the evolving tangents of the music. After all, when it comes to fusion, Davis is the fountainhead and the leading innovator. After all, who else but the legendary trumpeter would be equally at home playing with Charlie Parker, John Coltrane, Wayne Shorter, John McLaughlin, or John Lee Hooker?

Miles Davis had an uncanny knack for discovering, developing, and employing talent. The roster of musical giants that passed through his ensembles since he began leading bands in the late forties is staggering—no hyperbole. Awe-inspiring names like John Coltrane, Bill Evans, Ron Carter, Billy Cobham, Robben Ford, Keith Jarrett, Cannonball Adderley, Gil Evans, Wynton Kelly, Gerry Mulligan, George Coleman,

Marcus Miller, John Scofield, and Jack DeJohnette are on the short list. In retrospect, a Davis anointing is one of the most elevating, desirable, and beneficial benchmarks in contemporary music. And that's where guitarist Mike Stern comes in.

First, a bit of history: It is postulated that jazz-rock unofficially began when Miles Davis imagined the possibilities of guitar avatar Jimi Hendrix in a new electrified, jazz-oriented ensemble. Davis had already stretched the envelope of modern jazz to the breaking point with his sixties quintet and was on the move again by decade's end toward something more innovative and striking. Had Jimi lived past 1970, it is presumed he and Davis would have made a recording and most likely performed together. At least, it makes for some fascinating pipe dreams. Instead, Jimi left us prematurely, and Miles's initial groundbreaking document *Bitches Brew* (1969) remains fusion's definitive document and its musical ground zero. This double album flaunted jazz improvisation—namely the amplified guitar of John McLaughlin, Wayne Shorter's sax, keyboards courtesy of Chick Corea, and Larry Young and the leader's distinctive horn playing—over an electrified combo driven by rock rhythms. The die was cast.

Davis explored enumerable possibilities of the electric guitar with succeeding combos. In this pursuit, his fusion explorations of the seventies ran the gamut from the high-tech virtuosity of McLaughlin to the purely rhythmic world of funk with, not one or two, but three guitarists (Reggie Lucas, Pete Cosey, and Dominique Mtume) on 1974's *Dark Magus*. Davis withdrew from the scene in 1975 following the release of *Agharta*. After a six-year hiatus, he boldly returned with his first comeback album, *The Man with the Horn* (1981), and a spirited jazz-rock ensemble featuring flamboyant newcomer Mike Stern on guitar.

Mike Stern did not emerge from a vacuum. He began playing as a pre-teen and in the ensuing years paid his dues in a string of anonymous bar bands. On the bandstand, he accomplished his goals of mastering the guitar and internalizing and applying the au courante blues-rock language of his forebears and contemporaries. Before his twenty-

© Jan Persson CTSIMAGES

first birthday, Stern enrolled in a very prestigious jazz vocation school: the Berklee College of Music in Boston. In the rarefied environment of Berklee, he sufficiently impressed many of his instructors, including Pat Metheny. Metheny gave Stern a coveted colleague recommendation, which resulted in the fortuitous gig with Blood, Sweat & Tears Stern held from 1976 to 1978. During this period, Stern played in a BS&T lineup that included bass virtuoso and future collaborator Jaco Pastorius.

Stern returned to Berklee to continue his studies in 1978 and during this period built a formidable reputation in the Boston-New York region. The pattern of player recommendations led to Stern hooking up with Michael and Randy Brecker, Billy Cobham, and finally Miles Davis. He debuted on *The Man with the Horn* in 1981 and stayed with Miles through the early eighties. Other notable releases with the trumpeter include the live album *We Want Miles* (1981) and 1982's *Star People*, on which he shared guitar duties with John Scofield. All are considered classics of the fusion genre.

Mike Stern officially began his solo career more than two decades ago with *Upside Downside* (Atlantic, 1986). A striking and auspicious debut, the recording married diverse musical tangents. It showcased Stern's myriad talents cast in electrified funky fusion grooves and atmospheric jazz-rock settings, guided by stellar guitarist/producer Hiram Bullock. The album featured Stern as player and composer and purveyed enduring favorites like "After You," "Mood Swings" and the title track. *Time in Place* (1987) proved an admirable sophomore effort, sporting the Stern classic "Chromazone," while 1988's *Jigsaw* found him venturing deeper into rock-oriented territory.

Since then, Stern has released a string of consistently excellent albums, including the much-lauded *Standards (and Other Songs)* (1992), *Between the Lines* (1996), and the wonderfully eclectic *Give and Take* (1997), which found him covering John Coltrane's "Giant Steps," Sonny Rollins's "Oleo," Cole Porter's "I Love You," and Jimi Hendrix's "Who Knows," and turning in a notable performance on his original swinging blues "That's What You Think." Finishing the decade, Stern shared the honors with fellow fusion guitarists Bill Frisell and John Scofield on his appropriately titled *Play* (1999).

In the new millennium, Stern reinforced his legacy with such albums as *Voices* (2001), his first foray into vocal music, *These Times* (2004), which marked his twelfth work as a leader and featured banjoist Bela Fleck, and *Who Let the Cats Out* (2006). Amidst tour dates and sessions, he found time to lend his playing to the Yellow Jackets' *Lifecycle* (2008), their first album in fifteen years to feature a guitarist, and to perform live with the influential fusion group. His recent opus *Big Neighborhood* (2009) was an eclectic extravaganza that flirted with world music and high-velocity rock guitar shredding as well as bebop, blues, and funk tangents. On it, Stern hosted appearances by guest guitar virtuosos Steve Vai and Eric Johnson.

INFLUENCES

Mike Stern is a self-described bebopper with an edge— or should we say, more accurately, edges? His background reveals an eclectic wealth of influences: B.B. King, Albert King, Buddy Guy, Eric Clapton, and Jimi Hendrix as well as Jim Hall, Wes Montgomery, Michael Brecker, McCoy Tyner, John Coltrane, and J.S. Bach.

Stern picked up the guitar at age twelve and as a teenager went through a succession of rock-based garage bands in and around his local Washington, D.C. area. At twenty, he enrolled in Boston's jazz-oriented Berklee College of Music and came into the orbit of player/teachers like guitarists Pat Metheny and Mick Goodrick and pianist Charlie Banacos. It was Banacos who helped Stern with his ear training and vocabulary. Ear training remains a vital element in the equation, as noted in a recent article wherein the interviewer in his home spied numerous CDs, half-speed cassette recorders, and piles of handwritten Stern transcriptions of music by Coltrane, Tyner, and Brecker.

STYLE

Fusion music is a slippery animal. On the fingerboard, jazz-rock can mean a number of things: John McLaughlin's aggressive million-note pentatonic approach, Al Di Meola's scalar, Spanish flamenco-tinged passage work, Allan Holdsworth's florid legato sax-like stylings, John Scofield's gritty blues-rock-funk, or Jeff Beck's progressive British rock interpretation. And then there's Mike Stern. Stern is unique in his hybrid mix and enviable command of straight-ahead modern jazz, funk, blues, and rock. That's his "fusion" conception; it has prompted him to develop a singular approach and carve a special niche in the big jazz-rock picture.

As a soloist, Stern is in a class of his own, striking a seemingly irreconcilable balance between genuine bebop improvisation, intricate modern jazz-rock scalar lines, post-bop angularity and dissonance, aggressive Hendrix-inspired blues-rock licks, and subtle melodic playing. Jazz-rock or rock jazz, or something else entirely—it depends on the cut.

Stern has absorbed a variety of influences that surface regularly and unpredictably in his multifarious style. He has the requisite blues-based guitar language and rock energy gleaned from Jimi Hendrix, Jeff Beck, Buddy Guy, Albert King, et al with stylistically correct string bending, vibrato, pentatonic and blues scale melody, pinch harmonics, and phrasing nuances. However, he also projects a true bebop-derived palette—the product of learning and internalizing countless standards and landmark solos of the jazz genre. Moreover, he conveys the fluidity, technical execution, and sophisticated harmonic approach of a post-bop saxophonist like Michael Brecker married to the dynamic rock attack of a Beck or Hendrix. In lesser hands this combination could result in an unwieldy hodgepodge of musical confusion—not so with Stern.

In addition to idiomatic bebop, blues, and rock melodies, Stern often plays ethnically tinged lines based on modes and synthetic scales. For example, in the intro of "Nardis" (on *Standards*), a darkly modal tune, Stern exploits passages derived from combining the Aeolian mode and the harmonic minor scale. These are arranged in long strings of eighth notes, phrased like a horn and decorated with chromatic neighbor notes, producing a genre-correct targeting sound. The effect is of Middle Eastern world music colliding with post-bop jazz and is musically exotic.

Many of Stern's improvisations fall into the category of the *post-bop* jazz language. This type of melodic approach has a harmonically fluid, equilibrium-upsetting effect favored by sax players like Coltrane and Brecker. In some cases, the lines are extremely dissonant, filled with chromatic digressions and angular wide-interval leaps, and only peripherally relate to a basic underlying chord. Moreover, in this regard, many of Stern's improvised phrases reflect a wind player's phrasing conception with quick rising flurries ascending to a prominent melody note—a favorite device—and long zigzagging lines, comparable to Coltrane's "sheets of sound." Like many modern jazz players, he exploits "riffs" in repeated sequences of four-note groups, often based on seventh chords or extensions, which on the guitar Stern moves around the fingerboard freely in the manner of a legato horn passage.

Stern's handling of evergreen standards from the Great American Songbook is exemplified by takes on classic tunes such as "I Love You," "Like Someone in Love," and "There Is No Greater Love." In this context, he is capable of generating lines similar to those found in the repertories of Joe Pass, Jim Hall, Pat Martino, and George Benson. Moreover, Stern often states melodies and solo lines in parallel octaves in the manner established by Wes Montgomery. However, these bopping melodies are often colored with Stern's chorused, echo drenched sound, which imparts a contemporary processed timbre akin to the Pat Metheny tone.

Stern's chordal style is informed by jazz keyboard moves and impressionistic orchestral sounds. He often chooses chords built on 4ths (*quartal harmony*) and modern sonorities favored by McCoy Tyner, Herbie Hancock, Larry Young, and Bill Evans to harmonize common melodies. This produces colorful modern suspensions and extensions in standard progressions. Stern also employs altered tensions (flatted and raised 9ths and 5ths in chords), extended voicings (ninth, eleventh, and thirteenth chords), and *polychords* (the use of triad-on-triad stacks). He also exploits *bi-tonal chords* over pedal points, as in "Upside Downside." In line with his penchant for wet effects processing, many of Stern's chord passages are colored with ethereal echo/delay effects and volume swells.

ESSENTIAL LISTENING

Mike Stern's work is powerful and definitive on every album he has released since his debut in 1986. His early albums are classics of modern jazz-rock fusion. *Jigsaw* and *Odds or Evens* are exemplary, as is *Upside Downside*. *Standards (and Other Songs)* and *Give and Take*, which reveal his take on challenging jazz pieces of the core repertory, are also highly recommended. Furthermore, Stern's playing with Miles Davis on *We Want Miles* (1981) and *Star People* (1983) is also essential listening for fans of fusion and modern jazz.

ESSENTIAL VIEWING

Mike Stern's exciting fusion style is well documented on *Mike Stern: The Paris Concert* (2004, New Morning/ Inaustik). Moreover, there are numerous diverse and illuminating video performance clips of Mike Stern online. Highlights include a Wes Montgomery-inspired B♭ blues at the 55 club, a duet rendition of "Autumn Leaves" with bassist Dave Zeigner, several informal but telling clinic appearances, an aggressive Jeff Beck-flavored bop-rock trio version of Miles Davis's "Jean-Pierre," and live versions of favorite originals like "Chromazone," "Still There," "Joan's Street," and "All Heart."

SOUND

The Mike Stern sound is as distinctive as his conception. Stern played a stock white, seventies Fender Stratocaster as his primary instrument with Miles Davis. He also used an old modified Fender Telecaster, once owned by Roy Buchanan, bought from Danny Gatton. Stern's Tele was fitted with a Seymour Duncan humbucker in the neck position and a single-coil Bill Lawrence blade pickup in the bridge position.

When both of these instruments were stolen, Stern turned to a homemade Tele built by Michael Aronson mated with a vintage 1950–1951 Broadcaster neck and fitted with similar electronics. This battle-scarred guitar became his trademark axe. In the late nineties, Stern lent his name to a Tele-style guitar marketed by Yamaha as part of their Pacifica line. This signature instrument, often seen in concert, has a figured ash body, a 22-fret maple fingerboard, a Seymour Duncan '59 humbucker in the neck position, and a Duncan Hot Rail in the bridge position.

From the outset of his solo career, Stern used a stereo amp rig, split with an eighties Yamaha SPX90 multi-effects rack unit generally set for stereo chorus (from a pitch change patch). Originally, one side employed a Peavey Musician head and a Guild/Hartke cabinet with four 10-inch speakers. The other side was fed into a solid-state Yamaha G100-212 combo amp (100 watts with two 12-inch Electro-Voice speakers). These days, Stern uses a stereo rig with a Pierce G-1 amp head and 4x12 JBL speaker configuration, housed in a Hartke 4x12 cabinet or two 2x12 cabinets, still split with an SPX90. His other side continues to exploit the now battered and road-worn Yamaha G100-212 combo amp he has been using for over twenty years. On the road, he often opts for reissue Fender '65 Twin Reverb combo amps.

Though electronic effects are unusual in jazz, it's not so in fusion, and Stern has always made deliberate and thoughtful use of processors throughout his repertory. He colors his ethereal clean sound with echo and chorus and relies on stomp-box overdrive for rock lead solos. In his early years, Stern preferred a Boss DS-1 distortion pedal for his dirty sound, an Ibanez digital delay, and on occasion a Boss OC-2 Octaver. His current pedalboard contains five Boss stomp boxes: two DS-1 Distortion units, two DD-2 digital delays, and an OC-2 Octaver.

Stern strings his guitar with Fender strings. He uses a standard rock 'n' roll set with a heavier high E string (from high to low: .011, .013, .015, .026, .032, .038).

LICKS

FIG. 1: ROCK-JAZZ

This telling Mike Stern phrase addresses his blues-rock side at the outset. It is played with his classic processed distortion tone, is set in a funk groove, and begins with a nod to an early idol, Albert King. But wait. What follows in measures 2–4 is his patented mix of bebop and post-bop lines. Note the use of modal, scalar, and chromatic melodies and the largely double-timed phrasing. Don't be misled by all of the individual tones; instead just assimilate this lick as a piece of the Stern jazz-rock vernacular in B♭ minor. The line concludes with a return to a Hendrix-inspired blues-rock passage.

FIG. 1.

Moderate Funk

B♭m11

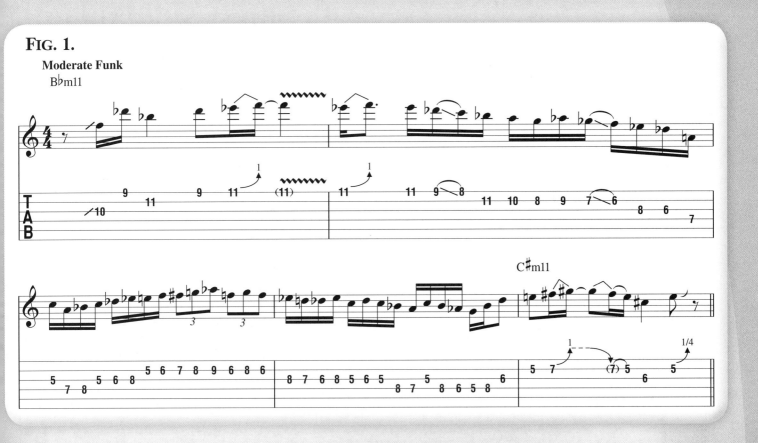

FIG. 2: MORE JAZZ THAN ROCK

This passage finds Stern inflecting a typical minor phrase with some favorite ingredients. The line is in C♯ minor and combines a number of ear-catching sounds. Note the rock-oriented entrance melody and the diatonic lick that follows. In measure 2, Stern inserts a nifty diminished arpeggio sound. Here, an A°7 outline adds a nice melodic contrast and functions as an *altered dominant sound* (G♯7♭9) within the passage. Stern's favorite chromatic embellishments distinguish the remainder of the line in measures 2 and 3 (beats 4 through 2) and set up a phrase ending in C♯ minor.

FIG. 2.

Moderate Funk

C♯m11

FIG. 3: PEDAL POINT PITCH AXIS CHORDS

This harmonically rich phrase illustrates one of Stern's most distinctive and exciting chordal patterns and is an example of his application of *quartal harmony*. Two ideas are at work in this tension-building excerpt. The first is the use of *pedal point*. The high D note is maintained throughout the passage as a melodic anchor or pedal tone. Below that, fixed-tone chords voiced as 4th-interval stacks are moved chromatically, forming a unique form of *pitch axis*. This is a prevalent figure in his playing. Stern uses it over a variety of tunes, from standards to funk grooves. It is heard prominently in his *Live in Paris* concert DVD.

FIG. 3.

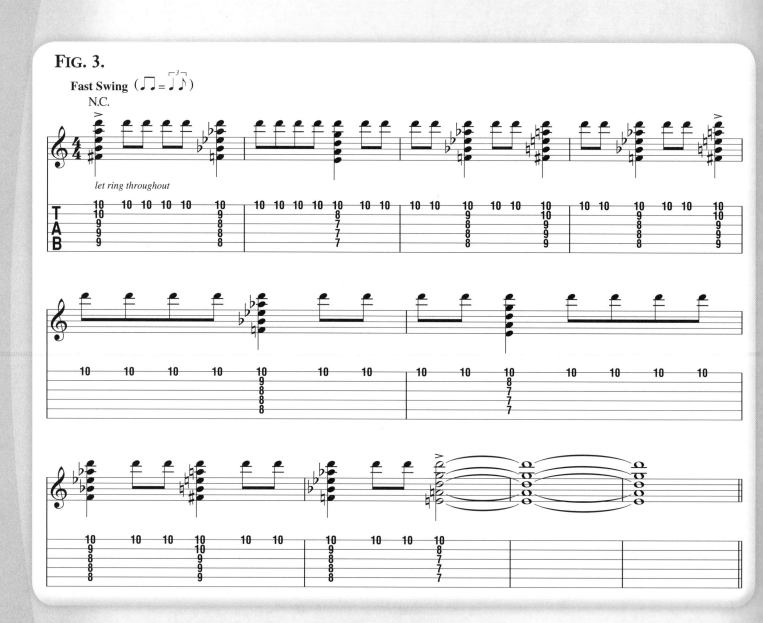

WOLF MARSHALL

Wolf Marshall is an internationally acclaimed guitarist and educator. *Guitar Player* and *The Wall Street Journal* have interviewed him in feature articles as have the *New York Times, Guitar World France, Vintage Guitar, Gitarist* (Holland), *Jazz Improv* and *Just Jazz Guitar*. Through his many products and performances, Wolf has attained a worldwide following and status.

Wolf set new standards for guitar education in the 1980s. His innovative books, audios, and videos created the basis for an industry which continues to boom. Wolf's voluminous magazine credits include articles, transcriptions, and columns in *Guitar Player, Guitar World, Guitar for the Practicing Musician, Guitar, Guitar School, Guitar Extra, Guitar Edge,* and *Guitar One.* His current Fretprints series has run monthly in *Vintage Guitar* since 2001.

Wolf's personal approach to teaching is featured in the *Wolf Marshall Guitar Method.* This comprehensive series (Hal Leonard) is considered to be the state-of-the-art in contemporary guitar education.

Wolf is an active performer, consultant, and composer. He has recently performed with Kenny Burrell, B.B. King, Dee Dee Bridgewater, and Burt Bacharach. He leads a highly successful jazz trio in Southern California. Over the years, companies as diverse as the Experience Music Project, World Vision and Floresta charities, Tristar films, D'Addario, Line 6 Guitar Port Online, and Sibelius software have employed Wolf's professional services. Wolf was invited by Kenny Burrell to join the music faculty of UCLA in 2007.

He currently teaches advanced jazz guitar studies at his alma mater alongside Mr. Burrell and Gerald Wilson. His many jazz publications include the much lauded *Best of Jazz Guitar, Best of Wes Montgomery, 101 Must-Know Jazz Licks* and *Giant Steps for Guitar.*

For more information please visit **www.wolfmarshall.com**.

Photo by Rick Gould

Guitar Notation Legend

Guitar music can be notated three different ways: on a *musical staff*, in *tablature*, and in *rhythm slashes*.

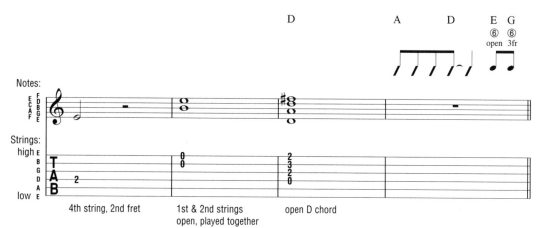

RHYTHM SLASHES are written above the staff. Strum chords in the rhythm indicated. Use the chord diagrams found at the top of the first page of the transcription for the appropriate chord voicings. Round noteheads indicate single notes.

THE MUSICAL STAFF shows pitches and rhythms and is divided by bar lines into measures. Pitches are named after the first seven letters of the alphabet.

TABLATURE graphically represents the guitar fingerboard. Each horizontal line represents a string, and each number represents a fret.

Definitions for Special Guitar Notation

HALF-STEP BEND: Strike the note and bend up 1/2 step.

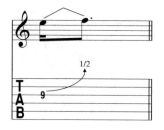

WHOLE-STEP BEND: Strike the note and bend up one step.

GRACE NOTE BEND: Strike the note and immediately bend up as indicated.

SLIGHT (MICROTONE) BEND: Strike the note and bend up 1/4 step.

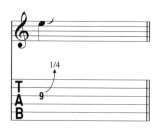

BEND AND RELEASE: Strike the note and bend up as indicated, then release back to the original note. Only the first note is struck.

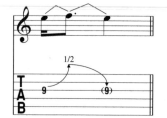

PRE-BEND: Bend the note as indicated, then strike it.

PRE-BEND AND RELEASE: Bend the note as indicated. Strike it and release the bend back to the original note.

UNISON BEND: Strike the two notes simultaneously and bend the lower note up to the pitch of the higher.

VIBRATO: The string is vibrated by rapidly bending and releasing the note with the fretting hand.

WIDE VIBRATO: The pitch is varied to a greater degree by vibrating with the fretting hand.

HAMMER-ON: Strike the first (lower) note with one finger, then sound the higher note (on the same string) with another finger by fretting it without picking.

PULL-OFF: Place both fingers on the notes to be sounded. Strike the first note and without picking, pull the finger off to sound the second (lower) note.

LEGATO SLIDE: Strike the first note and then slide the same fret-hand finger up or down to the second note. The second note is not struck.

SHIFT SLIDE: Same as legato slide, except the second note is struck.

TRILL: Very rapidly alternate between the notes indicated by continuously hammering on and pulling off.

TAPPING: Hammer ("tap") the fret indicated with the pick-hand index or middle finger and pull off to the note fretted by the fret hand.

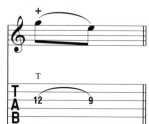

NATURAL HARMONIC: Strike the note while the fret-hand lightly touches the string directly over the fret indicated.

Harm.

T
A
B
12

PINCH HARMONIC: The note is fretted normally and a harmonic is produced by adding the edge of the thumb or the tip of the index finger of the pick hand to the normal pick attack.

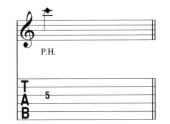

P.H.

T
A
B
5

HARP HARMONIC: The note is fretted normally and a harmonic is produced by gently resting the pick hand's index finger directly above the indicated fret (in parentheses) while the pick hand's thumb or pick assists by plucking the appropriate string.

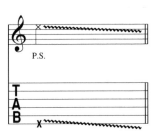

8va---

H.H.

T
A
B
7(19)

PICK SCRAPE: The edge of the pick is rubbed down (or up) the string, producing a scratchy sound.

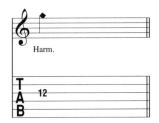

P.S.

T
A
B
X

MUFFLED STRINGS: A percussive sound is produced by laying the fret hand across the string(s) without depressing, and striking them with the pick hand.

T
A
B
X
X

PALM MUTING: The note is partially muted by the pick hand lightly touching the string(s) just before the bridge.

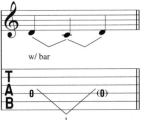

P.M. ---------------

T
A
B
0   0   0   0

RAKE: Drag the pick across the strings indicated with a single motion.

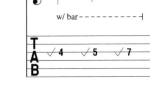

rake ---

T
A
B
5
X
X

TREMOLO PICKING: The note is picked as rapidly and continuously as possible.

T
A
B
5   7

ARPEGGIATE: Play the notes of the chord indicated by quickly rolling them from bottom to top.

T
A
B
5
5
5

VIBRATO BAR DIVE AND RETURN: The pitch of the note or chord is dropped a specified number of steps (in rhythm), then returned to the original pitch.

w/ bar

T
A
B
0   (0)
-1

VIBRATO BAR SCOOP: Depress the bar just before striking the note, then quickly release the bar.

w/ bar ----------

T
A
B
4   5   7

VIBRATO BAR DIP: Strike the note and then immediately drop a specified number of steps, then release back to the original pitch.

-1/2   -1/2   -1/2

w/ bar ----------

-1/2   -1/2   -1/2

T
A
B
7   7   7

Additional Musical Definitions

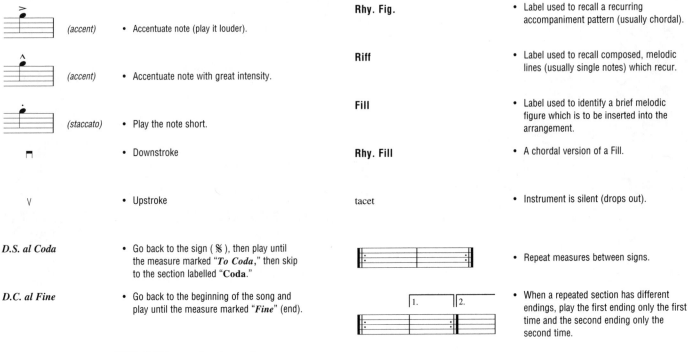

(accent) • Accentuate note (play it louder).

(accent) • Accentuate note with great intensity.

(staccato) • Play the note short.

⊓ • Downstroke

V • Upstroke

D.S. al Coda • Go back to the sign (𝄋), then play until the measure marked "*To Coda*," then skip to the section labelled "*Coda*."

D.C. al Fine • Go back to the beginning of the song and play until the measure marked "*Fine*" (end).

Rhy. Fig. • Label used to recall a recurring accompaniment pattern (usually chordal).

Riff • Label used to recall composed, melodic lines (usually single notes) which recur.

Fill • Label used to identify a brief melodic figure which is to be inserted into the arrangement.

Rhy. Fill • A chordal version of a Fill.

tacet • Instrument is silent (drops out).

• Repeat measures between signs.

1.   2.

• When a repeated section has different endings, play the first ending only the first time and the second ending only the second time.

NOTE: Tablature numbers in parentheses mean:
1. The note is being sustained over a system (note in standard notation is tied), or
2. The note is sustained, but a new articulation (such as a hammer-on, pull-off, slide or vibrato) begins, or
3. The note is a barely audible "ghost" note (note in standard notation is also in parentheses).

IMPROVE YOUR IMPROV
AND OTHER JAZZ TECHNIQUES WITH BOOKS FROM HAL LEONARD

JAZZ GUITAR

HAL LEONARD GUITAR METHOD

by Jeff Schroedl

The Hal Leonard Jazz Guitar Method is your complete guide to learning jazz guitar. This book uses real jazz songs to teach the basics of accompanying and improvising jazz guitar in the style of Wes Montgomery, Joe Pass, Tal Farlow, Charlie Christian, Pat Martino, Barney Kessel, Jim Hall, and many others.

00695359 Book/CD Pack... $19.99

AMAZING PHRASING

50 WAYS TO IMPROVE YOUR
IMPROVISATIONAL SKILLS • *by Tom Kolb*

This book/CD pack explores all the main components necessary for crafting well-balanced rhythmic and melodic phrases. It also explains how these phrases are put together to form cohesive solos. Many styles are covered – rock, blues, jazz, fusion, country, Latin, funk and more – and all of the concepts are backed up with musical examples.

00695583 Book/CD Pack.. $19.95

BEST OF JAZZ GUITAR

by Wolf Marshall • Signature Licks

In this book/CD pack, Wolf Marshall provides a hands-on analysis of 10 of the most frequently played tunes in the jazz genre, as played by the leading guitarists of all time. Each selection includes technical analysis and performance notes, biographical sketches, and authentic matching audio with backing tracks.

00695586 Book/CD Pack.. $24.95

CHORD-MELODY PHRASES FOR GUITAR

by Ron Eschete • REH ProLessons Series

Expand your chord-melody chops with these outstanding jazz phrases! This book covers: chord substitutions, chromatic movements, contrary motion, pedal tones, inner-voice movements, reharmonization techniques, and much more. Includes standard notation and tab, and a CD.

00695628 Book/CD Pack.. $17.99

CHORDS FOR JAZZ GUITAR

THE COMPLETE GUIDE TO COMPING,
CHORD MELODY AND CHORD SOLOING • *by Charlton Johnson*

This book/CD pack will teach you how to play jazz chords all over the fretboard in a variety of styles and progressions. It covers: voicings, progressions, jazz chord theory, comping, chord melody, chord soloing, voice leading and many more topics. The CD includes 98 full-band demo tracks. No tablature.

00695706 Book/CD Pack.. $19.95

CRASH COURSE ON JAZZ GUITAR VOICINGS

THE ESSENTIAL GUIDE FOR ALL GUITARISTS

by Hugh Burns • Artemis Editions

This ultimate beginner's guide to jazz guitar covers: jazz harmony explained simply, easy essential jazz shapes to get you playing right away, classic jazz progressions, vamps, turnarounds and substitutions and more.

00695815 Book/CD Pack.. $9.95

FRETBOARD ROADMAPS – JAZZ GUITAR

THE ESSENTIAL GUITAR PATTERNS

THAT ALL THE PROS KNOW AND USE • *by Fred Sokolow*

This book/CD pack will get guitarists playing lead & rhythm anywhere on the fretboard, in any key! It teaches a variety of lead guitar styles using moveable patterns, double-note licks, sliding pentatonics and more, through easy-to-follow diagrams and instructions. The CD includes 54 full-demo tracks.

00695354 Book/CD Pack.. $14.95

JAZZ IMPROVISATION FOR GUITAR

by Les Wise • REH ProLessons Series

This book/CD will allow you to make the transition from playing disjointed scales and arpeggios to playing melodic jazz solos that maintain continuity and interest for the listener. Topics covered include: tension and resolution, major scale, melodic minor scale, and harmonic minor scale patterns, common licks and substitution techniques, creating altered tension, and more! Features standard notation and tab, and a CD.

00695657 Book/CD Pack.. $16.95

JAZZ RHYTHM GUITAR

THE COMPLETE GUIDE

by Jack Grassel

This book/CD pack will help rhythm guitarists better understand: chord symbols and voicings, comping styles and patterns, equipment, accessories and set-up, the fingerboard, chord theory, and much more. The accompanying CD includes 74 full-band tracks.

00695654 Book/CD Pack.. $19.95

JAZZ SOLOS FOR GUITAR

LEAD GUITAR IN THE STYLES OF TAL FARLOW,
BARNEY KESSEL, WES MONTGOMERY, JOE PASS, JOHNNY SMITH

by Les Wise

Examine the solo concepts of the masters with this book including phrase-by-phrase performance notes, tips on arpeggio substitution, scale substitution, tension and resolution, jazz-blues, chord soloing, and more. The CD includes full demonstration and rhythm-only tracks.

00695447 Book/CD Pack.. $17.95

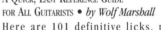

101 MUST-KNOW JAZZ LICKS

A QUICK, EASY REFERENCE GUIDE
FOR ALL GUITARISTS • *by Wolf Marshall*

Here are 101 definitive licks, plus a demonstration CD, from every major jazz guitar style, neatly organized into easy-to-use categories. They're all here: swing and pre-bop, bebop, post-bop modern jazz, hard bop and cool jazz, modal jazz, soul jazz and postmodern jazz. Includes an introduction, tips for using the book/CD, and a list of suggested recordings.

00695433 Book/CD Pack.. $17.95

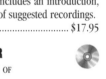

SWING AND BIG BAND GUITAR

FOUR-TO-THE-BAR COMPING IN THE STYLE OF
FREDDIE GREEN • *by Charlton Johnson*

This unique package teaches the essentials of swing and big band styles, including chord voicings, inversions, substitutions; time and groove, reading charts, chord reduction and expansion; sample songs, patterns, progressions, and exercises; chord reference library; and a CD with over 50 full-demo examples. Uses chord grids – no tablature.

00695147 Book/CD Pack.. $19.99